UNITED STATES POSTAL SERVICE

W9-BNI-212

The Postal Service Guide to U.S. Stamps

11th Edition
U.S. Stamps in Full Color
1985 Stamp Values

United States Postal Service
Washington, D.C.   20260-6355
Item No. 821

IMPORTANT INFORMATION

The United States Postal Service sells only the commemoratives released during the past few years and current regular and special stamps and postal stationery.

Prices listed in this book are called "catalog prices" by collectors and serve only as a guide to market prices for Fine specimens when offered by an informed dealer to an informed buyer.

Prices in regular type for single unused and used stamps are taken from the latest Scott 1985 Standard Postage Stamp Catalogue, Volume I © 1984, whose editors have based these values on the current stamp market. Prices quoted for unused and used stamps are for "Fine" condition, except where Fine is not available. If no value is assigned, market value is individually determined by condition of the stamp, scarcity and other factors.

Prices for Plate Blocks, Line Pairs, First Day Covers and Postal Cards are taken from Scott's Specialized Catalogue of U.S. Stamps, 1984 Edition, © 1983 The Scott numbering system for stamps is used in this book.

Prices for Souvenir Cards have been taken from the Catalog of United States Souvenir Cards, by Franklin R. Bruns, Jr., and James H. Bruns, published by Washington Press.

Prices for American Commemorative Panels are from Frank Riolo, Delray Beach, Florida. Souvenir Pages prices are from Charles D. Simmons of Buena Park, California.

Prices of actual stamp sales are dependent upon supply and demand, change in popularity, local custom, quality of the stamp itself and many other factors.

Library of Congress Catalogue Card Number 84-50114.
ISBN: 0-9604756-4-8
Printed in the United States of America

Editorial and Design: Mobium Corporation for Design and Communication, Chicago, IL
Printing: R.R. Donnelley and Sons Co., Crawfordsville, IN
Photo Credit: Dan Morrill, pages 28-29

TABLE OF CONTENTS

HOW TO USE THE POSTAL SERVICE GUIDE TO U.S. STAMPS

The Postal Service Guide to U.S. Stamps is a color catalog of postage stamps of the United States, designed to put all the vital information you need in one handy reference line.

Each line listing contains the following information:

		Un	U	PB/LP	#	FDC	Q
2054	20¢ Metropolitan Opera, Sept. 14	.00	.00	0.00	(6)	0.00	000,000,000

↑	↑	↑	↑	↑	↑	↑	↑
Scott Catalog Number	Denomination	First Day of Issue	Unused Catalog Price	Plate Block Price or Line Pair Price	First Day Cover Price	Quantity Issued	
	Description		Used Catalog Price		# of stamps in Plate Block		

2054

The Postal Service Guide to U.S. Stamps also lists philatelic details such as watermarks, perforations and years of issue. These will aid you in identifying stamps of similar design. Watermarks (Wmk.) are designs incorporated in the paper on which certain stamps are printed. Perforations are the number of small holes in a two centimeter space on the edge of the stamp. A stamp which has 12 such holes is listed as Perf. 12 (perforated 12), while a stamp with no perforations is listed as Imperf. (imperforate). Coil stamps are perforated on two sides only, either horizontally or vertically. **When a perforation, year of issue, or watermark is mentioned, the description applies to all succeeding issues until a change is noted.**

Illustration Numbers. Some of the stamps cataloged in this book are not shown. The illustrations for such stamps are identified by a number in parentheses. For example, in the listings which appear below, Scott No. 247 has the same illustration as Scott No. 246.

246   1¢ Franklin
247   1¢ blue Franklin (246)

How to Order Stamps. When ordering stamps from a dealer, identify items wanted by country of issue, Scott No., and condition (unused or used).

Condition is an important factor of price. Prices are for stamps in fine condition. Off center, heavily cancelled, faded or stained stamps usually sell at large discounts. Values in italics indicate latest auction prices, infrequent sales or fluctuating market values.

Suppose someone asked you, "What is the most popular hobby in the world?" Since you're reading this book, you can probably guess the answer. That's right. It's stamp collecting. In the United States alone, about 22 million people are stamp collectors. And there are millions more around the world.

What makes stamps so fascinating? Some people think of stamps as tiny windows on the world. Most countries have stamps that show people or things or events that their citizens think are very important, or valuable, or beautiful. So when you look at a postage stamp, you learn something about the country it comes from.

Another reason people like to collect stamps is that many stamps are really works of art. Talented artists and photographers design the stamps. They are printed with great care and skill. Having a collection of beautiful stamps is like having an art gallery of your own.

Another thing that makes stamp collecting so popular is that there is no special age for it. You can enjoy stamp collecting just as much when you're 70 years old as when you're 10. In stamp collecting, you never run out of something to do. If you started now, and collected stamps for the rest of your life, you'd probably not be able to collect all the stamps in the world. The first postage stamp was issued in 1840. Since then, hundreds of thousands of different stamps have been issued by the countries of the world. But rather than trying to collect as many different kinds of stamps from as many places as you can, you'll probably find some types of stamps that are particularly interesting to *you*—and concentrate on collecting those.

Stamps can help with schoolwork. They can be used in special projects in classes like history, geography, and science. Also, stamp collecting is a merit badge activity for Scouts.

Stamp collecting doesn't have to be an expensive hobby. Of course, you could spend many thousands of dollars on stamps, but you can also be a collector without spending much money at all.

You can start out by asking your family and your friends to save used stamps for you. Just ask them to save the used stamps on envelopes they receive in the mail at their homes or businesses. As you gather stamps, you'll want to put them in order so you can show them to other people. A ring binder with loose leaf paper can be your first stamp album. But don't paste or tape your stamps into the album! That would destroy their value.

You'll find out how to handle your stamps throughout this section. But first, look at the next page. There you'll discover some stamps that are very famous or very rare. If you are just starting to collect stamps, this bit of history will give you a feeling for the past and for some of the interesting stories you'll discover as you continue collecting.

Every stamp collector hopes to some day own a stamp that has been made important by being rare. There is always the hope that you will be the one to pick up an old envelope hidden away for years that carries a stamp that everyone else wants. Of course, not everyone can be that lucky, but learning about rare and famous stamps can be both fun and fascinating on its own. The rarest stamps all have their own history and have an attraction for collectors that can make them spend large sums for their acquisition. The very names of these stamps are lovingly recalled as unattainable dreams: Mauritius 1847, United States Boscawen Provisional, Penny Black, Sweden 1855 3 skilling-Banco.

Sometimes a stamp has become rare merely because the collecting community wasn't aware of its existence until years after its issue. In 1980, two copies of a set of stamps called the Hawaiian Missionaries each brought a price of over $200,000. These stamps have a history as interesting and strange as their name. Christian Missionaries came to Hawaii in 1820 and within 30 years had converted most of the population to Christianity. They also brought writing to the islands. In 1851 when stamps were first issued on the islands, it was mostly for the use of the missionaries who needed them to communicate from island to island or to write to colleagues, friends and family back in the United States. As these stamps have almost always been found on missionary correspondence, they've acquired the name Hawaiian Missionaries. The stamps, issued in 2 ¢, 5 ¢ and 13 ¢ face values, weren't noticed by collectors until 1864, and even then there was some uncertainty about their value to philatelists—the rarest, the 2 ¢, wasn't accepted until the 1890s. But then it quickly gained in value and in notoriety. In 1892, a French collector was found murdered in his apartment. The motive? His 2 ¢ Missionary was missing from his collection. As you might guess, another collector was discovered with the missing stamp. In his confession he told how he had tried to purchase the stamp, and, when turned down, had committed murder to acquire it.

Rarities are created in many different ways and become valuable to collectors for many different reasons. Interestingly enough, it isn't always the most rare stamps that bring the highest prices. Stamps have their fashions as well as other things do and sometimes stamps that are not especially few in number can be worth more than others that are very difficult to obtain but just do not catch the imagination of collectors.

A rare Hawaiian cover with 2¢ and 5¢ Missionaries and other U.S postage.

Many people who know about stamp collecting suggest that you shouldn't decide right away what kind of stamps you are going to collect. At first, they say, just get together as many different stamps as you can. United States stamps. Stamps from some other countries. Stamps that feature special subjects—birds, dogs, famous women, or Scouts, for example. (Stamps of this type are called *topicals,* because they are about one *topic*.) Then, after you've been collecting for a while, you'll have a better idea about what kind of stamps you want to specialize in. Just be sure to pick a type that has a lot of stamps, so you'll be able to get enough for a good-sized collection. U.S. commemoratives are an easy way to start.

Regular or Definitive Stamps These are the stamps you'll find on most mail. They are printed in unlimited quantities and sold by the Postal Service for long periods of time—several years, usually.

Regular or Definitive

Commemorative Stamps These stamps are issued to honor an important event, person, or special subject. They are usually larger and more colorful than definitives. They are sold for only a certain length of time—a few months, maybe, and are printed in limited quantities.

Coil Stamps These stamps are issued in rolls. Each stamp has two straight edges and two perforated edges.

Coil

Commemorative

Airmail Stamps U.S. airmail stamps are used for sending mail overseas.

Postage Due Stamps Postage due stamps are put on mail at the post office to show that the postage already paid was not enough. The amount shown on the stamp must be paid by the receiver of the mail.

Airmail

Postage Due

Special Delivery Stamps These stamps were sold to the sender for extra-fast delivery of the letter or package. They are not currently being produced by the Postal Service.

WHAT KIND OF ALBUM?

A simple ring binder with loose-leaf pages will do very nicely for your first album. But after a while you may want to buy a special stamp album. It's usually best to buy an album with loose-leaf pages. Then you can add more pages as your collection grows.

There is a kind of album that does not have pictures of the stamps that are to go on the pages. It just has plastic pockets on the pages. This type of album is called a *stock book*. The pages can be placed in a binder. You can buy as many pages as you need to hold your stamps.

How to Remove Stamps from Covers

To get stamps off paper, you'll need a small pan with some warm (not hot) water in it, some newspapers or paper towels, and your tongs. Place a few stamps face down in the water. Wait a little while, until the stamps float off the paper. The stamps will sink to the bottom. The paper will float. As soon as the stamps are free, lift them out with the tongs, one by one. Place them face down on the newspaper or paper towel. If they dry flat, you can put them in your album. Follow carefully the next directions. If the stamps are curled up when they are dry, put them between the pages of a telephone directory or another big, heavy book. Put another heavy book or some other kind of weight on top. Leave the stamps overnight. The next day they should be flat and ready to place in your album.

Putting Stamps in Your Album

You can use either folded or unfolded hinges to put stamps in your album. The shiny side is the gummed side. If you are using a folded hinge, lightly touch your tongue to the short side. Then, press the short side to the back of the stamp. Next, while holding the stamp with your tongs, touch your tongue to the long side of the hinge. Now put the stamp in its place on the album page, pressing it down with a blotter. (*Never* handle stamps with your fingers. Even if your hands are clean, oil from your skin may damage the stamps.) Finally, gently lift the corners of the stamp with the tongs to be sure it has not stuck to the page.

If you are collecting unused (called *uncancelled or mint*) stamps, you should use plastic mounts to put them in your album. Mounts will protect your stamps better than hinges. A mount is a small envelope that covers the whole stamp. It keeps air, grease, and dirt from damaging the stamp.

EQUIPMENT FOR STAMP COLLECTING

Suppose you have begun collecting stamps—from friends, family, businesses, and visiting the post office to look for new U.S. issues. You also have some kind of album. What else will you need for your hobby?

A. Tongs for moving a stamp from one place to another, especially when handling unused stamps, to prevent damage.

B. Hinges for attaching stamps to the pages of your album. Hinges come either folded or unfolded.

C. Mounts are small plastic envelopes. They cost more money than hinges, but are necessary to protect unused stamps.

D. A package of glassine (glass-ene) **envelopes** to hold different kinds of stamps until you are ready to put them in an album. Glassine is a special kind of thin paper that keeps grease and air from damaging stamps.

E. Stamp catalog to help you identify stamps and give you other information about them, including their value, used and unused.

F. Magnifying glass, four- or six-power, to help you distinguish stamps that seem to be the same.

G. Perforation gauge to help you identify stamps. It is used to measure the size and number of perforations (cuts or holes along the edges) on stamps.

H. Watermark fluid and a watermark tray of black glass or plastic. The stamp is placed face down in the tray and covered with a few drops of the watermark fluid. Then the watermark shows up. Watermark fluid can be dangerous, so be careful in following the directions.

Adhesive A gummed stamp made to be attached to mail.

Aerophilately The hobby of collecting airmail stamps, covers and other postal materials that are delivered by balloon, airplane, or other types of aircraft.

APS Abbreviation for American Philatelic Society.

Approvals Stamps sent by a dealer to a collector for examination. Approvals must either be bought or returned to the dealer within a certain time.

ATA Abbreviation for American Topical Association.

Autographed Cover A cover sheet or envelope signed by a person who had something to do with the event that is being commemorated—for example, the pilot of the plane that carried the material. Or an envelope addressed to a famous person, and signed by that person.

Block An attached group of stamps at least two stamps high and two stamps wide.

Booklet Pane A small sheet of stamps especially cut and printed to be sold in booklets.

Cachet (ka-shay') A design on a first day cover (envelope).

Cancellation A mark placed on a stamp to show that the stamp has been used.

Centering The position of the design on a postage stamp. On perfectly centered stamps the design is exactly in the middle of the stamp.

Coils Stamps issued in rolls for use in dispensers, affixers or vending machines.

Commemoratives Stamps that honor anniversaries, important people, or special events. Commemoratives are usually sold for only a certain length of time.

Condition The state of a stamp in regard to such things as centering, freshness, color, gum, and hinge marks.

Cover The envelope or wrapping in which a letter has been sent through the mail.

Definitives Regular issues of stamps—not commemoratives. Regular issues are usually sold over long periods of time.

Face Value The value of a stamp as printed on the stamp.

First Day Cover An envelope with a new stamp and a cancellation showing the date the stamp was first sold.

Gum The adhesive on the back of a stamp.

Hinges Small strips of paper gummed on one side and used by collectors to put their stamps in albums.

Imperforate Stamps Stamps printed in sheets without perforations or other means of separating them. Users had to cut the stamps apart with scissors or a knife. These stamps were usually early issues. They were printed before machines to make perforations had been invented.

Mint Sheet A sheet of unused stamps.

Mint Stamp A postage stamp that is in the same condition as when it was purchased from a post office.

Overprint A regular issue stamp that has some printing on top of the original design. Sometimes stamps are overprinted when there has been a change of government or when one country takes over another in a war.

Pane Part of an original large printed sheet of stamps. Sheets are cut into panes so that they are easier to handle and sell at post offices.

Pen Cancellation A cancellation made before modern post office equipment was used. Postmasters drew a line in ink across stamps, initialed them, or wrote their names on them.

Perforations Lines of small cuts or holes between two rows of stamps so that the stamps are easy to separate.

Philately (fi-lat'-el-lee) The collecting and study of postage stamps and other postal material.

Plate The metal base from which stamps are printed.

Plate Block (or number plate block) A block of stamps with the plate number or numbers in the margin.

Postal Stationery Envelopes, postal cards, aerogrammes, and wrappers with stamps printed or embossed on them.

Postmark A mark put on envelopes and other mailing pieces, showing the date and the name of the post office where it was mailed.

Postmaster Provisionals Stamps made by local postmasters. They were used before the government of the country began issuing stamps, or when the post office ran out of regular stamps.

Precancels Stamps with cancellations applied before the material was mailed.

Reissue An official reprinting of a stamp that was no longer being printed.

Revenue Stamps Stamps issued for use in collecting taxes on special papers or products. Not used for postage.

Selvage The paper around panes of stamps. Sometimes called the margin.

Se-tenant An attached pair, strip or block of stamps which differ in value, design or surcharge.

Surcharge An overprint which alters or restates the face value or denomination of the stamp to which it is applied.

Tagging Marking stamps with chemicals to be read by machines that sort mail and turn letters face-up for cancellation.

Thin Spot A thinning of the paper on the back of a stamp where a hinge was carelessly removed.

Tied On A stamp is "tied on" when the cancellation or postmark goes across the stamp to the envelope.

Topicals A group of stamps all with the same subject—space travel, for example.

Unused A stamp with or without original gum that has no cancellation or other sign of use.

Used A stamp that has been cancelled.

Want List A list of stamp numbers or philatelic items needed by a collector.

Watermark A design or pattern pressed into paper during its manufacture.

Overprint

Precancel

Perforate

Se-tenant

Imperforate

Coils

Surcharge

11

Specialty collecting hasn't anything to do with the subject matter of the stamps you collect. (Collecting stamps that have a particular subject is called **topical** collecting.) A specialty collection is a particular form of stamps, such as:

Blocks of Four A square block of four unused (mint), unseparated stamps, with two stamps above and two below. A block can come from anywhere on a sheet of stamps. This is the easiest block to collect.

Plate Blocks Usually plate blocks are four corner stamps with the printing plate number in the margin (selvage) of the sheet. On January 1, 1981, the Postal Service started a new plate number system. Each color plate first used in the production of a stamp is represented by a number 1 in the group of numbers in the margin. Whenever a plate is worn out and replaced during the printing process, a number 2 replaces the number 1. The color of the number is the same as the color of the plate it stands for.

Copyright Blocks The U.S. Postal Service now copyrights all new stamp designs. The copyright C in a circle, followed by "United States Postal Service" or "USPS" and the year, appears in the margin of each sheet of stamps. The first copyright notice appeared January 6, 1978, in the margin of sheets of the Carl Sandburg stamp. Most copyrights are collected in blocks of four.

Booklet Panes Stamp booklets were first issued in 1898. Usually six or more of the same stamps are on a page, called a pane. Several pages of stamps are stapled in a cover. Most collections are of an entire pane.

Covers Covers (envelopes) stamped and postmarked with the date of the stamp's first day of issue are collected by a large number of people. On page 20 you'll find more information about first day covers and how to order them.

Souvenir Cards These 6″ x 8″ cards are issued as souvenirs of the philatelic (stamp collecting) events. They are distributed by the United States Postal Service, or the Bureau of Engraving and Printing. Some are available cancelled. They cannot be used for postage. Of special interest to American stamp collectors is the annual souvenir card for National Stamp Collecting Month each October, first issued in 1981.

Mr. ZIP Blocks The Zoning Improvement Plan—better known as ZIP Code—helps the Postal Service handle and deliver mail quickly. A Mr. ZIP cartoon and slogan were first printed on the Sam Houston stamp of 1964. Mr. ZIP blocks have become quite popular with collectors.

The U.S. Postal Service encourages people to collect stamps and helps them with their hobby. One of the ways it does this is through the Benjamin Franklin Stamp Clubs. These are clubs that are sponsored by the U.S. Postal Service in schools and libraries across the country. They are for students in third through seventh grade.

Benjamin Franklin Stamp Clubs were first started in 1974. Since then more than 5 million students have been introduced to stamp collecting through these clubs. There are about 50,000 Ben Franklin Stamp Clubs now. Why are these clubs named after Benjamin Franklin? Because he was a leader in organizing our postal system. He was the first Postmaster General, in 1775.

1474

How does a Benjamin Franklin Stamp Club get started?
At the beginning of the school year, a person who works for the U.S. Postal Service in your area telephones schools and libraries to see if they are interested in having a stamp club. If the answer is yes, the person goes to the school or library to tell the teachers, librarians, and students about the Ben Franklin clubs. Sometimes a film about stamp collecting is shown. Usually a teacher, librarian, or parent agrees to be the club's advisor.

The U.S. Postal Service gives some materials to the Benjamin Franklin Stamp Clubs. Each of the members gets a free Treasury of Stamps album every year. This album has places for most of the new U.S. postage stamps that will be issued during the school year. Each member also gets a membership card. And every month during the school year, a newsletter called *Stamp Fun* is sent to the club. The advisor gets other free materials to help get the club started and keep it going. Films, slide-tape programs, and filmstrips are also available free from the Postal Service. The Postal Service representative will give other help to the club as it needs it.

What are some activities of the Ben Franklin Stamp Clubs?
If possible, the club meets every week. One of the most important activities, of course, is collecting, showing, and trading stamps. The club might arrange to have a stamp show. There might be a trip to visit a post office. Older stamp collectors in the community might visit the club, show their collections, and talk about them. Stamp dealers are often invited to meet with the clubs.

A new activity of the Benjamin Franklin Stamp Clubs is the Pen Pal Program. Clubs that want to write letters to other Ben Franklin clubs send their club names, addresses, and identification numbers to the Benjamin Franklin Stamp Club headquarters in Washington, D.C. A club can say in which states it wants Ben Franklin club pen pals. Then headquarters will send to the club addresses of pen pals in those states. Clubs write letters to their pen pal clubs about their activities. They also exchange "want lists" of stamps members need for their collections. Stamps can be traded or even bought this way.

Three items of postal stationery are popular with stamp collectors. These are embossed stamped envelopes, postal cards, and aerogrammes. You can buy these items at post offices.

Stamped Envelopes On stamped envelopes, the stamp is not printed separately. It is printed and embossed (made with a raised design) right on the envelope. Stamped envelopes are made for the Postal Service by a private contractor. They are made in several sizes and styles, including the window type. The embossed designs are sometimes commemoratives in more than one color.

Stamped envelopes were first issued in 1853. Today the average issue of stamped envelopes in one year is more than 1 million.

Postal Cards Postal cards are made of a heavier paper than envelopes. Plain and simple one-color postal cards were first issued in 1873. They stayed plain and simple until 1956. Then the first U.S. commemorative postal card came out. Usually several different postal cards are issued during a year. About 800 million are printed each year. For a listing of postal card values, please see page 285.

Aerogrammes An aerogramme (air letter) is a flat sheet of paper that's made to be a letter and an envelope in one. It's specially stamped, marked for folding, and gummed. After you write your letter, fold up the aerogramme and seal it. It's meant for foreign air mail only. An aerogramme will carry your message anywhere in the world at a lower postage rate than regular airmail.

Just as is the case with stamped envelopes and postal cards, the Postal Service has in recent years increased the use of commemorative designs on aerogrammes.

Olympics 84
USA
30c

USPS 1983

AEROGRAMME • VIA AIRMAIL • PAR AVION

③ Seal top flap last

③ Seal

Do not use tape or sticker

Additional message area

← ① Fold first at notches →

...rmitted

Small Business USA 20c

aerogramme

stamped envelope

15

The value of a stamp depends mostly on two things: how rare it is—that is, how few of them there are—and what condition it's in. You can get an idea of how rare a stamp is by the price listed for it in a catalog. But a stamp may sell for more or less than the catalog price, depending on its condition. A very rare stamp may be quite expensive even though it's in poor condition. For a while anyway, you'll probably be collecting stamps that aren't very expensive. But still, you should try to get stamps that are in the best condition you can.

Here are some of the things to look for when you are judging the condition of a stamp. Look at the front of the stamp. Are the colors bright? Or is the stamp dirty, stained, or faded? Is the design in the center of the paper, or is it a little crooked or off to the side? Are the edges in good condition? Or are some of the perforations missing? A stamp with a light cancellation mark is in better condition than one with heavy marks across it.

Now look at the back of the stamp. Is there a thin spot in the paper? It may have been caused by careless removal of paper or a hinge. Can you see marks from hinges? Stamps that have the original gum and have never been hinged are more valuable.

Stamp dealers put stamps into categories according to their condition. The worst is "Poor" or "Spacefiller." Most stamps you see will be in the categories "Superb," "Fine," and "Good." You can look at the examples on the next page to see the differences among stamps in these big categories.

Catalog prices listed in *The Postal Service Guide to U.S. Stamps* are for used and unused stamps in Fine condition that have been hinged. A stamp that has not been hinged and has excellent centering and color will cost more. A stamp in less than Fine condition that has been heavily cancelled will cost less than the catalog price.

You may see a stamp listed as mint. A mint stamp is one that is in the same condition as it was when purchased from the post office. An unused stamp is one that has not been cancelled. It may not have any gum on it or it may be damaged in some way. Stamps in mint condition are usually more valuable than in unused condition.

Light Cancel-Very Fine

Medium Cancel-Fine

Heavy Cancel

Superb

Very Fine

Fine

Good

Most stamp catalogs are printed only in black and white, not colors. That makes it hard to imagine what the stamps really look like, because most of them are in colors. Sometimes, to help you, the catalogs give the names of the colors on the stamps shown.

On these pages are some popular names for stamp colors, along with examples of stamps that are printed in those colors. The stamp colors shown here are not 100% accurate because printing processes such as the one used for this **Guide** don't use the same kinds of inks and paper as the original stamps. So the colors here may not look quite the same.

When you become an experienced stamp collector, you'll be able to recognize a stamp whose color makes it rare and valuable. In the meantime, you can use this guide to get a better idea of what stamps in a catalog really look like.

Blue

Dark Blue

Ultramarine

Bright Blue

Purple

Violet

Carmine

Rose Lake

Peach Blossom

 Henna Brown

 Brown

 Bistre Brown

Red

 Sepia

 Gray Brown

 Dark Gray

 Black

 Light Green

 Green

 Olive

 Light Olive Green

 Blue Green

 Yellow Gold

 Orange

Deep Orange   Yellow-Black-Green

A first day cover is an envelope that has a new stamp cancelled with the date of the first day it was issued. For each new postal stamp or stationery issue, the Postal Service names one post office that is related in some way to the subject of the stamp. First day cover ceremonies are conducted at this post office to honor the subject of the stamp.

Here's how you can get a first day cover through the Postal Service. You will get faster service if you buy the stamp yourself, and then send it to the first day post office for cancellation. When a new stamp goes on sale at your post office (usually the next day after the first day of issue), you can buy one and put it on your own envelope. Put the address in the lower right-hand corner. Leave plenty of room for the stamp and the cancellation. You can use a peelable address label if you don't want the address to remain on the envelope. Put your first day envelope inside another envelope. Mail it to "Customer Affixed Envelopes" in care of the postmaster of the first day city. The post office will cancel your envelope and return it to you through the mail. You may do this for 30 days after the issue date of the stamp.

Or, you can send an envelope addressed to yourself, but without a stamp. Put the addressed envelope into another envelope. Address the outside envelope to the name of the stamp, in care of the postmaster of the first day city. You must also include payment for the stamp or stamps that are to be put on your envelope. Do not send cash. You may send a check, a bank draft, or a U.S. Postal money order. Make it out to the U.S. Postal Service.

Do not send requests more than 60 days prior to the issue date. Usually you will receive your cancelled cover within three weeks after the first day of issue. If you don't, write to the postmaster of the first day city. Tell how the envelope was addressed, what kind of design or cachet it had, and how many stamps were ordered. If you ever get a first day cover that is damaged, send it back to the postmaster. A new one will be sent to you.

The U.S. Postal Service tries to get the first day covers into the mail just as soon as possible. To do this, it sends a special team of workers to a first day post office. Their job is just to work on first day covers. Of course, they can't do all that work on one day. Often it takes weeks. When there's an especially popular stamp issue, it may take even longer than usual to get all the first day covers out. For example, for the 1982 State Birds and Flowers issue 12,070,206 first day covers were cancelled.

The Bureau of Engraving and Printing in Washington, D.C. prints U.S. stamps and money. The Bureau has tours for visitors, and is a popular spot with tourists. To see the printing presses in operation can be very interesting, especially for stamp collectors. Stamps produced in the United States are the most carefully made and inspected in the world.

Several types of printing are used in the production of stamps.

Typography, or letterpress In this process, the design that is to appear on the stamp is raised above the metal printing plate. It is coated with ink and then pressed against the paper to print the design.

Intaglio (in-tal'yo) In this type of printing, the design is cut into the metal printing plate. The ink flows down into the lines. Then damp paper is forced onto the plate to pick up the ink.

Gravure This process is a form of intaglio. The design is photographed through a very fine screen. The screen breaks the image up into patterns of small dots. The photograph is then cut into a metal plate. The tiny dots made by the screen become holes that catch and hold the ink. The deeper the holes are, the more ink they will hold. When paper is pressed against the printing plate, it collects the ink from the holes. In this way, the design is printed on the paper.

Offset This printing process is based on the fact that water and grease do not mix. The stamp design is put on a metal printing plate by a photographic process. The part of the design that is to print (the image area) is made so that it will accept the greasy ink. The plate is wet with acid and water. When the plate is inked, the greasy ink sticks only to the image area. If paper were pressed against the plate at this point, the design would print backward. So the design is first "offset" onto a rubber blanket, and then onto the paper.

In all these processes, a separate printing plate is made for each color in the stamp.

Sometimes when a stamp is complicated, different printing processes are combined. For example, the International Peace Garden commemorative of 1982 was printed by a combination of offset and intaglio presses. The offset colors in this stamp are yellow, red, green, and black. The intaglio colors are black, brown, and green. Each pane (sheet) of 50 stamps has two groups of plate numbers. The four-number group is for the offset plates. The three-number group is for the intaglio plates.

2014

These four colorful stamps were issued in 1975 to celebrate the 200th birthday of the U.S. Postal Service. They show an early stagecoach and a modern trailer truck, old and new locomotives, an early mail plane and a jet, and a satellite for sending mailgrams. All have been carriers of the mail in this country during the past 200 years.

1572−1575

But, of course, people had been sending and receiving mail long before Ben Franklin became this country's first Postmaster General. About 4,000 years ago, a system of writing was first developed in countries around the Mediterranean Sea. The writing was cut into soft clay tablets. Then the tablets were baked and hardened. Sometimes the writing was a message to someone, and the tablets were carried by runners. The messengers' job became a little easier after the Egyptians began making a kind of paper out of the papyrus plant about 2400 B.C. Papyrus was easier to write on—and easier to carry. It was the most common writing material for 3,000 years.

The Romans developed some of the best methods of travel and correspondence in ancient times. Their mail system was so good that they had messenger stations every five to twelve miles. Sometimes the messengers rode one horse and had another to carry letter bags. Ships, too, carried mail across the Mediterranean to other parts of the Roman empire.

The Chinese emperor Kublai Khan built a postal system with 10,000 stations that were connected by good roads. The unusual thing about the Khan's system was that it could be used for private letters as well as for government mail. Most other systems of that time could be used only to carry mail sent by rulers, military commanders, and government officials. Of course, if you were an ordinary citizen, your letter went by slow-moving camel, while the Khan's went by swift horses. But at least the mail was delivered.

The Aztec and Inca Indians also had a delivery service that was used by the public. They didn't have horses, so runners carried the knotted cords that had the message in a kind of code.

In 1533 in England, King Henry VIII established regular postal routes and schedules. Private citizens could send letters by this service, but only if there was room in the bag after all the government mail was put in. And then the official mail went free. The private letters had to pay for the entire postal service. This made sending a letter very costly.

When colonists first settled in North America, there was no regular mail service. What little communication there was went between the new settlements and the countries the colonists had come from. That meant mail had to be carried by ships across the Atlantic Ocean. Government mail was carried by warships. Private citizens sent letters and packages with captains of trading ships. In 1639, Fairbank's Tavern in Boston was named as the place in Massachusetts where the transatlantic mail was to be collected.

The need for transportation of mail grew as the colonies grew. Several colonial governments set up postal services in cooperation with the British government. But these early postal services were not dependable. Sometimes the mail ships sailed when they were supposed to. Sometimes they didn't. Riders and mail coaches faced many dangers and delays.

As new types of transportation were developed, the mail services used them. Steamboats carried mail on the big rivers. By the 1830s, railroads began carrying mail.

About this time, back in England, Rowland Hill had an idea about the postal service. He was an inventor and teacher. His idea was that letters should be charged for by how much they weighed, not by the distance they were carried. For two years he argued for the "penny post." A fee of one penny would take a half-ounce letter to any part of the kingdom. And the person who sent the letter would pay the penny, not the person who received it. Finally, Hill's program was made into law. He was appointed to be in charge of the new service. So the first gummed postage stamp came into being. It was the "Penny Black," called that because it cost a penny, and it was black in color.

Five years later, in 1845, the Congress of the United States set new postal rates that were much like those in England. And on July 1, 1847, there was the first issue of U.S. postage stamps. The brown 5-cent stamp had a picture of Benjamin Franklin. The black 10-cent stamp showed George Washington. These stamps were not perforated. This means they did not have lines of holes between the rows of stamps. The user had to cut them apart. Before the U.S. stamps were issued, postmasters in some places had their own stamps printed. These stamps are called "postmasters' provisionals," and they are very valuable.

As settlers moved westward across the United States, attempts were made to set up a regular mail service from the Atlantic coast to the Pacific coast. The most famous overland mail service was the Pony Express. Relay stations were set up every 15 miles. There the riders got fresh horses.

The first western Pony Express trip was in April, 1860. A rider left St. Joseph, Missouri, on April 3, and the mail arrived in San Francisco, California, eleven days later. This service lasted only a year and a half. When the telegraph line across the country was completed, the Pony Express stopped.

1154

After the Civil War there were several improvements in mail service. In large cities, letter carriers began delivering mail to people's homes and businesses. Before that, a person had to go to the post office to pick up mail. Also, letter boxes were placed on street corners so that people could easily mail letters.

A new fast railroad mail service carried mail by train even to small towns. The mail went from St. Louis, Missouri, to San Francisco in five days—half as long as it took the Pony Express. Even if the train didn't stop at a town, mail was exchanged. A letter bag was handed by a postal worker to another postal worker on the train. And a letter bag was handed off the train to the postal worker standing beside the track. The train slowed, but didn't stop. Later, cranes were developed to help in the exchanging of mail with a moving train. The Fast Mail trains began in 1875 and continued in service until the United States entered World War I in 1917. These trains actually had post office cars.

One of the problems the postal service has had is keeping costs down while continuing to give dependable, fast service. In an effort to keep the price of stamps down, the federal government's Bureau of Engraving and Printing began printing all stamps in 1893. Before that, stamps were printed by private companies.

During the 1890s rural free delivery of mail was started. Until that time, people who did not live in cities, but on farms and in the countryside, had to go to the post office for their mail. In those days, more than half the American people lived in these rural areas. At first the rural carriers delivered mail with a horse and wagon. But beginning in 1902, automobiles were used more and more.

For city mail service, many kinds of transportation have been used. There have been postal street cars, in which the mail was collected and sorted. Some big cities had pneumatic tube lines. Mail was moved by air pressure through the tubes between main post offices and smaller ones. In New York and San Francisco postal boats picked up foreign mail from mail steamers in the harbor and took it to a nearby railroad. And there have been a few postal subway systems, in which mail was moved through underground passages. But since the 1950s, trucks have been the most popular way to move mail on the ground.

After the automobile, the next great advance in carrying the mail was the airplane. During World War I the airplane proved that it could be a means of transportation. After the war, airmail service was started. The planes used for the first airmail service were military training planes called Curtiss Jennies. The 24-cent airmail stamp issued in 1918 shows a Curtiss Jenny in flight. This stamp became one of the most famous because of a mistake. One sheet of the stamps was printed with the plane flying upside down. A recent catalog priced one of these stamps (#C3a) at $145,000!

The first airmail pilots had to have been daredevils. They often had engine trouble or ran into bad weather. The landing fields didn't have lights, and they had only road maps to fly by. Charles A. Lindbergh was one of these first airmail pilots. He flew a route between Springfield, Illinois,

C10

and St. Louis, Missouri. In 1927 he became famous for a private flight he made —the first nonstop flight from New York to Paris, made by a person flying alone. Other airmail-carrying craft shown on stamps include a dirigible, a "flying boat," propeller airplanes, and a jet. In 1977, airplanes became the standard way to move mail from city to city. Since then, it has not been necessary to buy a special airmail stamp to have your letter carried by this super-fast transportation. Today, machines, computers, and electronics help postal workers handle and carry mail.

PANES SUBSCRIPTION SERVICE

New Service Offers Superior Panes of Stamps

The U.S. Postal Service Philatelic Sales Division is offering a new Panes Subscription Service that lets subscribers pick the type of service they want and assures them superior quality panes as well.

The U.S. Bureau of Engraving and Printing selects the panes, checking each pane for paper quality, centering, gum, color, registration, perforations and marginal markings. These mint condition panes are then delivered in acetate mounts that are both safe and attractive. In addition, the Postal Service's guarantee allows you to return any panes within 30 days for a full refund.

Subscriptions run for a full year, beginning whenever the subscriber's account is first established. All issues for that year are automatically mailed. Subscribers may order all commemoratives, all definitives, or both in three types of service levels. A minimum deposit is required that covers the first six stamp issues. Remaining panes are prebilled at the face value of the stamps.

Service A supplies you with one full Pane of each U.S. stamp issued, either commemorative or definitive or both. The advance deposit is $60.
Service B provides four Panes of each issue—all four Panes with matching plate block numbers. The advance deposit is $240.
Service C gives you everything—four Panes with four-position matching plate block numbers for each plate block number made available to the Philatelic Sales Division. The advance deposit is $240.

In addition, the complete set of Official Mail Stamps is also being offered for $623. Official stamps are for use by Government Agencies and are not to be used for public mail.

The Panes Subscription Service means that you get the best panes of each new issue while making sure you never miss an issue, and you won't need to go to the Post Office to get them. For further information write to the U.S. Postal Service's Philatelic Sales Division, Washington, D.C. 20265-9997.

The STS-8 Flight Cover

On August 30, 1983, the Space Shuttle *Challenger* took off on its third flight, the eighth NASA shuttle mission. It also made philatelic history by carrying into orbit a number of specialty designed cacheted covers (envelopes) commemorating NASA's 25th anniversary. The cover was unique because it was the first to record flight into space bearing both launch date (August 30, 1983) and landing date (September 5, 1983) postal cancellations.

The cachet is a reproduction of the official "patch" design of STS-8, NASA's official designation for the eighth shuttle flight. Besides a picture of the *Challenger* rising above the earth, it bears the names of the five astronauts. *Challenger* carried 260,899 covers in its cargo bay, which were later placed on sale, and 1,001 covers in the crew cabin, which the Postal Service will retain for official display purposes. The large numbers of covers that were placed in special containers in the cargo bay were meant to insure that a sufficient quantity would be available so that all interested collectors could acquire one.

The stamp affixed to the cover is of interest as well. The striking American Eagle design, (#1909) was issued on August 12, 1983, at the Kennedy Space Center, Florida. The Commemorative "Space Mail" cancellation incorporates NASA's official 25th anniversary logo and bears an August 14, 1983, cancellation date because that was the day STS-8 was originally scheduled to be launched. This special $9.35 stamp is intended primarily for use on Express Mail Next Day Service packages.

Sending stamps and envelopes into space involved some special preflight measures to make sure the joint USPS/NASA venture would succeed. Special tests were made on the paper, ink and gum to determine whether they would be able to withstand the extremes of temperature, moisture and atmospheric pressure that would occur on the journey. On the shuttle's return, special tests were made just in case the covers had absorbed any radioactivity while in space. None was detected, and the Space Shuttle cover was a grand success.

All the Space Shuttle covers bear a serial number. Serial number "0," which has a cylinder "die" proof stamp affixed, will be on display at the new philatelic museum, "The Hall of Stamps," which was opened in 1984 at the Postal Service's L'Enfant Plaza headquarters building in Washington, D.C.

Computer Philately

Computers are entering our lives in a variety of ways and the stamp world is no exception. Many tasks at the USPS that were formerly done by hand are now performed by computers. Plans are under consideration to increase this use even further. Large scale stamp brokers feed computers with the latest stamp auction information so they can calculate stamp values that are more current than those featured in stamp catalogs that are published only annually. And now, with so many people buying computers for their homes or small businesses, many stamp collectors are finding that computers are a convenient way to help keep accurate records of their collections.

How can a computer help a stamp collector? Computers are very efficient at handling and storing large amounts of information and then presenting that information in rearranged sequences or formats. Collectors find that by using file management programs, they can store data about their stamps in a computer's "memory" and then use the computer to bring to light different aspects of their stamp collection.

A typical file management system works as follows. You create a number of "files" in your computer's memory. Each particular file can contain as much information about one particular stamp as the program allows. That information can then be broken up into categories. Thus, for each stamp, you might have room for five categories (most programs would allow you more): 1) Catalog Number; 2) Stamp Type or Description; 3) Stamp Condition; 4) Acquisition Price; 5) Catalog Value. You would create a separate file for each stamp.

Also, you can "see" your stamp holdings from a number of different perspectives. For example, you could ask your program for a list of all your stamps falling between Scott #1400 and #1500; the program would display all of your stamps, falling between those numbers in order. If properly programmed ahead of time, you can also call up data based on any of the categories you specified, or any portion of a category: i.e., all stamps in very fine condition; all stamps that are commemoratives; all stamps that cost above a certain amount.

Again, with the proper programming it is also possible to call up information to compare two or more categories. For instance, you might want to ask for all stamps that have appreciated in value since you purchased them. The computer would compare the category "Acquisition Price" with the category "Catalog Value" and display a list of any items in which the value increased.

DUCK STAMPS

There are other kinds of stamps issued by the government besides the ones that get your letter or package through the mails. Various government departments issue revenue stamps to register the payment of a tax or fee. The longest running annual series of revenue stamps is that issued by the U.S. Department of the Interior—the Migratory Bird Hunting and Conservation Stamps, or, as they are more popularly known, the Duck stamps.

The year 1984, in fact, is the 50th anniversary of the Duck stamp, and the U.S. Postal Service has honored the occasion by issuing a 20-cent commemorative.

The first Duck stamp was issued in 1934. In that year conservationists were successful in getting Congress to pass the Migratory Bird Hunting and Conservation Stamp Act. Long droughts and uncontrolled hunting in the early Thirties were causing a marked decrease in the populations of wild ducks and geese. It was hoped that the stamps would both regulate hunting and raise funds for the purchase and maintenance of wetlands and other wildlife habitats. Under the Act, every person over the age of 16 who hunts waterfowl must carry a current Duck stamp. The stamps were successful, and, in their 50-year history, over 75 million have sold. It is expected that some $15 million will be raised from the sale of the stamps in 1984.

Jay "Ding" Darling, a noted conservationist and a Pulitzer-Prize winning cartoonist, produced the artwork for the first Duck stamp. His drawing of two mallards landing in a windy marsh also served as the basis of the 1984 commemorative postage stamp, which was issued at Des Moines, Iowa, where Jay Darling spent his most prolific years as a cartoonist.

The revenue Duck stamp, which is issued each year on or about July 1, almost always carries a picture of one or more ducks, hence its name. Artwork for the stamp is chosen each year in an open competition, a contest that is the federal government's only ongoing art competition. The 1984 Duck stamp featured the winning design of an Alabama artist William C. Morris. His peaceful rendition of a pair of American Wigeons wading in a pool of deep blue water was chosen from among 1,582 entries.

Philatelists who specialize in revenue stamps began showing interest in the Duck stamps shortly after the first issue, but general collectors have become increasingly attracted to the series. The fine quality of the artwork in the series and the growing public concern over conservation have combined to recommend the Duck stamps to collectors. Purchase of the Duck stamps by non-hunting collectors is a convenient way to both obtain a handsome stamp and to contribute to the Department of the Interior's conservation efforts.

1934-1946

RW1
Mallards

RW2
Canvasbacks

RW3
Canada Geese

RW4
Scaup Ducks

RW5
Pintails

RW6
Teal

RW7
Mallards

RW8
Ruddy Ducks

RW9
Baldpates

RW10
Wood Ducks

RW11
Geese

RW12
Shovellers

RW13
Redheads

30

1947-1959

RW14
Snow Geese

RW15
Buffleheads

RW16
Goldeneyes

RW17
Swans

RW18
Gadwalls

RW19
Harlequins

RW20
Teal

RW21
Ring-neckeds

RW22
Blue Geese

RW23
Merganser

RW24
Eider

RW25
Canada Geese

RW26
Retriever Carrying Drake

1960-1972

RW27
Redhead Ducks

RW28
Mallard Hen & Ducklings

RW29
Pintail Ducks

RW30
Pair of Brant Landing

RW31
Hawaiian Nene Geese

RW32
Canvasback Ducks

RW33
Whistling Swans

RW34
Old Squaw Ducks

RW35
Hooded Mergansers

RW36
White-winged Scoters

RW37
Ross's Geese

RW38
Cinnamon Teals

RW39
Emperor Geese

32

1973-1983

RW40
Steller's Eiders

RW41
Wood Ducks

RW42
Decoy & Canvasbacks

RW43
Canada Geese

RW44
Pair of Ross's Geese

RW45
Hooded Merganser Drake

RW46
Green-winged Teal

RW47
Mallards

RW48
Ruddy Ducks

RW49
Canvasbacks

RW50
Pintails

33

Among the many commemorative stamps issued by the USPS is the ongoing Black Heritage USA Series of stamps. A new stamp has appeared in this series each year since 1978. Each commemorative marks the achievement of a black American whose accomplishments have enriched our society. With the 1984 issue, there are now seven stamps in the series, each following a similar format. All were designed by Jerry Pinkney, a member of the Citizens Stamp Advisory Committee.

2073

This year's 20-cent commemorative was issued on February 1, 1984, the first day of Black History Month. It honors black historian Carter G. Woodson. Woodson was born in 1875, the son of a poor family of former slaves. Despite his poverty and the few educational opportunities open to blacks at the time, Woodson went on to become one of the most respected historians in his field. He is best known for his 35-year editorship of the *Journal of Negro History.* He brought standards of excellence to his teaching, research and writing that have influenced the study of black history ever since.

1744

Harriet Tubman was born into slavery around 1820 in Maryland. In 1849, she escaped to the North by following the "Underground Railroad," a secret network designed to help fugitive slaves. Once free, she bravely decided to risk her new-found freedom by returning to the South to help other blacks escape as well. Between 1850 and the outbreak of the Civil War, she became one of the most active "conductors" of the "railroad," making the dangerous journey into the South some 20 times. During the war, she continued to risk her life and freedom by serving in the Union Army both as a scout and as a spy behind Confederate lines.

1771

Martin Luther King, Jr. organized and led the first mass civil rights movement in U.S. history. An eloquent and persuasive speaker, Rev. King was able to gather active support from both blacks and whites for his program of nonviolent protest against discrimination and segregation. His 1963 March on Washington brought 200,000 peaceful demonstrators to the steps of the Lincoln Memorial. He was awarded the Nobel Peace Prize in 1964 for his success in applying the principles of nonviolent resistance to the struggle for racial equality. Martin Luther King, Jr., was tragically slain in Memphis, Tennessee, on April 4, 1968.

1804

Benjamin Banneker (1731-1806) was a free-born son of freed slaves. He had little formal schooling, but he read widely on his own and became exceptionally skilled in mathematics and astronomy. He gained notice after he accurately predicted the solar eclipse that occurred in 1789. Also in that year, he was appointed a member of the surveying team that set the boundaries of the future Washington, D.C. His careful observations of the stars and planets led him to develop a series of almanacs for the years 1792-1802 which were praised by scientists in both America and Europe. He also became known for his essays and pamphlets against slavery and war.

1875

Whitney Moore Young, Jr., (1921-1971) was a black activist who was particularly successful in promoting aid for the black urban poor. He was a major force in persuading government and industry to institute equal opportunity employment practices and convinced many major corporations and foundations to finance self-help programs for the urban poor. He was head of the National Urban League from 1961 until his untimely death in 1971. As a consultant to President Lyndon B. Johnson on racial matters, he strongly influenced the federal anti-poverty programs of the 1960s.

2016

Jackie Robinson showed early promise as a superior athlete. He received an athletic scholarship to UCLA where he excelled in four varsity sports. In 1945, Robinson broke the color barrier in the baseball minor leagues when he was signed on to play for the Montreal Royals. His success there led to his signing with the Brooklyn Dodgers in 1947, when he became the first black to play in the major leagues. He was an immediate baseball success and was named that year's "Rookie of the Year." Because Jackie Robinson took the first step, the ranks of all professional sports were eventually opened to black athletes.

2044

The music called "ragtime" was America's most popular music during the early 20th century, and its most famous composer was the "King of Ragtime," Scott Joplin (1868-1917). As a young man, he played piano in cafes and honky-tonks in St. Louis and other Missouri towns, where he learned the black music of the Mississippi Valley and the newly emerging form of ragtime. At the Maple Leaf Club in Sedalia, Missouri, Joplin began composing his own rags. His successful *Maple Leaf Rag* in 1899 helped make ragtime popular outside the Midwest. Joplin went on to write rags of all sorts, including two rag operas and a folk ballet.

First U.S. Maximum Cards

In 1983, the U.S. Postal Service ventured into the Maximum Card field for the first time in its history.

What is a Maximum Card? It is a pictorial postcard that generally leaves space on the view side for both a stamp and a cancellation. Maximum Cards become especially interesting when picture, stamp and cancellation all relate to a common theme, usually the subject of the stamp.

The 1984 U.S. series of Olympic Maximum Cards carried the same artwork as the commemorative series of stamps honoring the 1984 Olympics. Also, each card was issued on the same date and at the same place as its stamp.

The maximum card originated in Europe over 40 years ago. Its name suggests two things about the card. First, there should be a *maximum* relationship between the card's illustration and that of the stamp affixed to it. Second, the size of the card is the maximum allowed to be mailed at the postal card rate by the Universal Postal Convention.

This interesting branch of collecting, sometimes called "maximaphily," has other creative possibilities as well. Some collectors have taken to making their own Maximum Cards out of commercial postcards that have illustrations related to U.S. stamps. For example, postcards can often be found with reproductions of famous paintings that have also been featured on postage stamps. Last year's Brooklyn Bridge commemorative (#2041) could have been affixed to a souvenir postcard that also showed the bridge and then sent to the Postal Service for a first day cancellation. Given the large number of commemoratives issued by the USPS, there are endless possibilities for matching stamps and postcards in interesting combinations. For more information on USPS Maximum Cards, please mail in the card between pages 288 and 289.

Art Students Design Stamps

If you were to design a postage stamp, what would it look like? Last year thousands of art students around the country were invited to try their hands at designing stamps. The occasion was a national competition sponsored by the U.S. Postal Service. Two student-inspired designs would be chosen to appear on 1984 postage stamps. The response was overwhelming. More than half a million elementary and high school art students submitted drawings to the project.

The National Art Education Association did the preliminary judging. Stressing simplicity of design and skill of execution, members of the association narrowed the field to 2,000 entries. These were turned over to the Citizens' Stamp Advisory Committee which submitted 85 drawings to Postmaster General William F. Bolger for final consideration. He chose 33 honorable mentions, 8 semifinalists and 2 finalists whose work would actually appear on 1984 stamps.

The two finalists and eight semifinalists were invited to a ceremony at postal headquarters in Washington, D.C., where their artwork was unveiled. In congratulating the students, Bolger remarked, "The greatest resource this nation has is its young people, and it is important to nourish their spirits with encouragement of their artistic ability." All the students received a certificate of achievement, a philatelic gift and an enlargement of their design for display in their local post offices and schools.

Finalist Molly LaRue, age 18, represented family unity with a series of stick figures whose bodies are red, white and blue hearts. The lettering of Molly's design was styled to match the artwork. Her drawing will be the basis of a 1984 stamp. She is a graduate of Shaker Heights High School in Shaker Heights, Ohio.

Finalist Danny LaBoccetta, age 8, created a cheerful Santa Claus with a sack of toys. Danny's drawing will appear on the 1984 contemporary issue Christmas stamp. He is a student at Our Lady of Perpetual Help School in Jamaica, New York.

39

Heather Gaucher, 11, from Spencer, Massachusetts, and a student at the Maple Street School, drew a bold, colorful message that says, "Letters Brighten Your Day."

Tommy Neyhard, 8, of Bloomsburg, Pennsylvania, and a second grade student in the Bloomsburg Memorial Elementary School, drew a colorful steamboat.

Lori Vassil, 18, who graduated in June from Central High School in Scranton, Pennsylvania, designed a love stamp showing an envelope with bright hearts emerging from it. Lori plans to be a nurse.

Jodie Booth, 13, of Cainsville, Missouri, and the daughter of a teacher of English in her school, the Cainsville R1 School, drew a black child and a white child with arms entwined and the moving message, "Friends Are Special."

Robin Malik, 18, who graduated in June from the Cresskill High School in Cresskill, New Jersey, featured a bright-eyed raccoon framed by holly leaves. She hopes to pursue an art career.

Shane Hillard, 6, was in kindergarten last year when he drew two bright red stick figures with the title "Love." Shane lives in Oquawka, Illinois, and attends Oquawka Elementary School.

Amber Evans, 17, and a senior this year at Upper Arlington High School in Columbus, Ohio, created an imaginary forest scene, with tree trunks reflected in a lake showing how they appeared before they were destroyed by fire.

Eddie Obuchowski, 9, a student at the Woodland Avenue School in Morristown, New Jersey, designed an imaginary view of the firmament. In addition to a fascination with space travel, he loves sports of all kinds.

A Preview of

The next international philatelic exhibition to be held in the United States will be AMERIPEX '86 in, of course, 1986. These annual "world's fairs" of stamps come to America every ten years and provide a showcase for stamps and collections from all over the world.

To get a preview of the big show, we spoke with Les Winick, a well-known philatelic writer who is one of the original seven organizers of AMERIPEX. Mr. Winick writes a stamp column for the *Chicago Tribune* and is a contributing editor to *Linn's Stamp News*. A collector himself, Mr. Winick specializes in space and rocket issues and Icelandic stamps. He is the author of *Catalog of Soviet Space Stamps* and is currently working on a stamp identifier for The Washington Press.

Q. For the record, Mr. Winick, where and when will AMERIPEX be held?

A. AMERIPEX '86 is scheduled to open on May 22, 1986, at the O'Hare Exposition Center (near O'Hare International Airport) and will run for 11 days through June 1. We're especially happy about the Exposition Center because its 350,000 square feet will let us put on the largest philatelic exhibition ever held in North America. All of the events will be on one level in a space the size of six football fields.

Q. Who will be there?

A. We are expecting over 100,000 visitors to AMERIPEX from all over the world. At this point, 42 countries have appointed commissioners to develop exhibits at AMERIPEX, and many more are expected. A number of foreign postal administrations are planning to show here, and the U.S. Postal Service has extended invitations to 166 members of the Universal Postal Union to come and sell their stamps. Visitors will be able to purchase stamps from all over the world at face value in one place.

Q. What can visitors expect to see?

A. We expect in excess of 60,000 pages to be shown in over 4,000 frames displaying stamps and philatelic material from every area of philately and every part of the world. We have invited the Queen of England, the Smithsonian Institution, the Bureau of Engraving and Printing and the Prince of Monaco to exhibit from their collections. The USPS is planning a major exhibit on the history of the U.S. post, ranging from its origins to the modern era of telecommunications. Thurn and Taxis, a family that began scheduled postal service as early as the 15th century in Europe, will bring an exhibit on the origins of the mails, showing early postal artifacts. This will be the first time this exhibit has been shown outside of Europe. Fifty renowned philatelists have been invited to judge the philatelic competitions, and they have each

42

been invited to display stamps and covers from their private collections. Many of the most famous stamps in the world will be on exhibit at AMERIPEX. We are planning films, lectures and seminars on subjects as different as beginning stamp collecting, postal history and buying and selling at auctions. In fact, there should be so much activity at AMERIPEX that visitors won't know what to do first.

Q. Tell us about some of your youth-oriented programs.

A. Admission to AMERIPEX will be free to young people. We want to encourage young stamp collectors and hope to make AMERIPEX fun, comfortable and informative. The U.S. Postal Service is sponsoring exhibits by the Ben Franklin Stamp Clubs, exhibits that have been developed especially for AMERIPEX. These will include "hands-on" exhibits with computer terminals and souvenir printouts. Animated shows are planned, and free field trips for neighboring Ben Franklin Clubs will be scheduled. Special competitions for young stamp collectors will be held as well.

Q. Will visitors be able to buy philatelic material at AMERIPEX?

A. There will be two major selling areas for the USPS. One will be accessible to purchasers who wish to buy stamps and other philatelic items without having to enter the Exposition Center. There will also be a large indoor selling area for the same purpose. As I mentioned earlier, foreign postal administrations will be selling stamps from their countries at the exhibition. We will have a bourse of 300 stands where dealers will be offering old and new issues and where visitors can get their want lists filled. Of these, 24 "super-booths" have been sold to some of the largest stamp dealers in the world. In addition, a number of auctions will be held, all of them open to the public, where collectors can bid on rare and famous stamps. With so much gathered under one roof, AMERIPEX will offer an unparalleled opportunity for visitors to add different and interesting philatelic items to their collections.

Q. Do you have any parting thoughts for our readers?

A. AMERIPEX '86 will be the biggest philatelic show ever held in the U.S. All special events, auctions, films, lectures and exhibitions will be open to the public. We're enthusiastic about the response we've had so far and can assure visitors that there will be something of interest from every area of stamp collecting. I want to invite everyone to AMERIPEX in Chicago in 1986.

1¢ Franklin Types I-IV of 1851-56

5

Bust of **5**

Detail of **7** Type II
Lower scrollwork incomplete
(lacks little balls).
Side ornaments are complete.

11

Bust of **5**

Detail of **6** Type Ia
Top ornaments and outer line
partly cut away.
Lower scrollwork is complete.

Bust of **5**

Detail of **8** Type III
Outer lines broken in the
middle.
Side ornaments are complete.

Detail of **8A** Type IIIa
Outer lines broken top or
bottom but not both.

Detail of **11**
THREE CENTS.
Type I. There is an outer frame
line at top and bottom.

Bust of **5**

Detail of **5** Type I
Has curved, unbroken lines
outside labels.
Scrollwork is complete, forms
little balls at bottom.

Detail of **5A** Type Ib
Lower scrollwork is incomplete,
the little balls are not so clear.

Bust of **5**

Detail of **9** Type IV
Outer lines recut top, bottom,
or both.

12

Detail of **12**
FIVE CENTS.
Type I. There are projections on
all four sides.

10¢ Washington Types I-IV of 1855

15

Detail of **13**
Type I. The "shells" at the lower corners are practically complete. The outer line below the label is very nearly complete. The outer lines are broken above the middle of the top label and the "X" in each upper corner.

Bust of **15** ↓

Detail of **14**
Type II. The design is complete at the top. The outer line at the bottom is broken in the middle. The shells are partly cut away.

Detail of **15**
Type III. The outer lines are broken above the top label and the "X" numerals. The outer line at the bottom and the shells are partly cut away, as in Type II.

Bust of **15** ↓

Detail of **16**
Type IV. The outer lines have been recut at top or bottom or both.
Types I, II, III and IV have complete ornaments at the sides of the stamps and three pearls at each outer edge of the bottom panel.

Bust of **5**

Detail of **24**
ONE CENT FRANKLIN
Type V. Similar to Type III of 1851-56 but with side ornaments partly cut away.

Bust of **11**

Detail of **26**
THREE CENTS WASHINGTON
Type II. The outer frame line has been removed at top and bottom. The side frame lines were recut so as to be continuous from the top to the bottom of the plate.

30A

↑

Detail of **30A**
FIVE CENTS JEFFERSON
Type II. The projections at top and bottom are partly cut away.

Detail of **35**
TEN CENTS WASHINGTON
(Two typical examples).
Type V. Side ornaments slightly cut away. Outer lines complete except over right X.

45

55   57

Detail of **67**
5¢. A leaflet has been added
to the foliated ornaments at
each corner.

Detail of **64**
3¢. Ornaments at corners have
been enlarged and end in a
small ball.

Issue of 1861

Detail of **55**

Detail of **57**

63   67

Issue of 1861-62

Detail of **63**
1¢. A dash has been added
under the tip of the ornament
at right of the numeral in upper
left corner.

56   58   68   69

Detail of **56**

Detail of **58**

62   64

Detail of **62**

Detail of **68**
10¢. A heavy curved line has
been cut below the stars and an
outer line has been added
to the ornaments above them.

Detail of **69**
12¢. Ovals and scrolls have
been added to the corners.

72

46

Detail of **72**
90¢. Parallel lines from an angle
above the ribbon with "U.S.
Postage"; between these lines
a row of dashes has been
added and a point of color to
the apex of the lower pair.

Detail of **134**

Detail of **138**

118

135   **136**   **139**   **140**

Detail of **118**
FIFTEEN CENTS.
Type I. Picture unframed.

Detail of **135**

Detail of **139**

Detail of **119**
Type II. Picture framed.
Type III. Same as Type I but
without fringe of brown shading
lines around central vignette.

Detail of **136**

Detail of **140**

Issue of 1870-71:
Printed by the National Bank
Note Company.
Issued without secret marks
(see Nos. 156-163).

134

137   **138**   **141**

Detail of **137**

Detail of **141**

1873: Printed by the Continental Bank Note Co.

Designs of the 1870-71 Issue with secret marks on the values from 1¢ to 15¢ as described and illustrated below.

159   **160**

Detail of 159
6¢. The first four vertical lines of the shading in the lower part of the left ribbon have been strengthened.

Detail of 160
7¢. Two small semi-circles are drawn around the ends of the lines which outline the ball in the lower right hand corner.

161   **162**

Detail of 161
10¢. There is a small semi-circle in the scroll, at the right end of the upper label.

Detail of 162
12¢. The balls of the figure "2" are crescent shaped.

163

Detail of 163
15¢. In the lower part of the triangle in the upper left corner two lines have been made heavier forming a "V". This mark can be found on some of the Continental and American (1879) printings, but not all stamps show it.
Secret marks were added to the dies of the 24¢, 30¢ and 90¢ but new plates were not made from them. The various printings of these stamps can be distinguished only by the shades and paper.

206   **207**

Detail of 206
1¢. Upper vertical lines have been deepened, creating a solid effect in parts of background. Upper arabesques have lines of shading.

Detail of 207
3¢. Shading at sides of central oval is half its previous width. A short horizontal dash has been cut below the "TS" of "CENTS".

208   **209**

Detail of 208
6¢. Has three vertical lines instead of four between the edge of the panel and the outside of the stamp.

Detail of **209**
10¢. Has four vertical lines
instead of five between left side
of oval and edge of the shield.
Horizontal lines in lower part of
background have been
strengthened.

$1 Perry
Types of 1894

261

283

2¢ Washington
Types I-III of 1894

Triangle of **248-250**
Type I. Horizontal lines of
uniform thickness run across
the triangle.

Detail of **261**
Type I. The circles enclosing $1
are broken.

Detail of **283**
Type II. The lips of the
ornaments break the curved
line below the "E" of "TEN" and
the "T" of "CENTS."

251

Detail of **261A**
Type II. The circles enclosing
$1 are complete.

282C

Watermark **191**

Triangle of **251**
Type II. Horizontal lines cross
the triangle, but are thinner
within than without.

Detail of **282C**
TEN CENTS
Type I. The tips of the foliate
ornaments do not impinge on
the white curved line below
"TEN CENTS."

USPS

Watermark **190**

Triangle of **252**
Type III. The horizontal lines do
not cross the double frame
lines of the triangle.

USPS

Watermark **191**

49

1847-1875

1

2

3

4

5

11

12

15

17

30A

37

39

		Un	U
Issues of 1847 to 1894 are Unwatermarked, Issue of 1847, Imperf.			
1	5¢ Benjamin		
	Franklin, July 1	5,000.00	800.00
2	10¢ George		
	Washington,		
	July 1	20,000.00	2,500.00
Issue of 1875, Reproductions of 1 & 2			
3	5¢ Franklin	1,650.00	—
4	10¢ Washington	2,000.00	—

Reproductions. The letters R. W. H. & E. at the bottom of each stamp are less distinct on the reproductions than on the originals.

5¢. On the original the left side of the white shirt frill touches the oval on a level with the top of the "F" of "Five." On the reproduction it touches the oval about on a level with the top of the figure "5."

10¢. On the reproduction, line of coat at left points to right of "X" and line of coat at right points to center of "S" of CENTS. On the original, line of coat points to "T" of TEN and between "T" and "S" of CENTS.

On the reproduction the eyes have a sleepy look, the line of the mouth is straighter, and in the curl of hair near the left cheek is a strong black dot, while the original has only a faint one.

		Un	U
Issue of 1851-56, Imperf.			
5	1¢ Franklin, type I	100,000.00	20,000.00
5A	1¢ Same, type Ib	10,500.00	3,500.00
Nos. 6-9: Franklin (5)			
6	1¢ dark blue,		
	type Ia	13,500.00	4,250.00
7	1¢ blue, type II	450.00	85.00
8	1¢ blue, type III	4,500.00	1,250,00
8A	1¢ pale blue,		
	type IIIA	1,550.00	525.00
9	1¢ blue, type IV	300.00	75.00
10	3¢ orange brown Washington,		
	type I (11)	1,250.00	65.00
11	3¢ Washington, type I	120.00	7.00

		Un	U
12	5¢ Jefferson, type I	9,000.00	1,300.00
13	10¢ green Washington,		
	type I (15)	7,500.00	675.00
14	10¢ green, type II (15)	1,500.00	275.00
15	10¢ Washington, type III	1,550.00	285.00
16	10¢ green, type IV (15)	9,500.00	1,350.00
17	12¢ Washington	1,850.00	250.00

		Un	U
Issue of 1857-61, Perf. 15			
Nos. 18-24: Franklin (5)			
18	1¢ blue, type I	675.00	325.00
19	1¢ blue, type Ia	8,500.00	2,000.00
20	1¢ blue, type II	425.00	120.00
21	1¢ blue, type III	3,250.00	950.00
22	1¢ blue, type IIIa	575.0p	200.00
23	1¢ blue, type IV	1,500.00	265.00
24	1¢ blue, type V	120.00	22.50

		Un	U
Nos. 25-26: Washington (11)			
25	3¢ rose, type I	650.00	27.50
26	3¢ dull red, type II	50.00	2.75
Nos. 27-29: Jefferson (12)			
27	5¢ brick red, type I	6,500.00	900.00
28	5¢ red brown, type I	1,350.00	275.00
28A	5¢ Indian red, type I	8,000.00	1,200.00
29	5¢ brown, type I	675.00	200.00
30	5¢ orange brown		
	Jefferson, type II (30A)	750.00	900.00
30A	5¢ Jefferson, type II	425.00	170.00
Nos 31-35: Washington (15)			
31	10¢ green type I	4,500.00	500.00
32	10¢ green, type II	1,400.00	150.00
33	10¢ green, type III	1,450.00	160.00
34	10¢ green, type IV	12,000.00	1,400.00
35	10¢ green type V	175.00	57.50
36	12¢ black Washington		
	(17)	300.00	75.00
37	24¢ Washington	650.00	200.00
38	30¢ Franklin	800.00	285.00
39	90¢ Washington	1,450.00	2,750.00
	90¢ Same, with pen cancel	—	1,000.00

Note: Beware of forged cancellations of No. 39. Genuine cancellations are rare.

		Un	U
1875: Government Reprints, Perf. 12, White Paper, Without Gum			
40	1¢ bright blue Franklin (5)	500.00	—
41	3¢ scarlet Washington (11)	2,750.00	—
42	5¢ orange brown		
	Jefferson (30A)	900.00	—
43	10¢ blue green		
	Washington (15)	2,250.00	—

		Un	U
1875 continued			
44	12¢ greenish black		
	Washington (17)	*2,450.00*	—
45	24¢ blackish violet		
	Washington (37)	*2,750.00*	—
46	30¢ yel. org. Franklin		
	(38)	*2,850.00*	—
47	90¢ deep blue		
	Washington (39)	*4,000.00*	—
Issue of 1861, Perf. 12			

Following the outbreak of the Civil War, the U.S. Government demonetized all previous issues.

55	1¢ Franklin	*16,500.00*	—
56	3¢ Washington	700.00	—
57	5¢ brown Jefferson	*12,000.00*	—
58	10¢ Washington	4,750.00	—
59	12¢ Washington	*35,000.00*	—
60	24¢ dk. vio. Washington		
	(70)	5,000.00	—
61	30¢ red org. Franklin		
	(71)	*15,000.00*	—
62	90¢ dull blue		
	Washington (72)	*19,000.00*	—
62B	10¢ dark green		
	Washington (58)	4,750.00	450.00

Nos. 55-62 were not used for postage and do not exist in a cancelled state. The paper they were printed on is thin and semi-transparent, that of the following issues is more opaque.

Issue of 1861-62, Perf. 12			
63	1¢ Franklin	100.00	17.50
64	3¢ Washington	3,250.00	250.00
65	3¢ rose Washington (64)	45.00	1.10
66	3¢ lake Washington (64)	*1,350.00*	—
67	5¢ Jefferson	3,850.00	350.00
68	10¢ Washington	235.00	32.50
69	12¢ Washington	425.00	45.00
70	24¢ Washington	475.00	60.00
71	30¢ Franklin	450.00	60.00
72	90¢ Washington	1,100.00	225.00
Issue of 1861-66, Perf. 12			
73	2¢ Andrew Jackson		
	("Black Jack")	110.00	20.00

		Un	U
74	3¢ scarlet Washington		
	(64)	*3,750.00*	—
75	5¢ red brown Jefferson		
	(67)	1,200.00	185.00
76	5¢ brn. Jefferson (67)	275.00	47.50
77	15¢ Abraham Lincoln	450.00	60.00
78	24¢ lilac Washington (70)	250.00	45.00

No. 74 was not regularly issued.

Grills on U.S. Stamps

Between 1867 and 1870, postage stamps were embossed with grills to prevent people from re-using cancelled stamps. The pyramid-shaped grills absorbed cancellation ink, making it virtually impossible to remove a postmark chemically.

Issue of 1867, With Grills, Perf. 12			
Grills A, B, C: Points Up			
A. Grill Covers Entire Stamp			
79	3¢ rose Washington		
	(64)	1,650.00	425.00
80	5¢ brn. Jefferson (67)	*40,000.00*	—
81	30¢ org. Franklin (71)	—	*32,500.00*
B. Grill about 18x15 mm.			
82	3¢ rose Washington (64)	—	*35,000.00*
C. Grill about 13x16 mm.			
83	3¢ rose Washington (64)	1,450.00	300.00
Grills, D, Z, E, F: Points Down			
D. Grill about 12x14 mm.			
84	2¢ blk. Jackson (73)	2,400.00	725.00
85	3¢ rose Washington (64)	1,100.00	325.00
Z. Grill about 11x14 mm.			
85A	1¢ bl. Franklin (63)	—	*110,000.00*
85B	2¢ blk. Jackson (73)	900.00	275.00
85C	3¢ rose Washington (64)	2,500.00	750.00
85D	10¢ green Washington		
	(68)	—	*23,500.00*
85E	12¢ black Washington		
	(69)	1,450.00	500.00
85F	15¢ blk. Lincoln (77)	—	*35,000.00*
E. Grill about 11x13 mm.			
86	1¢ blue Franklin (63)	625.00	200.00
87	2¢ black Jackson (73)	300.00	65.00
88	3¢ rose Washington (64)	200.00	9.50
89	10¢ grn. Washington (68)	1,000.00	150.00
90	12¢ blk. Washington (69)	1,200.00	170.00

861-1875

55 56 57 58 59

62 63 64 67 68 69

2 113 114 115 116

7 118 120 121 122

135 136 137 138

	1867 continued	Un	U
91	15¢ black Lincoln (77)	2,400.00	400.00
	F. Grill about 9x13 mm.		
92	1¢ blue Franklin (63)	225.00	75.00
93	2¢ black Jackson (73)	110.00	22.50
94	3¢ red Washington (64)	75.00	2.50
95	5¢ brown Jefferson (67)	750.00	185.00
96	10¢ yellow green		
	Washington (68)	550.00	85.00
97	12¢ black Washington		
	(69)	600.00	90.00
98	15¢ black Lincoln (77)	600.00	100.00
99	24¢ gray lilac		
	Washington (70)	1,100.00	425.00
100	30¢ orange Franklin (71)	1,250.00	325.00
101	90¢ blue Washington		
	(72)	3,500.00	850.00

Reissues of 1861-66 in 1875, Without Grill, Perf. 12

		Un	U
102	1¢ blue Franklin (63)	*475.00*	*650.00*
103	2¢ black Jackson (73)	*2,500.00*	*3,250.00*
104	3¢ brown red		
	Washington (64)	*3,000.00*	*4,000.00*
105	5¢ brown Jefferson (67)	*1,600.00*	*1,850.00*
106	10¢ grn. Washington (68)	*2,100.00*	*2,500.00*
107	12¢ blk. Washington (69)	*2,850.00*	*3,350.00*
108	15¢ black Lincoln (77)	*2,850.00*	*3,500.00*
109	24¢ deep violet		
	Washington (70)	*3,500.00*	*5,500.00*
110	30¢ brownish orange		
	Franklin (71)	*4,250.00*	*6,500.00*
111	90¢ blue Washington (72)	*5,500.00*	*9,500.00*

Issue of 1869, With Grill Measuring 9½x9 mm., Perf. 12

		Un	U
112	1¢ Franklin	225.00	60.00
113	2¢ Post Horse & Rider	160.00	25.00
114	3¢ Locomotive	135.00	5.50
115	6¢ Washington	775.00	85.00
116	10¢ Shield and Eagle	850.00	95.00
117	12¢ *S.S. Adriatic*	750.00	85.00
118	15¢ Columbus		
	Landing, type I	1,750.00	235.00
119	15¢ brown and blue		
	Columbus Landing,		
	type II (118)	850.00	115.00

		Un	U
119b	Center		
	inverted	*130,000.00*	*17,000.00*
120	24¢ Declaration of		
	Independence	2,500.00	500.00
120b	Center		
	inverted	*100,000.00*	*16,500.00*
121	30¢ Shield, Eagle		
	and Flags	2,250.00	250.00
121b	Flags inverted	115,000.00	*45,000.00*
122	90¢ Lincoln	8,000.00	1,250.00

Reissues of 1869 in 1875, Without Grill, Hard White Paper, Perf. 12

		Un	U
123	1¢ Buff (112)	325.00	200.00
124	2¢ brown (113)	375.00	325.00
125	3¢ blue (114)	3,000.00	1,400.00
126	6¢ blue (115)	850.00	500.00
127	10¢ yellow (116)	1,400.00	1,000.00
128	12¢ green (117)	1,500.00	1,000.00
129	15¢ brown and blue		
	Columbus Landing,		
	type III (118)	1,300.00	500.00
130	24¢ grn. & vio. (120)	1,250.00	500.00
131	30¢ bl. & car. (121)	1,750.00	1,000.00
132	90¢ car. & blk. (122)	5,500.00	*8,000.00*

Reissues of 1869 in 1880, Soft, Porous Paper, Perf. 12

		Un	U
133	1¢ buff (112)	200.00	135.00

Issue of 1870-71, With Grill, White Wove Paper, Perf. 12

		Un	U
134	1¢ Franklin	425.00	50.00
135	2¢ Jackson	300.00	30.00
136	3¢ Washington	225.00	8.50
137	6¢ Lincoln	1,400.00	250.00
138	7¢ Edwin M. Stanton	1,000.00	225.00
139	10¢ Jefferson	1,350.00	375.00
140	12¢ Henry Clay	*11,500.00*	1,500.00
141	15¢ Daniel Webster	1,600.00	675.00
142	24¢ General Winfield		
	Scott	—	*10,500.00*

It is generally accepted as fact that the Continental Bank Note Co. printed and delivered a quantity of 24¢ stamps. They are impossible to distinguish from those printed by the National Bank Note Co.

	Un	U

1870-71 continued

		Un	U
143	30¢ Alexander		
	Hamilton	3,750.00	800.00
144	90¢ Commodore Perry	5,000.00	700.00

Without Grill, White Wove Paper, Perf. 12

		Un	U
145	1¢ ultra. Franklin (134)	135.00	6.50
146	2¢ red brn. Jackson		
	(135)	40.00	4.50
147	3¢ green Washington		
	(136)	90.00	.40
148	6¢ carmine Lincoln (137)	185.00	11.00
149	7¢ verm. Stanton (138)	300.00	50.00
150	10¢ brown Jefferson (139)	185.00	12.00
151	12¢ dull violet Clay (140)	475.00	45.00
152	15¢ bright orange Webster		
	(141)	450.00	50.00
153	24¢ purple W. Scott (142)	525.00	65.00
154	30¢ black Hamilton (143)	900.00	80.00
155	90¢ carmine Perry (144)	1,100.00	150.00

Issue of 1873, Without Grill, Perf. 12, White Wove Paper, Thin to Thick

		Un	U
156	1¢ Franklin	45.00	1.75
157	2¢ Jackson	130.00	7.00
158	3¢ Washington	35.00	.15
159	6¢ Lincoln	160.00	8.00
160	7¢ Stanton	375.00	50.00
161	10¢ Jefferson	165.00	8.25
162	12¢ Clay	550.00	55.00
163	15¢ Webster	475.00	45.00
165	30¢ Hamilton (143)	475.00	45.00
166	90¢ Perry (144)	1,150.00	160.00

Issue of 1875, Special Printing, Hard, White Wove Paper, Without Gum

		Un	U
167	1¢ ultra. Franklin (156)	5,500.00	—
168	2¢ dark brown		
	Jackson (157)	3,000.00	—
169	3¢ blue green		
	Washington (158)	8,500.00	—
170	6¢ dull rose Lincoln		
	(159)	7,000.00	—
171	7¢ reddish vermilion		
	Stanton (160)	1,850.00	—
172	10¢ pale brown		
	Jefferson (161)	6,000.00	—

		Un	U
173	12¢ dark violet Clay		
	(162)	2,350.00	—
174	15¢ bright orange		
	Webster (163)	6,500.00	—
175	24¢ dull purple		
	W. Scott (142)	1,650.00	—
176	30¢ greenish black		
	Hamilton (143)	6,000.00	—
177	90¢ violet car. Perry		
	(144)	6,000.00	—

Although perforated, these stamps were usually cut apart with scissors. As a result, the perforations are often much mutilated and the design is frequently damaged.

Yellowish Wove Paper

		Un	U
178	2¢ vermilion Jackson		
	(157), June 21	125.00	4.00
179	5¢ Zachary Taylor,		
	June 21	135.00	7.50

Special Printing, Hard, White Wove Paper, Without Gum

		Un	U
180	2¢ carmine verm.		
	Jackson (157)	17,000.00	—
181	5¢ bright blue Taylor		
	(179)	31,500.00	—

Issue of 1879. Printed by the American Bank Note Company. Soft, Porous Paper Varying from Thin to Thick.

		Un	U
182	1¢ dark ultramarine		
	Franklin (156)	90.00	1.20
183	2¢ vermilion Jackson		
	(157)	50.00	1.20
184	3¢ green Washington		
	(158)	37.50	.10
185	5¢ blue Taylor (179)	175.00	7.50
186	6¢ pink Lincoln (159)	400.00	10.00
187	10¢ brown Jefferson (139)		
	(no secret mark)	600.00	12.00
188	10¢ brown Jefferson (161)		
	(with secret mark)	400.00	13.00
189	15¢ red orange		
	Webster (163)	150.00	13.50
190	30¢ full black Hamilton		
	(143)	425.00	21.00
191	90¢ carmine Perry (144)	1,000.00	140.00

1870-1879

143

144

156

157

158

159

160

161

162

163

179

205

 206

 207

 208

 209

 210

 211

 212

 219

 219D

 221

 222

 223

 224

 225

 226

227

228

229

		Un	U
Issue of 1880, Special Printing, Soft, Porous Paper, Without Gum			
192	1¢ dark ultramarine		
	Franklin (156)	8,000.00	—
193	2¢ black brown		
	Jackson (157)	4,500.00	—
194	3¢ blue green		
	Washington (158)	11,500.00	—
195	6¢ dull rose Lincoln		
	(159)	8,500.00	—
196	7¢ scarlet vermilion		
	Stanton (160)	2,250.00	—
197	10¢ deep brown		
	Jefferson (161)	7,500.00	—
198	12¢ blackish purple		
	Clay (162)	4,250.00	—
199	15¢ orange Webster		
	(163)	7,000.00	—
200	24¢ dark violet		
	W. Scott (142)	2,350.00	—
201	30¢ greenish black		
	Hamilton (143)	6,250.00	—
202	90¢ dull car. Perry (144)	6,250.00	—
203	2¢ scarlet vermilion		
	Jackson (157)	16,000.00	—
204	5¢ deep blue Taylor		
	(179)	27,500.00	—
Issue of 1882			
205	5¢ Garfield, Apr. 10	90.00	4.00
Special Printing. Soft, Porous Paper, Without Gum			
205C	5¢ gray brown (205)	16,500.00	—
Issue of 1881-82, Designs of 1873 Re-engraved.			
206	1¢ Franklin	30.00	.40
207	3¢ Washington	35.00	.12
208	6¢ Lincoln	235.00	40.00
209	10¢ Jefferson	67.50	2.25
Issue of 1883			
210	2¢ Washington, Oct. 1	28.50	.08
211	4¢ Jackson, Oct. 1	140.00	7.00
Special Printing. Soft, Porous Paper.			
211B	2¢ pale red brown		
	Washington (210)	675.00	—

		Un	U
211D	4¢ deep blue green		
	Jackson (211) no gum	13,000.00	—
Issue of 1887			
212	1¢ Franklin	50.00	.65
213	2¢ green Washington		
	(210)	20.00	.08
214	3¢ vermilion		
	Washington (207)	42.50	32.50
Issue of 1888, Perf. 12			
215	4¢ carmine Jackson		
	(211)	140.00	10.00
216	5¢ indigo Garfield (205)	120.00	6.00
217	30¢ orange brown		
	Hamilton (143)	350.00	70.00
218	90¢ purple Perry (144)	725.00	130.00
Issue of 1890-93, Perf. 12			
219	1¢ Franklin	20.00	.10
219D	2¢ Washington	150.00	.45
220	2¢ carmine (219D)	16.50	.05
1890-93 continued			
221	3¢ Jackson	55.00	4.50
222	4¢ Lincoln	52.50	1.50
223	5¢ Ulysses S. Grant	52.50	1.50
224	6¢ Garfield	52.50	13.00
225	8¢ William T. Sherman	40.00	8.50
226	10¢ Webster	100.00	1.50
227	15¢ Clay	150.00	15.00
228	30¢ Jefferson	225.00	18.50
229	90¢ Perry	375.00	85.00

	1893 continued	Un	U	PB/LP	#	FDC	Q
	Columbian Exposition Issue, 1893, Perf. 12						
230	1¢ Columbus Sights Land	25.00	.30	500.00	(6)	2,600.00	449,195,550
231	2¢ Landing of Columbus	22.50	.06	450.00	(6)	2,000.00	1,464,588,750
232	3¢ The Santa Maria	50.00	15.00	850.00	(6)	6,000.00	11,501,250
233	4¢ Fleet of Columbus ultramarine	75.00	6.00	1,100.00	(6)	6,000.00	19,181,550
233a	4¢ blue (error) (233)	6,500.00	2,500.00				
234	5¢ Columbus Seeking Aid	85.00	7.00	1,600.00	(6)	6,250.00	35,248,250
235	6¢ Columbus at Barcelona	75.00	20.00	1,300.00	(6)	6,750.00	4,707,550
236	8¢ Columbus Restored to Favor	50.00	8.00	850.00	(6)		10,656,550
237	10¢ Columbus Presenting Indians	130.00	6.50	3,500.00	(6)	7,500.00	16,516,950
238	15¢ Columbus Announcing						
	His Discovery	225.00	65.00	5,750.00	(6)		1,576,950
239	30¢ Columbus at La Rabida	325.00	90.00	8,500.00	(6)		617,250
240	50¢ Recall of Columbus	400.00	140.00	12,000.00	(6)		243,750
241	$1 Isabella Pledging Her Jewels	1,100.00	575.00	23,500.00	(6)		55,050
242	$2 Columbus in Chains	1,250.00	500.00	25,000.00	(6)	14,000.00	45,550
243	$3 Columbus Describing His						
	Third Voyage	2,600.00	900.00	55,000.00	(6)		27,650
244	$4 Isabella and Columbus	3,500.00	1,300.00	110,000.00	(6)		26,350
245	$5 Portrait of Columbus	3,750.00	1,500.00	120,000.00	(6)		27,350

The First U.S. Commemoratives

In the early 1890's, the United States decided to celebrate the 400th anniversary of America's discovery with a grand, international exhibition. The world was invited to Chicago to see what resulted from Christopher Columbus's voyages — a young, energetic continent. Planning was on such a large scale that the World's Columbian Exposition had to open in 1893, rather than the actual anniversary year of 1892.

230

The Post Office joined the celebration, making philatelic history by issuing its first set of commemorative stamps. Sixteen stamps were engraved with scenes from Columbus's story (#230-#245). These handsome depictions proved immensely popular, and many collectors still consider the Columbians to be the most attractive and desirable of all commemoratives.

The success of the Columbians began the practice of commemorating events by issuing official U.S. postage stamps. It had another effect, too. Before this set, stamps had mainly featured portraits of famous people. One attempt had been made in 1869 to circulate stamps with other kinds of pictures, but public disapproval caused the stamps to be withdrawn in less than a year. In 1893, opinion had shifted; the Columbian issue was the precursor of the great variety of pictorial matter we see on stamps today.

1893

230 231 232

233 234 235

236 237 238

239 240 241

242 243 244

245

246 251 253 254 255 256

257 258 259 260 261 262

263

	Un	U	PB/LP	#	FDC		Q

Bureau Issues

Starting in 1894, the Bureau of Engraving and Printing at Washington has produced all U.S. postage stamps except Nos. 909-921 (Overrun Countries), 1335 (Eakins painting), 1355 (Disney), 1410-1413 (Anti-Pollution), 1414-1418 (Christmas, 1970), 1789 (John Paul Jones), 1804 (Benjamin Banneker), 1825 (Veterans Administration), 1833 (American Education), 2023 (Francis of Assisi), 2038 (Joseph Priestley), 2065 (Martin Luther), 2066 (Alaska Statehood) and 2080 (Hawaii Statehood).

Issue of 1894, Perf. 12, Unwmkd.

		Un	U	PB/LP	#
246	1¢ Franklin	21.00	3.00	325.00	(6)
247	1¢ blue Franklin (246)	52.50	1.25	650.00	(6)
248	2¢ Washington, type I	17.50	2.00	225.00	(6)
	Nos. 249-252; Washington (251)				
249	2¢ carmine lake, type I	125.00	1.35	1,250.00	(6)
250	2¢ carmine, type I	21.00	.25	325.00	(6)
251	2¢ carmine, type II	165.00	2.50	2,500.00	(6)
252	2¢ carmine, type III	85.00	3.25	1,200.00	(6)
253	3¢ Jackson	80.00	6.25	1,000.00	(6)
254	4¢ Lincoln	90.00	2.50	1,250.00	(6)
255	5¢ Grant	70.00	3.50	875.00	(6)
256	6¢ Garfield	135.00	14.00	1,600.00	(6)
257	8¢ Sherman	100.00	10.00	1,000.00	(6)
258	10¢ Webster	185.00	6.50	2,750.00	(6)
259	15¢ Clay	275.00	45.00	4,250.00	(6)
260	50¢ Jefferson	375.00	75.00	7,000.00	(6)
261	$1 Commodore Perry, type I	950.00	225.00	16,500.00	(6)
261A	$1 black Perry, type II (261)	2,000.00	450.00	27,500.00	(6)
262	$2 James Madison	2,400.00	550.00	40,000.00	(6)
263	$5 John Marshall	3,750.00	1,000.00	—	(6)

Issue of 1895, Perf. 12, Wmkd. 191

		Un	U	PB/LP	#
264	1¢ blue Franklin (264)	6.00	.10	185.00	(6)
	Nos. 265-267; Washington (251)				
265	2¢ carmine, type I	25.00	.65	375.00	(6)
266	2¢ carmine, type II	22.50	2.50	425.00	(6)
267	2¢ carmine, type III	4.50	.05	135.00	(6)
268	3¢ purple Jackson (253)	32.50	1.00	650.00	(6)
269	4¢ dk. brown Lincoln (254)	35.00	1.10	650.00	(6)
270	5¢ chocolate Grant (255)	32.50	1.75	650.00	(6)
271	6¢ dull brn. Garfield (256)	75.00	3.50	1,250.00	(6)
272	8¢ vio. brn. Sherman (257)	35.00	1.00	700.00	(6)
273	10¢ dk. green Webster (258)	60.00	1.20	1,300.00	(6)
274	15¢ dark blue Clay (259)	185.00	8.25	3,500.00	(6)
275	50¢ orange Jefferson (260)	265.00	20.00	6,750.00	(6)
276	$1 black Perry, type I (261)	625.00	65.00	11,500.00	(6)
276A	$1 blk. Perry, type II (261)	1,350.00	120.00	23,500.00	(6)
277	$2 brt. blue Madison (262)	975.00	250.00	21,000.00	(6)
278	$5 dk. grn. Marshall (263)	2,100.00	375.00	60,000.00	(6)

	Issue of 1898, Perf. 12	Un	U	PB/LP	#	FDC	Q
279	1¢ dp. green Franklin (246)	10.00	.06	185.00	(6)		
279B	2¢ red Washington, type III (251)	9.00	.05	175.00	(6)		
280	4¢ rose brn. Lincoln (254)	30.00	.70	700.00	(6)		
281	5¢ dark blue Grant (255)	37.50	.65	800.00	(6)		
282	6¢ lake Garfield (256)	45.00	2.00	1,100.00	(6)		
282C	10¢ Webster, type I	160.00	2.00	3,250.00	(6)		
283	10¢ Webster, type II	100.00	1.75	1,800.00	(6)		
284	15¢ olive green Clay (259)	120.00	6.75	2,750.00	(6)		
	Trans-Mississippi Exposition Issue, June 17, Perf. 12						
285	1¢ Marquette on the Mississippi	30.00	5.50	265.00	(4)	5,250.00	70,993,400
286	2¢ Farming in the West	27.50	1.50	250.00	(4)	4,500.00	159,720,800
287	4¢ Indian Hunting Buffalo	150.00	22.50	1,500.00	(4)		4,924,500
288	5¢ Fremont on the Rocky Mts.	125.00	20.00	1,400.00	(4)	5,500.00	7,694,180
289	8¢ Troops Guarding Train	180.00	40.00	2,400.00	(4)	8,000.00	2,927,200
290	10¢ Hardships of Emigration	200.00	20.00	3,000.00	(4)		4,629,760
291	50¢ Western Mining Prospector	800.00	165.00	18,500.00	(4)	9,250.00	530,400
292	$1 Western Cattle in Storm	2,000.00	600.00	45,000.00	(4)		56,900
293	$2 Mississippi River Bridge						
	at St. Louis	3,000.00	825.00	90,000.00	(4)		56,200
	Pan-American Exposition Issue, 1901, May 1, Wmkd. 191						
294	1¢ Great Lakes Steamer	22.50	4.00	325.00	(6)	3,500.00	91,401,500
294a	Center inverted	11,000.00	3,000.00	48,500.00	(3)		
295	2¢ An Early Locomotive	22.50	1.10	325.00	(6)	3,000.00	209,759,700
295a	Center inverted	50,000.00	12,000.00				
296	4¢ Closed Coach Automobile	105.00	19.00	3,000.00	(6)	4,250.00	5,737,100
296a	Center inverted	14,000.00	—	75,000.00	(4)		
297	5¢ Bridge at Niagara Falls	120.00	20.00	3,250.00	(6)	4,500.00	7,201,300
298	8¢ Sault Ste. Marie Canal Locks	150.00	75.00	6,000.00	(6)		4,921,700
299	10¢ American Line Steamship	225.00	35.00	8,750.00	(6)		5,043,700

The Trans-Mississippi Commemoratives

Fifty years after the California Gold Rush, the Trans-Mississippi International Exposition was held in Omaha, Nebraska. It celebrated the exploration and settlement of America west of the Mississippi River. The Post Office used the occasion to issue its second set of commemoratives (#285-#293). Nine pictorial stamps were issued showing both the hardships and the wonders of western life.

These lovely stamps were all adapted from pre-existing artwork and were originally to be printed in two colors. But suddenly the Spanish-American war broke out. At the Bureau of Printing and Engraving, the presses were now needed to print revenue stamps for the war effort. To have the postage stamps ready at the opening of the Exposition, there was just time to print them in one color only. This last minute change was disappointing—yet the stamps themselves have always been prized by collectors for their great variety of subject matter and the exceptional quality of their artwork.

1898-1901

282C   283   285   286

287   288   289

290   291   292

293   294   294a   295

295a   296   296a   297

298   299

300   301   302   303   304

305   306   307   308   309   310

311   312   313   319

323   324   325   326

	Issue of 1902-03, Perf. 12, Wmkd. 191	Un	U	PB/LP	#	FDC	Q
300	1¢ Franklin, 1903	10.00	.05	185.00	(6)		
301	2¢ Washington, 1903	12.50	.05	200.00	(6)	2,750.00	
302	3¢ Jackson, 1903	55.00	3.00	1,100.00	(6)		
303	4¢ Grant, 1903	55.00	1.00	1,100.00	(6)		
304	5¢ Lincoln, 1903	65.00	1.00	1,250.00	(6)		
305	6¢ Garfield, 1903	70.00	2.25	1,250.00	(6)		
306	8¢ Martha Washington, 1902	40.00	2.00	875.00	(6)		
307	10¢ Webster, 1903	70.00	1.50	1,500.00	(6)		
308	13¢ Benjamin Harrison, 1902	40.00	8.50	700.00	(6)		
309	15¢ Clay, 1903	160.00	6.00	4,500.00	(6)		
310	50¢ Jefferson, 1903	525.00	25.00	9,500.00	(6)		
311	$1 David G. Farragut, 1903	900.00	55.00	18,500.00	(6)		
312	$2 Madison, 1903	1,200.00	175.00	27,500.00	(6)		
313	$5 Marshall, 1903	3,000.00	625.00	70,000.00	(6)		

For listings of 312 and 313 with Perf. 10, see Nos. 479 and 480.

	Issues of 1906-08, Imperf.						
314	1¢ blue green Franklin (300),-06	35.00	21.00	300.00	(6)		
314A	4¢ brown Grant (303), 1908	17,500.00	9,000.00				
315	5¢ blue Lincoln (304), 1908	650.00	300.00	5,750.00	(6)		

No. 314A was issued imperforate, but all copies were privately perforated with large oblong perforations at the sides. (Schermack type III).

	Coil Stamps, Perf. 12 Horizontally						
316	1¢ blue green pair						
	Franklin (300), 1908	22,500.00		55,000.00			
317	5¢ blue pair Lincoln (304),-08	4,500.00		6,750.00			
	Perf. 12 Vertically						
318	1¢ blue green pair Franklin						
	(300), 1908	3,500.00	—	5,250.00			
	Issue of 1903, Perf. 12, Shield-shaped Background						
319	2¢ Washington, Nov. 12	7.00	.05	125.00	(6)		
	Issue of 1906, Nos. 320-322; Washington (319), Imperf.						
320	2¢ carmine, Oct 2	32.50	20.00	350.00	(6)		
	Issue of 1908, Coil Stamps, Perf. 12, Horizontally						
321	2¢ carmine pair	35,000.00	—				
	Perf. 12 Vertically						
322	2¢ carmine pair	4,750.00	—	7,000.00			
	Issue of 1904, Perf. 12, Louisiana Purchase Exposition Issue, Apr. 30						
323	1¢ Robert R. Livingston	30.00	5.00	225.00	(4)	3,500.00	79,779,200
324	2¢ Thomas Jefferson	27.50	1.50	225.00	(4)	3,250.00	192,732,400
325	3¢ James Monroe	90.00	35.00	750.00	(4)	3,750.00	4,542,600
326	5¢ William McKinley	120.00	22.50	900.00	(4)	4,750.00	6,926,700

	1904 continued	Un	U	PB/LP	#	FDC	Q
327	10¢ Map of Louisiana Purchase	225.00	35.00	2,400.00	(4)	7,000.00	4,011,200
	Issue of 1907, Perf. 12, Jamestown Exposition Issue						
328	1¢ Captain John Smith	22.50	4.00	325.00	(6)	2,500.00	77,728,794
329	2¢ Founding of Jamestown	30.00	2.50	475.00	(6)	2,750.00	149,497,994
330	5¢ Pocahontas	130.00	27.50	3,500.00	(6)		7,980,594
	Regular Issues of 1908-09, Perf. 12, Wmkd. 191						
331	1¢ Franklin, 1908	8.00	.05	90.00	(6)		
331a	Booklet pane of 6	150.00	35.00				
332	2¢ Washington, 1908	7.50	.05	80.00	(6)		
332a	Booklet pane of 6	120.00	35.00				
333	3¢ Washington, type I, 1908	27.50	3.00	350.00	(6)		
	Nos. 334-342; Washington (333)						
334	4¢ orange brown, 1908	30.00	1.00	400.00	(6)		
335	5¢ blue, 1908	40.00	2.00	650.00	(6)		
336	6¢ red orange, 1908	50.00	4.50	1,000.00	(6)		
337	8¢ olive green, 1908	32.50	2.50	550.00	(6)		
338	10¢ yellow, 1909	65.00	1.50	1,150.00	(6)		
339	13¢ blue green, 1909	35.00	22.50	550.00	(6)		
340	15¢ pale ultramarine, 1909	60.00	5.75	750.00	(6)		
341	50¢ violet, 1909	325.00	15.00	8,000.00	(6)		
342	$1 violet brown, 1909	500.00	85.00	12,000.00	(6)		
	Imperf.						
343	1¢ green Franklin (331), 1908	8.00	3.50	90.00	(6)		
344	2¢ car. Washington (332), 1908	11.00	3.00	170.00	(6)		
	Nos. 345-347; Washington (333)						
345	3¢ deep violet, type I, 1909	22.50	13.50	300.00	(6)		
346	4¢ orange brown, 1909	40.00	20.00	450.00	(6)		
347	5¢ blue, 1909	60.00	35.00	750.00	(6)		
	Coil Stamps of 1908-10						
	Nos. 350-351, 354-356: Washington (333), Perf. 12 Horizontally						
348	1¢ green Franklin (331), 1908	22.50	12.00	175.00			
349	2¢ car. Washington (332), 1909	45.00	5.50	225.00			
350	4¢ orange brown, 1910	110.00	57.50	750.00			
351	5¢ blue, 1909	130.00	75.00	750.00			
	1909, Perf. 12 Vertically						
352	1¢ green Franklin (331), 1909	55.00	17.50	250.00			
353	2¢ car. Washington (332), 1909	45.00	5.50	250.00			
354	4¢ orange brown, 1909	120.00	45.00	130.00			
355	5¢ blue, 1909	130.00	65.00	1,200.00			
356	10¢ yellow, 1909	1,200.00	350.00	7,250.00			
	Issues of 1909, Bluish Paper, Perf. 12						
	Nos. 359-366: Washington (333)						
357	1¢ green Franklin (331)	110.00	100.00	1,250.00	(6)		
358	2¢ car. Washington (332)	100.00	75.00	1,250.00	(6)		

1904-1910

327   328   329   330

331   332   333   334

335   336   337   338   342

1909-1913

367 368 370 371

372 373

	1909 continued	Un	U	PB/LP	#	FDC	Q
359	3¢ deep violet, type I	1,450.00	1,000.00	16,500.00	(6)		
360	4¢ orange brown	14,000.00	—	60,000.00	(3)		
361	5¢ blue	3,500.00	4,000.00	35,000.00	(6)		
362	6¢ red orange	950.00	600.00	11,000.00	(6)		
363	8¢ olive green	14,000.00	—	55,000.00	(3)		
364	10¢ yellow	975.00	650.00	12,000.00	(6)		
365	13¢ blue green	2,000.00	1,000.00	18,500.00	(6)		
366	15¢ pale ultramarine	950.00	650.00	10,000.00	(6)		
	Lincoln Memorial Issue, Feb. 12						
367	2¢ Lincoln, Perf. 12	8.50	2.75	200.00	(6)	350.00	148,387,191
368	2¢ Lincoln, Imperf.	40.00	30.00	375.00	(6)	1,900.00	1,273,900
369	2¢ Lincoln, Perf. 12, Bluish Paper	300.00	175.00	4,750.00	(6)		637,000
	Alaska-Yukon Exposition Issue						
370	2¢ William Seward, Perf. 12	13.00	2.25	325.00	(6)	1,800.00	152,887,311
371	2¢ William Seward, Imperf.	55.00	35.00	450.00	(6)		525,400
	Hudson-Fulton Celebration Issue, Sep. 25						
372	2¢ Half Moon and Clermont, Perf. 12	16.00	4.75	375.00	(6)	950.00	72,634,631
373	2¢ Half Moon and Clermont, Imperf.	60.00	35.00	600.00	(6)	2,350.00	216,480
	Issues of 1910-13, Perf. 12, Wmkd. 190						
	Nos. 376-382: Washington (333)						
374	1¢ green Franklin (331), 1910	7.50	.06	95.00	(6)		
374a	Booklet pane of 6	135.00	30.00				
375	2¢ car. Washington (332), 1910	7.00	.05	85.00	(6)		
375a	Booklet pane of 6	110.00	25.00				
376	3¢ deep violet, type I, 1911	17.50	1.50	185.00	(6)		
377	4¢ brown, 1911	25.00	.50	250.00	(6)		
378	5¢ blue, 1911	25.00	.50	285.00	(6)		
379	6¢ red orange, 1911	35.00	.75	525.00	(6)		
380	8¢ olive green, 1911	115.00	12.50	2,000.00	(6)		
381	10¢ yellow, 1911	105.00	4.00	1,450.00	(6)		
382	15¢ pale ultramarine, 1911	250.00	15.00	3,000.00	(6)		
	Imperf.						
383	1¢ green Franklin (331), 1911	4.00	3.00	85.00	(6)		
384	2¢ car. Washington (332), 1911	6.00	1.50	250.00	(6)		
	Coil Stamps, Perf. 12 Horizontally						
385	1¢ green Franklin (331), 1910	25.00	12.00	200.00			
386	2¢ car. Washington (332), 1910	37.50	10.00	325.00			
	Perf. 12 Vertically						
387	1¢ green Franklin (331), 1910	75.00	20.00	325.00			
388	2¢ car. Washington (332), 1910	550.00	70.00	3,750.00			
389	3¢ dp. vio. Washington,						
	type I (333), 1911	12,000.00	4,250.00	—			
	Perf. 8½ Horizontally						
390	1¢ green Franklin (331), 1910	4.50	2.75	27.50			

	1910-13 continued	Un	U	PB/LP	#	FDC	Q
391	2¢ car. Washington (332), 1910	32.50	7.50	*200.00*			
	Perf. 8½ Vertically, Nos. 394-396; Washington (333)						
392	1¢ green Franklin (331), 1910	20.00	14.00	*110.00*			
393	2¢ car. Washington (332), 1910	40.00	5.00	*200.00*			
394	3¢ deep violet, type I, 1911	50.00	25.00	*325.00*			
395	4¢ brown, 1912	50.00	25.00	*325.00*			
396	5¢ blue, 1913	50.00	25.00	*325.00*			
	Panama Pacific Exposition Issue, 1913, Perf. 12						
397	1¢ Balboa	20.00	1.75	190.00	(6)	*3,500.00*	167,398,463
398	2¢ Locks, Panama Canal	22.50	.50	*375.00*	(6)		251,856,543
399	5¢ Golden Gate	90.00	11.00	2,900.00	(6)	*4,500.00*	14,544,363
400	10¢ Discovery						
	of San Francisco Bay	165.00	25.00	4,000.00	(6)		8,484,182
400A	10¢ orange (400)	275.00	18.50	*11,500.00*	(6)		
	1914-15, Perf. 10						
401	1¢ green Balboa (397), 1914	30.00	6.50	450.00	(6)		167,398,463
402	2¢ carmine Canal Locks (398),-15	95.00	1.50	2,500.00	(6)		251,856,543
403	5¢ blue Golden Gate (399),-15	210.00	17.50	5,750.00	(6)		14,544,363
404	10¢ orange Discovery of						
	San Francisco Bay (400), 1915	1,550.00	72.50	*19,000.00*	(6)		8,484,182
	Issues of 1912-14						
	Nos. 405-413: Washington (333), Perf. 12						
405	1¢ green, 1912	7.00	.06	115.00	(6)		
405b	Booklet pane of 6	65.00	7.50				
406	2¢ carmine, type I, 1912	6.00	.05	140.00	(6)		
406a	Booklet pane of 6	70.00	17.50				
407	7¢ black, 1914	100.00	7.00	1,500.00	(6)		
408	1¢ green, Imperf., 1912	1.50	.60	30.00	(6)		
409	2¢ carmine, type I, Imperf., 1912	1.65	.60	60.00	(6)		
	Coil Stamps, Perf. 8½ Horizontally						
410	1¢ green, 1912	6.25	3.00	35.00			
411	2¢ carmine, type I, 1912	7.75	3.25	42.50			
	Perf. 8½ Vertically						
412	1¢ green, 1912	21.00	5.00	90.00			
413	2¢ carmine, type I, 1912	35.00	.50	200.00			
	Perf. 12, Nos. 415-421; Franklin (414)						
414	8¢ Franklin, 1912	35.00	1.25	575.00	(6)		
415	9¢ salmon red, 1914	47.50	13.50	850.00	(6)		
416	10¢ orange yellow, 1912	35.00	.30	650.00	(6)		
417	12¢ claret brown, 1914	37.50	4.00	550.00	(6)		
418	15¢ gray, 1912	75.00	3.00	825.00	(6)		
419	20¢ ultramarine, 1914	175.00	15.00	2,350.00	(6)		
420	30¢ orange red, 1914	120.00	15.00	2,150.00	(6)		

1910-1915

397 398 399 400

405 406 414 420

1912-1916

	1912-14 continued	Un	U	PB/LP	#	FDC		Q
421	50¢ violet, 1914	525.00	15.00	10,000.00	(6)			
	Nos. 422-423: Franklin (414), Perf. 12							
422	50¢ violet, Feb. 12, 1912	275.00	15.00	6,750.00	(6)			
423	$1 violet brown, Feb. 12, 1912							
	Wmkd. 191	625.00	70.00	*12,500.00*	(6)			
	Issues of 1914-15, Perf. 10, Wmkd. 190							
	Nos. 424-430: Washington (333)							
424	1¢ green, 1914	3.00	.06	60.00	(6)			
424d	Booklet pane of 6	4.00	.75					
425	2¢ rose red, type I, 1914	2.75	.05	40.00	(6)			
425e	Booklet pane of 6	15.00	3.00					
426	3¢ deep violet, type I, 1914	12.50	1.25	150.00	(6)			
427	4¢ brown, 1914	32.50	.40	450.00	(6)			
428	5¢ blue, 1914	27.50	.40	350.00	(6)			
429	6¢ red orange, 1914	37.50	1.20	325.00	(6)			
430	7¢ black, 1914	90.00	4.25	1,050.00	(6)			
	Nos. 431-440: Franklin (414)							
431	8¢ pale olive green, 1914	35.00	1.50	400.00	(6)			
432	9¢ salmon red, 1914	47.50	7.50	575.00	(6)			
433	10¢ orange yellow, 1914	45.00	.25	625.00	(6)			
434	11¢ dark green, 1915	20.00	5.50	200.00	(6)			
435	12¢ claret brown, 1914	22.50	3.75	250.00	(6)			
437	15¢ gray, 1914	125.00	6.25	900.00	(6)			
438	20¢ ultramarine, 1914	250.00	3.50	3,200.00	(6)			
439	30¢ orange red, 1914	300.00	12.00	4,850.00	(6)			
440	50¢ violet, 1914	850.00	15.00	11,500.00	(6)			
	Coil Stamps, Perf. 10, 1914							
441	1¢ green	1.00	.75	*7.50*				
442	2¢ carmine, type I	10.00	6.50	55.00				
443	1¢ green	22.50	5.00	110.00				
444	2¢ carmine, type I	35.00	1.00	175.00				
445	3¢ violet, type I	225.00	100.00	1,200.00				
446	4¢ brown	140.00	32.50	650.00				
447	5¢ blue	47.50	20.00	225.00				
	Coil Stamps, Washington (333), 1915-16, Perf. 10 Horizontally							
448	1¢ green, 1915	6.50	2.75	45.00				
449	2¢ red, type I, 1915	1,500.00	130.00	7,000.00				
450	2¢ carmine, type III, 1916	12.00	2.75	75.00				
	1914-16, Perf. 10 Vertically							
452	1¢ green, 1914	10.00	1.50	80.00				
453	2¢ red, type I, 1914	120.00	3.75	700.00				

		Un	U	PB/LP	#	FDC	Q
	Coil Stamps, 1914-16 Issues, continued						
454	2¢ carmine, type II, 1915	125.00	13.50	800.00			
455	2¢ carmine, type III, 1915	11.00	.85	85.00			
456	3¢ violet, type I, 1916	300.00	85.00	1,250.00			
457	4¢ brown	32.50	15.00	60.00			
458	5¢ blue	32.50	15.00	185.00			
	Issue of 1914 Washington (333), Imperf., Coil						
459	2¢ carmine, type I, June 30	475.00	*600.00*	2,850.00			
	Issues of 1915, Perf. 10, Wmkd. 191						
460	$1 violet black Franklin						
	(414), Feb. 8	950.00	85.00	13,500.00	(6)		
	Perf. 11						
461	2¢ pale carmine red, type I.						
	Washington (333), June 17	90.00	80.00	1,000.00	(6)		
	Privately perforated copies of No. 409 have been made to resemble No. 461.						
	From 1916 all postage stamps except Nos. 519 and 832b are on unwatermarked paper.						
	Issues of 1916-17, Perf. 10						
	Nos. 462-469: Washington (333)						
462	1¢ green, 1916	7.50	.20	160.00	(6)		
462a	Booklet pane of 6	12.00	*1.00*				
463	2¢ carmine, type I, 1916	4.25	.10	110.00	(6)		
463a	Booklet pane of 6	75.00	*15.00*				
464	3¢ violet, type I, 1916	90.00	11.00	1,600.00	(6)		
465	4¢ orange brown, 1916	45.00	1.50	850.00	(6)		
466	5¢ blue, 1916	80.00	1.40	1,100.00	(6)		
467	5¢ car. (error in plate of 2¢), 1917	800.00	525.00	135.00	(6)		
468	6¢ red orange, 1916	95.00	7.50	1,150.00	(6)		
469	7¢ black, 1916	125.00	12.00	1,500.00	(6)		
470	8¢ olive green, 1916	50.00	5.00	600.00	(6)		
471	9¢ salmon red, 1916	57.50	15.00	700.00	(6)		
472	10¢ orange yellow, 1916	110.00	1.00	1,600.00	(6)		
473	11¢ dark green, 1916	27.50	15.00	325.00	(6)		
474	12¢ claret brown, 1916	47.50	4.25	600.00	(6)		
475	15¢ gray, 1916	175.00	10.00	2,500.00	(6)		
476	20¢ light ultramarine, 1916	275.00	11.00	3,750.00	(6)		
477	50¢ light violet, 1917	1,500.00	67.50	*25,000.00*	(6)		
478	$1 violet black, 1916	950.00	15.00	*13,500.00*	(6)		
	Issues of 1917, Perf. 10, Mar. 22						
479	$2 dark blue Madison (312), 1917	550.00	40.00	6,500.00	(6)		
480	$5 light green Marshall (313), 1917	450.00	42.50	5,250.00	(6)		

		Un	U	PB/LP	#	FDC	Q
	Issues of 1916-17, Washington (333), Imperf.						
481	1¢ green, 1916	1.10	.75	16.50	(6)		
482	2¢ carmine, type I, 1916	1.50	1.50	32.50	(6)		
483	3¢ violet, type I, 1917	18.00	8.50	200.00	(6)		
484	3¢ violet, type II, 1917	12.00	4.00	150.00	(6)		
485	5¢ carmine (2¢ error), 1917			250.00	(6)		
	Coil Stamps, Washington (333), 1916-19, Perf. 10 Horizontally						
486	1¢ green, 1918	1.00	.15	4.50			
487	2¢ carmine, type II, 1919	20.00	2.50	165.00			
488	2¢ carmine, type III, 1917	3.50	1.50	30.00			
489	3¢ violet, type I, 1917	5.50	1.00	42.50			
	1916-22, Perf. 10 Vertically						
490	1¢ green, 1916	.75	.15	4.75			
491	2¢ carmine, type II, 1916	1,450.00	185.00	7,000.00			
492	2¢ carmine, type III, 1916	10.00	.15	60.00			
493	3¢ violet, type I, 1917	22.50	3.00	160.00			
494	3¢ violet, type II,1918	12.50	.60	100.00			
495	4¢ orange brown, 1917	12.50	3.50	100.00			
496	5¢ blue, 1919	4.50	.60	30.00			
497	10¢ or. yel. Franklin (414), 1912	26.50	8.50	150.00		1,350.00	
	Issues of 1917-19, Perf. 11						
	Nos. 498-507: Washington (333)						
498	1¢ green, 1917	.25	.05	18.00	(6)		
498e	Booklet pane of 6	1.75	.35				
499	2¢ rose, type I, 1917	.25	.05	14.00	(6)		
499e	Booklet pane of 6	2.00	.50				
500	2¢ deep rose, type Ia, 1917	275.00	120.00	2,500.00	(6)		
501	3¢ light violet, type I, 1917	15.00	.10	190.00	(6)		
501b	Booklet pane of 6	75.00	15.00				
502	3¢ dark violet, type II, 1917	18.50	.25	250.00	(6)		
502b	Booklet pane of 6, 1918	50.00	10.00				
503	4¢ brown, 1917	13.00	.20	200.00	(6)		
504	5¢ blue, 1917	9.00	.08	165.00	(6)		
505	5¢ rose (error in plate of 2¢),-17	550.00	400.00	35.00	(6)		
506	6¢ red orange, 1917	15.00	.30	250.00	(6)		
507	7¢ black, 1917	32.50	1.20	375.00	(6)		
	Nos. 508-518: Franklin (414)						
508	8¢ olive bistre, 1917	13.50	.70	250.00	(6)		
509	9¢ salmon red, 1917	17.50	2.25	250.00	(6)		

1917-1920

	1917-19 continued	Un	U	PB/LB	#	FDC	Q
510	10¢ orange yellow, 1917	20.00	.10	300.00	(6)		
511	11¢ light green, 1917	10.00	3.25	150.00	(6)		
512	12¢ claret brown, 1917	10.50	.45	150.00	(6)		
513	13¢ apple green, 1919	13.00	7.00	150.00	(6)		
514	15¢ gray, 1917	47.50	1.00	800.00	(6)		
515	20¢ light ultramarine, 1917	60.00	.30	875.00	(6)		
516	30¢ orange red, 1917	50.00	.95	750.00	(6)		
517	50¢ red violet, 1917	100.00	.65	1,750.00	(6)		
518	$1 violet brown, 1917	85.00	1.75	1,300.00	(6)		
	Issue of 1917, Perf. 11, Wmkd. 191						
519	2¢ carmine Washington						
	(332), Oct. 10	250.00	225.00	2,500.00	(6)		
	Privately perforated copies of No. 344 have been made to resemble No. 519.						
	Issues of 1918, Unwmkd., Perf. 11						
523	$2 orange red and black						
	Franklin (547), Aug. 19	1,300.00	175.00	*22,500.00*	(8)		
524	$5 deep green and black						
	Franklin (547), Aug. 19	500.00	25.00	*8,500.00*	(8)		
	Issues of 1918-20, Washington (333)						
	Perf. 11						
525	1¢ gray green, 1918	225.00	.60	35.00	(6)		
526	2¢ carmine, type IV, 1920	30.00	4.00	250.00	(6)	825.00	
527	2¢ carmine, type V, 1920	17.50	1.00	160.00	(6)		
528	2¢ carmine, type Va, 1920	9.00	.15	65.00	(6)		
528A	2¢ carmine, type VI, 1920	45.00	1.00	375.00	(6)		
528B	2¢ carmine, type VII, 1920	20.00	.12	170.00	(6)		
529	3¢ violet, type III, 1918	2.25	.10	60.00	(6)		
530	3¢ purple, type IV, 1918	.70	.06	15.00	(6)		
	Imperf.						
531	1¢ green, 1919	10.00	8.00	100.00	(6)		
532	2¢ car. rose, type IV, 1919	40.00	25.00	350.00	(6)		
533	2¢ carmine, type V, 1919	275.00	65.00	2,500.00	(6)		
534	2¢ carmine, type Va, 1919	13.50	9.00	130.00	(6)		
534A	2¢ carmine, type VI, 1919	40.00	25.00	400.00	(6)		
534B	2¢ carmine, type VII, 1919	1,750.00	425.00	*14,500.00*	(6)		
535	3¢ violet, type IV, 1918	10.00	6.50	90.00	(6)		
	Issues of 1919						
	Perf. 12½						
536	1¢ gray green Washington						
	(333), Aug. 15	15.00	12.50	200.00	(6)		

	1919 continued	Un	U	PB/LP	#	FDC	Q
	Perf. 11						
537	3¢ Allied Victory, Mar. 3	12.50	4.25	175.00	(6)	*700.00*	99,585,200
	Nos. 538-546: Washington (333), 1919, Perf. 11x10						
538	1¢ green	10.00	9.00	100.00	(4)		
539	2¢ carmine rose, type II	2,150.00	675.00	15,000.00	(4)		
540	2¢ carmine rose, type III	11.00	9.00	110.00	(4)		
541	3¢ violet, type II	37.50	35.00	450.00	(4)		
	1920, Perf. 10x11						
542	1¢ green, May 26	6.50	1.00	135.00	(6)	*525.00*	
	1921, Perf. 10						
543	1¢ green	.50	.06	20.00	(4)		
	1921, Perf. 11						
544	1¢ green, 19x22½mm	*6,500.00*	*1,500.00*				
545	1¢ green, 19½—20mmx22mm	150.00	90.00	1,100.00	(4)		
546	2¢ carmine rose, type III	100.00	70.00	900.00	(4)		
	Issues of 1920, Perf. 11						
547	$2 Franklin	450.00	35.00	*9,500.00*	(8)		
	Pilgrims 300th Anniv. Issue, Dec. 21						
548	1¢ Mayflower	6.50	3.00	80.00	(6)	*700.00*	137,978,207
549	2¢ Pilgrims Landing	10.00	2.25	110.00	(6)	*625.00*	196,037,327
550	5¢ Signing of Compact	60.00	18.50	900.00	(6)		11,321,607
	Issues of 1922-25, Perf. 11						
551	½¢ Nathan Hale, 1925	.15	.05	8.50	(6)	*25.00*	
552	1¢ Franklin (19x22mm), 1923	2.50	.07	35.00	(6)	*37.50*	
552a	Booklet pane of 6	5.50	*.50*				
553	1½¢ Harding, 1925	4.00	.20	55.00	(6)	*40.00*	
554	2¢ Washington, 1923	2.00	.05	35.00	(6)	*50.00*	
554c	Booklet pane of 6	7.00	*1.00*				
555	3¢ Lincoln, 1923	22.50	1.25	300.00	(6)	*42.50*	
556	4¢ Martha Washington, 1923	22.50	.20	300.00	(6)	*55.00*	
557	5¢ Theodore Roosevelt, 1922	22.50	.06	325.00	(6)	*110.00*	
558	6¢ Garfield, 1922	42.50	.85	600.00	(6)	*200.00*	
559	7¢ McKinley, 1923	10.00	.75	95.00	(6)	*110.00*	
560	8¢ Grant, 1923	55.00	.85	1,100.00	(6)	*110.00*	
561	9¢ Jefferson, 1923	17.00	1.25	250.00	(6)	*110.00*	
562	10¢ Monroe, 1923	23.50	.10	425.00	(6)	*110.00*	
563	11¢ Rutherford B. Hayes, 1922	2.25	.25	60.00	(6)	*550.00*	
564	12¢ Grover Cleveland, 1923	9.00	.08	100.00	(6)	*150.00*	
565	14¢ American Indian, 1923	6.00	.85	85.00	(6)	*350.00*	
566	15¢ Statue of Liberty, 1922	24.00	.06	325.00	(6)	*350.00*	
567	20¢ Golden Gate, 1923	27.50	.06	*325.00*	(6)	*400.00*	
568	25¢ Niagara Falls, 1922	27.50	.50	325.00	(6)	*600.00*	
569	30¢ Buffalo, 1923	45.00	.35	500.00	(6)	*700.00*	

1919-1925

 537

 547

 548

 549

 550

 551

 552

553

554

555

 556

 557

558

 559

560

 561

 562

 563

 564

 565

 566

 567

 568

 569

79

570   571   572   573

610   611

	1922-25 continued	Un	U	PB/LP	#	FDC	Q
570	50¢ Arlington Amphitheater, 1922	80.00	.12	1,450.00	(6)	900.00	
571	$1 Lincoln Memorial, 1923	60.00	.45	600.00	(6)	4,250.00	
572	$2 U.S. Capitol, 1923	175.00	9.50	2,000.00	(6)	8,500.00	
573	$5 Head of Freedom, Capitol Dome, 1923	425.00	15.00	6,500.00	(8)	11,000.00	
	Issues of 1923-25, Imperf.						
575	1¢ green Franklin (552), 1923	11.00	3.50	145.00	(6)		
576	1½¢ yel. brown Harding (553),-25	2.50	1.75	45.00	(6)	50.00	
577	2¢ carmine Washington (554)	3.00	2.00	40.00	(6)		

For listings of other perforated stamps of issues 551-573 see:

Nos. 578 and 579	Perf. 11x10	
Nos. 581 to 591	Perf. 10	
Nos. 594 and 595	Perf. 11	
Nos. 622 and 623	Perf. 11	
Nos. 632 to 642, 653, 692 to 696	Perf. 11x10½	
Nos. 697 to 701	Perf. 10½x11	

	Perf. 11x10				
578	1¢ green Franklin (552)	80.00	65.00	850.00	(4)
579	2¢ carmine Washington (554)	57.50	50.00	450.00	(4)

	Issues of 1923-26, Perf. 10	Un	U	PB/LP	#	FDC	Q
581	1¢ green Franklin (552), 1923	7.00	.65	120.00	(4)	2,000.00	
582	1½¢ brown Harding (553), 1925	5.00	.60	45.00	(4)	52.50	
583	2¢ carmine Washington (554), 1924	2.50	.05	30.00	(4)		
583a	Booklet pane of 6	75.00	25.00				
584	3¢ violet Lincoln (555), 1925	30.00	1.75	325.00	(4)	62.50	
585	4¢ yellow brown						
	M. Washington (556)	17.00	.40	200.00	(4)		
586	5¢ blue T. Roosevelt (557), 1925	16.00	.18	200.00	(4)	62.50	
587	6¢ red orange Garfield (558), 1925	9.00	.40	65.00	(4)	77.50	
588	7¢ black McKinley (559), 1926	11.50	5.00	120.00	(4)	75.00	
589	8¢ olive green Grant (560), 1926	30.00	3.00	325.00	(4)	80.00	
590	9¢ rose Jefferson (561), 1926	5.50	2.25	45.00	(4)	85.00	
591	10¢ orange Monroe (562), 1925	65.00	.06	750.00	(4)	110.00	
	Perf. 11						
594	1¢ green Franklin,						
	19¾x22¼mm (552)	7,000.00	1,850.00				
595	2¢ carmine Washington,						
	19¾x22¼mm (554)	200.00	150.00	1,750.00	(4)		
596	1¢ green Franklin,						
	19¼x22¾mm (552)	—	13,500.00				
	Coil Stamps 1923-29, Perf. 10 Vertically						
597	1¢ green Franklin (552), 1923	.35	.06	2.25		450.00	
598	1½ ¢ brown Harding (553), 1925	.75	.10	5.25		60.00	
599	2¢ carmine Washington,						
	type I (554), 1929	.30	.05	2.00		750.00	
599A	2¢ carmine Washington,						
	type II (554), 1929	140.00	10.00	800.00			
600	3¢ violet Lincoln (555)	8.00	.08	40.00		80.00	
601	4¢ yellow brown						
	M. Washington (556), 1923	4.00	.40	30.00			
602	5¢ dark blue						
	Theodore Roosevelt (557), 1924	1.50	.18	10.00		85.00	
603	10¢ orange Monroe (562), 1924	4.00	.08	27.50		105.00	
	Coil Stamps 1923-25 Perf. 10 Horizontally						
604	1¢ yel. grn. Franklin (552), 1924	.25	.08	3.50		95.00	
605	1½¢ yel. brn. Harding (553), 1925	.30	.15	2.50		60.00	
606	2¢ carmine Washington (554), 1923	.30	.12	2.00		90.00	
	Harding Memorial Issue, 1923, Flat Plate Printing (19¼x22¼mm)						
610	2¢ Harding, Perf. 11, Sept. 1	.85	.10	40.00	(6)	40.00	1,459,487,085
611	2¢ Harding Imperf., Nov. 15	15.00	6.00	185.00	(6)	100.00	770,000
	Rotary Press Printing (19¼x22¾mm)						
612	2¢ black, Perf. 10 (610), Sept. 12	25.00	2.50	425.00	(4)	110.00	99,950,300
613	2¢ black Perf. 11 (610)	—	13,500.00				

		Un	U	PB/LP	#	FDC	Q
	Huguenot-Walloon 300th Anniv. Issue, 1924, May 1						
614	1¢ Ship *New Netherland*	5.50	5.00	65.00	(6)	40.00	51,378,023
615	2¢ Landing at Fort Orange	9.50	3.50	115.00	(6)	55.00	77,753,423
616	5¢ Huguenot Monument, Florida	55.00	22.50	575.00	(6)	100.00	5,659,023
	Lexington-Concord Issue, 1925, Apr. 4						
617	1¢ Washington at Cambridge	5.50	5.50	60.00	(6)	40.00	15,615,000
618	2¢ Birth of Liberty	10.00	7.50	125.00	(6)	50.00	26,596,600
619	5¢ Statue of Minute Man	50.00	20.00	450.00	(6)	90.00	5,348,800
	Norse-American Issue, 1925, May 18						
620	2¢ Sloop *Restaurationen*	9.00	5.00	325.00	(8)	32.50	9,104,983
621	5¢ Viking Ship	30.00	22.50	1,000.00	(8)	55.00	1,900,983
	Issues of 1925-26						
622	13¢ Benjamin Harrison, 1926	20.00	.65	250.00	(6)	35.00	
623	17¢ Woodrow Wilson, 1925	27.50	.35	275.00	(6)	35.00	
	Issues of 1926						
627	2¢ Independence,						
	150th Anniv., May 10	4.25	.60	70.00	(6)	17.50	307,731,900
628	5¢ Ericsson Memorial, May 29	11.00	5.00	120.00	(6)	30.00	20,280,500
629	2¢ Battle of White Plains, Oct. 18	2.75	2.25	70.00	(6)	7.00	40,639,485

Huguenots and Walloons in America

In 1624, a Dutch ship, the New Netherland (#614), brought 30 families of French-speaking Protestants to the young colonies in North America. They called themselves Walloons and most of them settled in the Dutch colony of New Netherlands, in what is now New York state. Their settlement near Fort Orange (#615) later became Albany, New York.

The Walloons thrived in the atmosphere of religious tolerance of the Dutch colony. In fact, the colony's first governor was a Walloon—Peter Minuit, who purchased Manhattan from the Indians in 1626. The Walloons continued as a distinct French-speaking group for many years, making up about half of Manhattan's population.

That, however, wasn't the first time French Protestants had sought freedom in the New World. In 1562, a group called the Huguenots had built a settlement on the St. John's River in Florida. Almost immediately, however, the settlers fell into bitter disagreements. Some left to start a short-lived settlement in South Carolina. Those who remained continued to fight among themselves. Many refused to work, and some began to abuse their Indian neighbors. Hunger and disease wracked the colony. Finally the Spaniards, who claimed Florida as their own territory, decided to remove this French presence. A Spanish army destroyed the Huguenot settlement and killed all of its inhabitants.

In May, 1924, the Daughters of the American Revolution erected a monument to the Huguenots at Mayport, Florida, and the Post Office used the occasion to memorialize these early colonizing efforts in their Huguenot-Walloon Tercentenary Issue (#614-#616).

1924-1926

614   615   616

617   618   619

620   621   622   623

627   629

628

83

631

633

643

644

645

646

647

648

649

650

		Un	U	PB/LP	#	FDC	Q
1926 continued							
International Philatelic Exhibition Issue, Oct. 18, Souvenir Sheet							
630	2¢ car. rose, sheet of 25 with						107,398
	selvage inscription (629)	525.00	425.00			1,500.00	
	Imperf.						
631	1½¢ Harding Aug. 27, 18½	2.50	2.10	80.00	(4)	40.00	
	Issues of 1926-27, Perf. 11x10½						
632	1¢ green Franklin (552), 1927	.15	.05	3.00	(4)	60.00	
632a	Booklet pane of 6, 1927	2.50	.25				
633	1½¢ Harding, 1927	2.75	.08	110.00	(4)	60.00	
634	2¢ carmine Washington, type I						
	(554) 1956	.15	.05	1.20	(4)	62.50	
634d	Booklet pane of 6, 1927	1.00	.15				
634A	2¢ carmine Washington, type II						
	(554) 1926	375.00	22.50	2,500.00	(4)		
635	3¢ violet Lincoln (555), 1934	.55	.05	9.00	(4)	52.50	
636	4¢ yellow brown						
	M. Washington (556), 1927	4.25	.08	140.00	(4)	60.00	
637	5¢ dark blue T. Roosevelt (557),-27	3.50	.05	25.00	(4)	60.00	
638	6¢ red orange Garfield (558), 1927	3.50	.05	25.00	(4)	72.50	
639	7¢ black McKinley (559), 1927	3.50	.08	25.00	(4)	75.00	
640	8¢ olive green, Grant (560), 1927	3.50	.05	25.00	(4)	77.50	
641	9¢ orange red Jefferson						
	(561), 1927	3.50	.05	25.00	(4)	95.00	
642	10¢ orange Monroe (562), 1927	5.75	.05	42.50	(4)	100.00	
	Issues of 1927, Perf. 11						
643	2¢ Vermont 150th Anniversary,						
	Aug. 3	1.65	1.65	60.00	(6)	5.00	39,974,900
644	2¢ Burgoyne Campaign, Aug. 3	5.50	3.75	85.00	(6)	20.00	25,628,450
	Issues of 1928						
645	2¢ Valley Forge, May 26	1.25	.65	65.00	(6)	5.00	101,330,328
	Perf. 11x10½						
646	2¢ Battle of Monmouth, Oct. 20	1.50	1.50	70.00	(4)	22.50	9,779,896
647	2¢ carmine , Aug. 13	7.00	6.00	200.00	(4)	22.50	5,519,897
648	5¢ Hawaii 150th Anniv., Aug. 13	21.00	20.00	400.00	(4)	40.00	1,459,897
	Aeronautics Conference Issue, Dec. 12, Perf.11						
649	2¢ Wright Airplane	1.50	1.40	22.50	(6)	12.00	51,342,273
650	5¢ Globe and Airplane	8.50	5.00	110.00	(6)	18.00	10,319,700
	Issues of 1929						
651	2¢ George Rogers Clark, Feb. 25	.85	.80	20.00	(6)	7.00	16,684,674
	Perf. 11x10½						
653	½¢ olive brown Nathan Hale (551)	.05	.05	1.00	(4)	30.00	
	Electric Light Jubilee Issue, Perf. 11						
654	2¢ Edison's First Lamp, June 5	1.00	1.00	50.00	(6)	11.00	31,679,200
	Perf. 11x10½						
655	2¢ carmine rose (654), June 11	.90	.25	75.00	(4)	77.50	210,119,474

	1929 continued	Un	U	PB/LP	#	FDC	Q
	Coil Stamp, Perf. 10 Vertically						
656	2¢ carmine rose (654), June 11	20.00	2.00	90.00		100.00	133,530,000
	Perf. 11						
657	2¢ Sullivan Expedition, June 17	1.00	.90	45.00	(6)	4.50	51,451,880
	Regular Issue of 1929						
	Perf. 11x10½, 658-668 Overprinted Kans.						
658	1¢ green Franklin	2.50	1.65	35.00	(4)	27.50	13,390,000
659	1½¢ brown Harding (553)	3.50	3.00	55.00	(4)	27.50	8,240,000
660	2¢ carmine Washington (554)	3.50	.65	55.00	(4)	27.50	87,410,000
661	3¢ violet Lincoln (555)	18.50	12.00	200.00	(4)	30.00	2,540,000
662	4¢ yellow brown						
	M. Washington (556)	18.50	7.50	185.00	(4)	32.50	2,290,000
663	5¢ deep blue T. Roosevelt (557)	14.00	9.00	200.00	(4)	35.00	2,700,000
664	6¢ red orange Garfield (558)	28.50	17.50	550.00	(4)	42.50	1,450,000
665	7¢ black McKinley (559)	30.00	22.50	450.00	(4)	42.50	1,320,000
666	8¢ olive green Grant (560)	85.00	72.50	850.00	(4)	80.00	1,530,000
667	9¢ light rose Jefferson (561)	14.00	11.00	225.00	(4)	72.50	1,130,000
668	10¢ orange yellow Monroe (562)	23.50	11.00	425.00	(4)	85.00	2,860,000
	669-679 Overprinted Nebr.						
669	1¢ green Franklin	2.50	2.00	35.00	(4)	27.50	8,220,000
670	1½¢ brown Harding (553)	3.25	2.25	50.00	(4)	25.00	8,990,000
671	2¢ carmine Washington (554)	2.25	.85	35.00	(4)	25.00	73,220,000
672	3¢ violet Lincoln (555)	12.50	8.75	200.00	(4)	32.50	2,110,000
673	4¢ yellow brown						
	M. Washington (556)	18.50	11.00	225.00	(4)	37.50	1,600,000
674	5¢ deep blue T. Roosevelt (557)	18.00	13.50	275.00	(4)	37.50	1,860,000
675	6¢ red orange Garfield (558)	40.00	19.00	600.00	(4)	55.00	980,000
676	7¢ black McKinley (559)	22.50	15.00	275.00	(4)	57.50	850,000
677	8¢ olive green Grant (560)	30.00	22.00	375.00	(4)	60.00	1,480,000
678	9¢ light rose Jefferson (561)	35.00	25.00	425.00	(4)	62.50	530,000
679	10¢ orange yellow Monroe (562)	110.00	17.50	1,000.00	(4)	70.00	1,890,000
	Warning: Excellent forgeries of the Kansas and Nebraska overprints exist.						
	Perf. 11						
680	2¢ Battle of Fallen Timbers,						
	Sept. 14	1.00	1.00	50.00	(6)	4.75	29,338,274
681	2¢ Ohio River Canal, Oct. 19	.80	.80	32.50	(6)	4.00	32,680,900
	Issues of 1930						
682	2¢ Mass. Bay Colony, Apr. 8	.80	.60	55.00	(6)	3.75	74,000,774
683	2¢ Carolina-Charleston, Apr. 10	1.75	1.60	85.00	(6)	4.00	25,215,574
	Perf. 11x10½						
684	1½¢ Warren G. Harding	.25	.05	1.25	(4)	4.75	
685	4¢ William H. Taft	.50	.06	8.50	(4)	10.00	

656 (Coil Pair)

657

658

669

669

680

681

682

683

684

685

688

689

690

702

703

704

705

706

707

708

709

710

711

712

	1930 continued	Un	U	PB/LP	#	FDC	Q
	Coil Stamps, Perf. 10 Vertically						
686	1½¢ brown Harding (684)	1.60	.07	6.00		7.50	
687	4¢ brown Taft (685)	2.75	.50	12.50		20.00	
	Perf. 11						
688	2¢ Braddock's Field, July 9	1.40	1.40	60.00	(6)	5.25	25,609,470
689	2¢ Von Steuben, Sept. 17	.80	.75	35.00	(6)	5.00	66,487,000
	Issues of 1931						
690	2¢ Pulaski, Jan. 16	.25	.18	25.00	(6)	4.00	96,559,400
	Perf. 11x10½						
692	11¢ light blue Hayes (563)	3.00	.10	19.00	(4)	80.00	
693	12¢ brown violet Cleveland (564)	6.50	.06	35.00	(4)	80.00	
694	13¢ yellow green Harrison (622)	2.75	.10	17.50	(4)	85.00	
695	14¢ dark blue Indian (565)	4.00	.30	25.00	(4)	85.00	
696	15¢ gray Statue of Liberty (566)	10.00	.06	60.00	(4)	95.00	
	Perf. 10½x11						
697	17¢ black Wilson (623)	5.25	.20	30.00	(4)	325.00	
698	20¢ car. rose Golden Gate (567)	13.00	.05	70.00	(4)	160.00	
699	25¢ blue green Niagara						
	Falls (568)	11.00	.08	60.00	(4)	350.00	
700	30¢ brown Buffalo (569)	18.50	.07	110.00	(4)	275.00	
701	50¢ lilac Amphitheater (570)	60.00	.07	325.00	(4)	400.00	
	Perf. 11						
702	2¢ Red Cross, May 21	.15	.12	2.50	(4)	4.00	99,074,600
703	2¢ Yorktown, Oct. 12	.40	.35	4.00	(4)	5.00	25,006,400
	Issues of 1932. Perf. 11x10½, Washington Bicentennial Issue , Jan. 1						
704	½¢ Portrait by Charles W. Peale	.08	.05	4.50	(4)	5.00	87,969,700
705	1¢ Bust by Jean Antoine Houdon	.13	.05	5.50	(4)	5.50	1,265,555,100
706	1½¢ Portrait by Charles W. Peale	.55	.08	25.00	(4)	5.50	304,926,800
707	2¢ Portrait by Gilbert Stuart	.10	.05	1.75	(4)	5.50	4,222,198,300
708	3¢ Portrait by Charles W. Peale	.60	.06	18.00	(4)	5.75	456,198,500
709	4¢ Portrait by Charles P. Polk	.30	.06	7.00	(4)	5.75	151,201,300
710	5¢ Portrait by Charles W. Peale	2.25	.10	24.00	(4)	6.00	170,565,100
711	6¢ Portrait by John Trumbull	5.00	.06	85.00	(4)	6.75	111,739,400
712	7¢ Portrait by John Trumbull	.35	.20	7.50	(4)	6.75	83,257,400
713	8¢ Portrait by Charles B.J.F.						
	Saint Memin	5.00	.90	100.00	(4)	6.75	96,506,100
714	9¢ Portrait by W. Williams	4.25	.25	65.00	(4)	7.75	75,709,200
715	10¢ Portrait by Gilbert Stuart	16.50	.10	160.00	(4)	10.00	147,216,000
	Perf. 11						
716	2¢ Olympic Games, Jan. 25	.50	.25	17.50	(6)	5.00	51,102,800
	Perf. 11x10½						
717	2¢ Arbor Day, Apr. 22	.18	.08	12.50	(4)	3.25	100,869,300

	1932 continued	Un	U	PB/LP	#	FDC	Q
	10th Olympic Games Issue, June 15						
718	3¢ Runner at Starting Mark	2.00	.06	25.00	(4)	5.75	168,885,300
719	5¢ Myron's Discobolus	3.25	.30	40.00	(4)	7.50	52,376,100
720	3¢ Washington, June 16	.15	.05	1.50	(4)	10.00	
720b	Booklet pane of 6	22.50	5.00				
	Coil Stamps, Perf. 10 Vertically						
721	3¢ deep violet (720), June 24	3.00	.08	14.00		20.00	
	Perf. 10 Horizontally						
722	3¢ deep violet (720), Oct. 12	1.85	.45	10.00		20.00	
	Perf. 10 Vertically						
723	6¢ red orange Garfield						
	(558), Aug. 18	12.50	.25	75.00		20.00	
	Perf. 11						
724	3¢ William Penn, Oct. 24	.35	.25	20.00	(6)	3.00	49,949,000
725	3¢ Daniel Webster, Oct. 24	.50	.40	32.50	(6)	3.00	49,538,500
	Issues of 1933						
726	3¢ Georgia 200th Anniv. Feb. 12	.35	.25	22.50	(6)	3.00	61,719,200
	Perf. 10½x11						
727	3¢ Peace of 1783, Apr. 19	.15	.10	7.00	(4)	3.50	73,382,400
	Century of Progress Issue, May 25						
728	1¢ Restoration of Ft. Dearborn	.12	.06	3.00	(4)	2.75	348,266,800
729	3¢ Fed. Building at Chicago 1933	.18	.05	4.00	(4)	2.75	480,239,300
	American Philatelic Society Issue, Souvenir Sheets, Aug. 25, Without Gum, Imperf.						
730	1¢ deep yellow green						
	sheet of 25 (728)	45.00	40.00			150.00	456,704
730a	Single stamp	1.00	.50			2.75	11,417,600

Lincoln as Postmaster

In 1835, Matthew Marsh wrote a letter to his brother back east. Life in New Salem, Illinois, as Marsh reported, was not entirely to his liking:

"The Post Master is very careless about leaving his office open and unlocked during the day. Half the time I go in and get my papers, etc., without anyone being there as was the case yesterday. The letter was only marked twenty-five (cents) and even if he had been there and known it was double he would not have charged me any more."

That Post Master was 26-year-old Abraham Lincoln, who had yet to distinguish himself in any career. He'd bought a store and bankrupted it; worked as a land surveyor, until the bank repossessed his horse and saddle; and made an unsuccessful run for the state legislature.

Yet none of young Lincoln's setbacks diminished his curiosity and ambition. During his years as village postmaster, 1833-1836, he began to study and practice law, which led to...well, you know the rest.

18   719   720   723   724   725

26   727   728   729

1933-1934

731

732

733

734

736

737

739

740

741

	1933 continued	Un	U	PB/LP	#	FDC	Q
731	3¢ deep violet, sheet of 25 (729)	40.00	37.50			150.00	441,172
731a	Single stamp	.85	.50			2.75	11,029,300
	Perf. 10½x11						
732	3¢ NRA, Aug. 15	.14	.05	2.00	(4)	3.00	1,978,707,300
	Perf. 11						
733	3¢ Byrd's Antarctic Expedition,						
	Oct. 9	.85	.85	30.00	(6)	7.00	5,735,944
734	5¢ Tadeusz Kosciuszko, Oct. 13	.85	.40	65.00	(6)	6.25	45,137,700
	Issues of 1934, National Stamp Exhibition Issue, Souvenir Sheet,						
	Feb. 10, Without Gum, Imperf.						
735	3¢ dk. blue sheet of 6 (733)	28.50	26.00			67.50	811,404
735a	Single stamp	3.00	2.50			6.75	4,868,424
	Perf. 11						
736	3¢ Maryland 300th Anniversary,						
	Mar. 23	.20	.20	15.00	(6)	2.00	46,258,300
	Mothers of America Issue, May 2, Perf. 11x10½						
737	3¢ Whistler's Mother	.15	.06	1.75	(4)	2.00	193,239,100
	Perf. 11						
738	3¢ deep violet (737)	.20	.20	7.25	(6)	2.00	15,432,200
739	3¢ Wisconsin 300th Anniversary,						
	July 7	.20	.12	7.00	(6)	2.00	64,525,400
	National Parks Issue						
740	1¢ El Capitan, Yosemite, Calif.	.10	.06	1.50	(6)	2.25	84,896,350
741	2¢ Grand Canyon, Arizona	.15	.06	2.00	(6)	2.25	74,400,200

Mesa Verde National Park

In the extreme southwestern corner of Colorado stands a high plateau of thick juniper and piñon forests. Spanish explorers named this area Mesa Verde, literally "green table." The high north end of the mesa offers a breathtaking vista of mountains, river valleys and other plateaus. From this vantage point, the viewer can look into four states: Colorado, Utah, Arizona and New Mexico.

A region of unquestioned natural beauty, Mesa Verde is also one of the most important archaeological preserves in the U.S. The agricultural Pueblo Indians occupied the area for some 700 years, up to the 13th century A.D. The development of their civilization can be traced through their habitations —from early cave dwellings to magnificent multi-storied buildings constructed beneath overhanging cliffs. Experts are still unsure why the Pueblo Indians abandoned these captivating structures.

The largest of these is the Cliff Palace, an enormous village sheltered in an immense cave. It wasn't discovered until 1888, when two cowboys came upon it in an unexplored canyon. This structure contains more than 220 rooms and a number of larger chambers. The Cliff Palace appears on a 1934 commemorative stamp (#743). The park, established in 1906, contains hundreds of these ruins, preserving our fullest record of early life in the American Southwest.

	1934 continued	Un	U	PB/LP	#	FDC	Q
742	3¢ Mt. Rainier and Mirror Lake,						
	Washington	.20	.06	3.50	(6)	2.50	95,089,000
743	4¢ Mesa Verde, Colorado	.55	.50	12.00	(6)	3.25	19,178,650
744	5¢ Old Faithful, Yellowstone,						
	Wyoming	1.10	.90	14.50	(6)	3.25	30,980,100
745	6¢ Crater Lake, Oregon	2.00	1.25	30.00	(6)	4.00	16,923,350
746	7¢ Great Head, Acadia Park,						
	Maine	1.00	1.00	20.00	(6)	4.00	15,988,250
747	8¢ Great White Throne,						
	Zion Park, Utah	2.85	2.50	35.00	(6)	4.25	15,288,700
748	9¢ Mt Rockwell and Two Medicine						
	Lake, Glacier National Park,						
	Montana	3.00	.90	32.50	(6)	4.50	17,472,600
749	10¢ Great Smoky Mountains,						
	North Carolina	5.00	1.35	57.50	(6)	7.50	18,874,300
	American Philatelic Society Issue, Souvenir Sheet, Imperf.						
750	3¢ deep violet sheet of six						
	(742), Aug. 28	45.00	35.00			65.00	511,391
750a	Single stamp	5.00	4.50			7.00	3,068,346
	Trans-Mississippi Philatelic Issue						
751	1¢ green sheet of six (740), Oct. 10	18.50	15.00			45.00	793,551
751a	Single stamp	2.00	1.75			4.50	4,761,306
	Special Printing (Nos. 752 to 771 inclusive), Issued March 15, 1935, Without Gum						
	Issues of 1935, Perf. 10½x11						
752	3¢ violet Peace of 1783 (727)						
	Issued in sheets of 400, Mar. 15	.20	.15	16.00	(4)	13.00	3,274,556
	Perf. 11						
753	3¢ blue Byrd's Antarctic						
	Expedition (733)	.60	.60	25.00	(6)	15.00	2,040,760
	Imperf.						
754	3¢ dp. vio. Whistler's Mother (737)	1.00	.60	40.00	(6)	15.00	2,389,288
755	3¢ deep violet Wisconsin						
	300th Anniversary (739)	1.00	.60	40.00	(6)	15.00	2,294,948
756	1¢ green Yosemite (740)	.30	.20	6.50	(6)	15.00	3,217,636
757	2¢ red Grand Canyon (741)	.40	.35	7.50	(6)	15.00	2,746,640
758	3¢ dp. vio. Mt. Rainier (742)	.75	.70	22.50	(6)	16.00	2,168,088
759	4¢ brown Mesa Verde (743)	2.00	2.00	27.50	(6)	16.00	1,822,684
760	5¢ blue Yellowstone (744)	3.00	2.25	37.50	(6)	16.00	1,724,576
761	6¢ dk. blue Crater Lake (745)	4.00	2.75	47.50	(6)	16.50	1,647,696
762	7¢ black Acadia (746)	3.00	2.50	45.00	(6)	16.50	1,682,948
763	8¢ sage green Zion (747)	3.50	2.75	60.00	(6)	17.00	1,638,644
764	9¢ red orange Glacier Nat'l Park						
	(748)	3.75	2.75	60.00	(6)	18.00	1,625,224
765	10¢ gray black Smoky Mts. (749)	6.25	5.50	80.00	(6)	20.00	1,644,900

742

743

744

745

746

747

748

749

772

773

774

775

776

777

778

782

783

784

	1935 continued	Un	U	PB/LP	#	FDC	Q
766	1¢ yellow green (728)	50.00	50.00				98,712
	Pane of 25						
766a	Single stamp	1.00	.50			11.00	2,467,800
767	3¢ violet (729)	45.00	40.00				85,914
	Pane of 25						
767a	Single stamp	.85	.50			11.00	2,147,850
768	3¢ dark blue (733)	32.50	25.00				
	Pane of 6						
768a	Single stamp	3.25	2.75			13.00	1,,603,200
769	1¢ green (740)	15.00	12.00				279,960
	Pane of 6						
769a	Single stamp	1.75	1.75			8.00	1,679,760
770	3¢ deep violet (742)	35.00	25.00				215,920
	Pane of 6						
770a	Single stamp	3.75	3.75			10.00	1,295,520
771	16¢ dark blue Seal of U.S. (CE2),						
	issued in sheets of 200	4.00	3.50	100.00	(6)	25.00	1,370,560
	Perf. 11x10½						
772	3¢ Connecticut 300th Anniv.,						
	Apr. 26	.15	.06	2.00	(4)	9.50	70,726,800
773	3¢ California-Pacific Exposition,						
	May 29	.12	.06	2.00	(4)	9.50	100,839,600
	Perf. 11						
774	3¢ Boulder Dam, Sep. 30	.12	.06	2.75	(6)	13.00	73,610,650
	Perf. 11x10½						
775	3¢ Michigan 100th Anniv., Nov. 1	.12	.06	2.00	(4)	9.00	75,823,900
	Issues of 1936						
776	3¢ Texas 100th Anniv., Mar. 2	.12	.06	2.00	(4)	9.00	124,324,500
	Perf.10½x11						
777	3¢ Rhode Island 300th Anniv.,						
	May 4	.15	.06	2.00	(4)	9.00	67,127,650
	Third International Philatelic Exhibition Issue, Souvenir Sheet, Imperf.						
778	Violet, sheet of 4 different stamps						
	(772, 773, 775 and 776), May 9	3.50	3.50			17.50	2,809,039
	Perf. 11x10½						
782	3¢ Arkansas 100th Anniv., June 15	.12	.06	2.00	(4)	9.00	72,992,650
783	3¢ Oregon Territory, July 14	.12	.06	2.00	(4)	9.00	74,407,450
784	3¢ Susan B. Anthony, Aug. 26	.10	.05	.75	(4)	17.50	269,522,200

1936-1937

	Issues of 1936-37	Un	U	PB/LP	#	FDC	Q
	Army Issue						
785	1¢ George Washington						
	and Nathanael Greene, 1936	.10	.06	1.00	(4)	6.00	105,196,150
786	2¢ Andrew Jackson and						
	Winfield Scott, 1937	.15	.06	1.10	(4)	6.00	93,848,500
787	3¢ Generals Sherman,						
	Grant and Sheridan, 1937	.20	.08	1.50	(4)	6.00	87,741,150
788	4¢ Generals Robert E. Lee						
	and "Stonewall" Jackson, 1937	.65	.15	13.00	(4)	6.75	35,794,150
789	5¢ U.S. Military Academy,						
	West Point, 1937	1.00	.15	15.00	(4)	8.00	36,839,250
	Navy Issue						
790	1¢ John Paul Jones						
	and John Barry, 1936	.10	.06	1.00	(4)	6.00	104,773,450
791	2¢ Stephen Decatur						
	and Thomas MacDonough, 1937	.15	.06	1.10	(4)	6.00	92,054,550
792	3¢ Admirals David G. Farragut						
	and David D. Porter, 1937	.20	.08	1.50	(4)	6.00	93,291,650
793	4¢ Admirals William T. Sampson,						
	George Dewey and Winfield						
	S. Schley, 1937	.65	.15	13.00	(4)	6.75	34,552,950
794	5¢ Seal of U.S. Naval Academy						
	and Naval Cadets, 1937	1.00	.15	15.00	(4)	8.00	36,819,050
	Issues of 1937						
795	3¢ Northwest Ordinance						
	150th Anniversary, July 13	.12	.06	2.00	(4)	8.50	84,825,25
	Perf. 11						
796	5¢ Virginia Dare, Aug. 18	.35	.25	11.50	(6)	9.50	25,040,40
	Society of Philatelic Americans, Souvenir Sheet, Imperf.						
797	10¢ blue green (749), Aug. 26	1.25	.85			8.00	5,277,44
	Perf. 11x10½						
798	3¢ Constitution 150th Anniv.,						
	Sept. 17	.15	.07	1.65	(4)	8.50	99,882,30
	Territorial Issues, Perf. 10½x11						
799	3¢ Hawaii, Oct. 18	.15	.07	2.00	(4)	9.50	78,454,45
	Perf. 11x10½						
800	3¢ Alaska, Nov. 12	.15	.07	2.00	(4)	9.50	77,004,20
801	3¢ Puerto Rico, Nov. 25	.15	.07	1.75	(4)	9.50	81,292,45
802	3¢ Virgin Islands, Dec. 15	.15	.07	2.00	(4)	9.50	76,474,55

785

786

787

788

789

790

791

792

793

794

795

796

798

799

800

801

802

1938

803   804   805   806

807   808   809   810   811   812

813   814   815   816   817

818   819   820   821   822   823

824   825   826   827   828   829

830   831   832   833   834

		Un	U	PB/LP	#	FDC	Q
	Presidential Issue, 1938						
803	½¢ Benjamin Franklin	.05	.05	.40	(4)	1.25	
804	1¢ George Washington	.06	.05	.25	(4)	1.35	
804b	Booklet pane of 6	1.75	.20				
805	1½¢ Martha Washington	.06	.05	.30	(4)	1.35	
806	2¢ John Adams	.06	.05	.35	(4)	1.65	
806b	Booklet pane of 6	4.25	.50				
807	3¢ Thomas Jefferson	.10	.05	.50	(4)	1.65	
807a	Booklet pane of 6	8.50	.50				
808	4¢ James Madison	.45	.05	1.80	(4)	1.65	
809	4½¢ White House	.20	.06	1.60	(4)	2.25	
810	5¢ James Monroe	.40	.05	1.80	(4)	2.25	
811	6¢ John Q. Adams	.45	.05	2.00	(4)	2.25	
812	7¢ Andrew Jackson	.50	.05	2.00	(4)	2.50	
813	8¢ Martin Van Buren	.65	.05	2.25	(4)	2.50	
814	9¢ William H. Harrison	.70	.05	2.75	(4)	2.65	
815	10¢ John Tyler	.50	.05	2.00	(4)	2.75	
816	11¢ James K. Polk	1.00	.08	4.50	(4)	2.75	
817	12¢ Zachary Taylor	1.65	.06	6.00	(4)	3.00	
818	13¢ Millard Fillmore	1.75	.08	5.50	(4)	3.00	
819	14¢ Franklin Pierce	1.75	.10	5.50	(4)	3.25	
820	15¢ James Buchanan	.75	.05	3.60	(4)	3.25	
821	16¢ Abraham Lincoln	1.75	.35	7.00	(4)	3.50	
822	17¢ Andrew Johnson	1.50	.12	7.00	(4)	3.75	
823	18¢ Ulysses S. Grant	3.00	.08	13.00	(4)	4.25	
824	19¢ Rutherford B. Hayes	1.85	.50	8.00	(4)	4.25	
825	20¢ James A. Garfield	1.20	.05	5.50	(4)	4.50	
826	21¢ Chester A. Arthur	2.25	.10	8.25	(4)	5.00	
827	22¢ Grover Cleveland	2.25	.50	8.25	(4)	5.25	
828	24¢ Benjamin Harrison	7.00	.25	26.50	(4)	5.25	
829	25¢ William McKinley	1.40	.05	7.25	(4)	6.50	
830	30¢ Theodore Roosevelt	9.00	.05	38.50	(4)	10.00	
831	50¢ William Howard Taft	13.50	.06	52.50	(4)	20.00	
	Perf. 11						
832	$1 Woodrow Wilson	15.00	.10	60.00	(4)	55.00	
832b	Wmkd. USIR	350.00	90.00				
833	$2 Warren G. Harding	37.50	6.00	200.00	(4)	100.00	
834	$5 Calvin Coolidge	140.00	5.50	675.00	(4)	175.00	

This series was in use for approximately 16 years when the Liberty Series began replacing it. Various shades of these stamps are in existence due to the numerous reprintings.

		Un	U	PB/LP	#	FDC	Q
	Issues of 1938, Perf. 11x10½						
835	3¢ Constitution Ratification,						
	June 21	.25	.08	6.00	(4)	8.50	73,043,650
	Perf. 11						
836	3¢ Swedish-Finnish 300th Anniv.,						
	June 27	.25	.10	6.00	(6)	8.50	58,564,368
	Perf. 11x10½						
837	3¢ Northwest Territory, July 15	.25	.08	16.50	(4)	8.50	65,939,500
838	3¢ Iowa Territory 100th Anniv.,						
	Aug. 24	.25	.08	9.50	(4)	8.50	47,064,300
	Issues of 1939, Coil Stamps, Perf. 10 Vertically						
839	1¢ green Washington (804)	.25	.06	1.20		7.00	
840	1½¢ bistre brown						
	M. Washington (805)	.30	.06	1.50		7.00	
841	2¢ rose car. Adams (806)	.30	.05	1.50		7.00	
842	3¢ deep violet Jefferson (807)	.75	.04	2.75		8.00	
843	4¢ red violet Madison (808)	9.00	.35	25.00		8.00	
844	4½¢ dk. gray White House (809)	.60	.45	4.00		8.00	
845	5¢ bright blue Monroe (810)	6.00	.35	25.00		9.00	
846	6¢ red orange J.Q. Adams (811)	1.10	.20	8.00		12.00	
847	10¢ brown red Tyler (815)	12.50	.40	52.50		15.00	
	Perf. 10 Horizontally						
848	1¢ green Washington (804)	.75	.12	3.00		7.00	
849	1½¢ bistre brown						
	M. Washington (805)	1.10	.40	3.75		7.00	
850	2¢ rose car. Adams (806)	2.50	.50	6.75		7.00	
851	3¢ deep violet Jefferson (807)	2.25	.45	6.50		8.00	
	Perf. 10½x11						
852	3¢ Golden Gate Exposition,						
	Feb. 18	.12	.06	1.65	(4)	7.50	114,439,600
853	3¢ New York World's Fair, Apr. 1	.15	.06	2.00	(4)	8.50	101,699,550
	Perf. 11						
854	3¢ Washington's Inauguration,						
	Apr. 30	.25	.10	4.75	(6)	7.50	72,764,550
	Perf. 11x10½						
855	3¢ Baseball Anniversary						
	100th, June 12	.22	.08	3.50	(4)	17.50	81,269,600
	Perf. 11						
856	3¢ Panama Canal, Aug. 15	.22	.08	6.00	(6)	7.50	67,813,350
	Perf. 10½x11						
857	3¢ 300th Anniv. of Printing,						
	Sept. 25	.12	.08	1.65	(4)	7.50	71,394,750
	Perf. 11x10½						
858	3¢ 50th Anniv. of Statehood,						
	Nov. 2	.12	.08	1.65	(4)	7.00	66,835,000

835

836

837

838

852

853

854

855

856

857

859   860   861   862   863

864   865   866   867   868

869   870   871   872   873

874   875   876   877   878

879   880   881   882   883

		Un	U	PB/LP	#	FDC	Q
Famous Americans Issue, 1940, Perf. 10½x11							
	Authors						
859	1¢ Washington Irving	.08	.06	1.10	(4)	2.00	56,348,320
860	2¢ James Fenimore Cooper	.10	.08	1.25	(4)	2.00	53,177,110
861	3¢ Ralph Waldo Emerson	.12	.06	2.00	(4)	2.00	53,260,270
862	5¢ Louisa May Alcott	.35	.30	12.00	(4)	5.00	22,104,950
863	10¢ Samuel L. Clemens						
	(Mark Twain)	2.50	2.35	55.00	(4)	8.25	13,201,270
	Poets						
864	1¢ Henry W. Longfellow	.12	.08	1.50	(4)	2.00	51,603,580
865	2¢ John Greenleaf Whittier	.10	.08	1.50	(4)	2.00	52,100,510
866	3¢ James Russell Lowell	.18	.06	3.50	(4)	2.00	51,666,580
867	5¢ Walt Whitman	.35	.25	12.00	(4)	4.50	22,207,780
868	10¢ James Whitcomb Riley	3.50	3.00	55.00	(4)	8.25	11,835,530
	Educators						
869	1¢ Horace Mann	.09	.08	1.50	(4)	2.00	52,471,160
870	2¢ Mark Hopkins	.10	.06	1.40	(4)	2.00	52,366,440
871	3¢ Charles W. Eliot	.30	.06	3.25	(4)	2.00	51,636,270
872	5¢ Frances E. Willard	.50	.35	13.00	(4)	4.75	20,729,030
873	10¢ Booker T. Washington	2.50	2.25	35.00	(4)	8.25	14,125,580
	Scientists						
874	1¢ John James Audubon	.08	.06	1.00	(4)	2.00	59,409,000
875	2¢ Dr. Crawford W. Long	.10	.06	1.20	(4)	2.00	57,888,600
876	3¢ Luther Burbank	.10	.06	2.00	(4)	2.00	58,273,180
877	5¢ Dr. Walter Reed	.30	.25	10.50	(4)	4.50	23,779,000
878	10¢ Jane Addams	2.00	2.00	35.00	(4)	8.25	15,112,580
	Composers						
879	1¢ Stephen Collins Foster	.08	.06	1.25	(4)	2.00	57,322,790
880	2¢ John Philip Sousa	.10	.06	1.25	(4)	2.00	58,281,580
881	3¢ Victor Herbert	.15	.06	1.75	(4)	2.00	56,398,790
882	5¢ Edward MacDowell	.60	.30	13.00	(4)	4.50	21,147,000
883	10¢ Ethelbert Nevin	5.50	2.25	50.00	(4)	7.75	13,328,000

	1940 continued	Un	U	PB/LP	#	FDC	Q
	Artists						
884	1¢ Gilbert Charles Stuart	.08	.06	1.10	(4)	2.00	54,389,510
885	2¢ James A. McNeill Whistler	.10	.06	1.10	(4)	2.00	53,636,580
886	3¢ Augustus Saint-Gaudens	.10	.06	1.25	(4)	2.00	55,313,230
887	5¢ Daniel Chester French	.40	.22	12.50	(4)	4.00	21,720,580
888	10¢ Frederic Remington	2.75	2.25	45.00	(4)	7.75	13,600,580
	Inventors						
889	1¢ Eli Whitney	.12	.08	2.50	(4)	2.00	47,599,580
890	2¢ Samuel F. B. Morse	.10	.06	1.50	(4)	2.00	53,766,510
891	3¢ Cyrus Hall McCormick	.20	.06	2.50	(4)	2.00	54,193,580
892	5¢ Elias Howe	1.50	.40	22.50	(4)	5.00	20,264,580
893	10¢ Alexander Graham Bell	15.50	3.25	135.00	(4)	13.50	13,726,580
	Issues of 1940, Perf. 11x10½						
894	3¢ Pony Express, Apr. 3	.50	.15	7.50	(4)	6.75	46,497,400
	Perf. 10½x11						
895	3¢ Pan American Union, Apr. 14	.40	.12	7.00	(4)	5.25	47,700,000
	Perf. 11x10½						
896	3¢ Idaho Statehood,						
	50th Anniversary, July 3	.20	.08	3.75	(4)	5.25	50,618,150
	Perf. 10½x11						
897	3¢ Wyoming Statehood,						
	50th Anniversary, July 10	.20	.08	3.25	(4)	5.25	50,034,400
	Perf. 11x10½						
898	3¢ Coronado Expedition, Sept. 7	.20	.08	3.25	(4)	5.25	60,943,700
	National Defense Issue, Oct. 16						
899	1¢ Statue of Liberty	.05	.05	.60	(4)	5.00	
900	2¢ Anti-aircraft Gun	.06	.05	.70	(4)	5.00	
901	3¢ Torch of Enlightenment	.12	.05	1.40	(4)	5.00	
	Perf. 10½x11						
902	3¢ Thirteenth Amendment,						
	Oct. 20	.25	.15	8.25	(4)	6.00	44,389,550
	Issue of 1941, Perf. 11x10½						
903	3¢ Vermont Statehood, Mar. 4	.22	.10	2.75	(4)	5.50	54,574,550
	Issues of 1942						
904	3¢ Kentucky Statehood, June 1	.15	.12	2.25	(4)	5.00	63,558,400
905	3¢ Win the War, July 4	.10	.05	.60	(4)	4.75	

884

885

886

887

888

889

890

891

892

893

894

895

896

897

898

899

900

901

902

903

904

905

1942-1944

906

907

908

909

910

911

912

913

914

915

916

917

918

919

920

921

922

923

	1942 continued	Un	U	PB/LP	#	FDC	Q
906	5¢ Chinese Resistance, July 7	.40	.30	25.00	(4)	7.00	21,272,800
	Issues of 1943						
907	2¢ Allied Nations, Jan. 14	.08	.05	.50	(4)	4.25	1,671,564,200
908	1¢ Four Freedoms, Feb. 12	.06	.05	1.00	(4)	4.25	1,227,334,200
	Overrun Countries Issue, 1943-44, Perf. 12						
909	5¢ Poland, June 22	.35	.20			5.75	19,999,646
910	5¢ Czechoslovakia, July 12	.30	.15			5.50	19,999,646
911	5¢ Norway, July 27	.25	.12			5.00	19,999,646
912	5¢ Luxembourg, Aug. 10	.25	.12			5.00	19,999,646
913	5¢ Netherlands, Aug. 24	.25	.12			5.00	19,999,646
914	5¢ Belgium, Sept. 14	.25	.12			5.00	19,999,646
915	5¢ France, Sept. 28	.25	.10			5.00	19,999,646
916	5¢ Greece, Oct. 12	.85	.60			5.00	14,999,646
917	5¢ Yugoslavia, Oct. 26	.50	.40			5.00	14,999,646
918	5¢ Albania, Nov. 9	.50	.40			5.00	14,999,646
919	5¢ Austria, Nov. 23	.30	.25			5.00	14,999,646
920	5¢ Denmark, Dec. 7	.50	.50			5.00	14,999,646
921	5¢ Korea, Nov. 2, 1944	.28	.25			6.50	14,999,646
	Inscribed "KORPA"	22.50	17.50				
	Issues of 1944, Perf. 11x10½						
922	3¢ Transcontinental Railroad,						
	May 10	.25	.15	2.50	(4)	6.75	61,303,000
923	3¢ Steamship, May 22	.15	.15	2.50	(4)	4.50	61,001,450

Our National Pastime

In February, 1939, stamp news made the sporting pages in every major newspaper in the country. At a Baseball Writers' Association dinner, Postmaster General James A. Farley announced the forthcoming issue of a stamp commemorating the 100th anniversary of baseball. Club owners and fans alike had wanted the Postal Department to honor baseball's birthday, but there was little agreement about what should go on the stamp.

855

At first, the Post Office had planned to feature Abner Doubleday, since he had set down the rules for baseball in 1839. But historians argued that others had actually invented the game. Then hundreds of suggestions poured in concerning the design of the stamp. Most of the proposed scenes wouldn't have fit on a postage stamp, or else they focused too narrowly on one aspect of baseball.

It was finally decided to picture the kind of baseball most people play: sandlot ball in a neighborhood park (#855). Artist William A. Roach of the Bureau of Engraving and Printing subtly honored PMG Farley, as well. His drawing of children playing ball is placed in Farley's home town, Grassy Point, New York.

	1944 continued	Un	U	PB/LP	#	FDC	Q
924	3¢ Telegraph, May 24	.12	.10	1.60	(4)	4.00	60,605,000
925	3¢ Philippines, Sept. 27	.12	.12	3.00	(4)	4.00	50,129,350
926	3¢ 50th Anniversary of						
	Motion Picture, Oct. 31	.12	.10	2.00	(4)	4.00	53,479,400
	Issues of 1945						
927	3¢ Florida Statehood, Mar. 3	.10	.08	1.00	(4)	4.00	61,617,350
928	5¢ United Nations Conference,						
	Apr. 25	.12	.08	.70	(4)	4.00	75,500,000
	Perf. 10½x11						
929	3¢ Iwo Jima (Marines), July 11	.10	.05	.60	(4)	5.00	137,321,000
	Issues of 1945-46, Perf. 11x10½						
	Franklin D. Roosevelt Issue						
930	1¢ F.D.R. and home at Hyde Park	.05	.05	.30	(4)	3.00	128,140,000
931	2¢ Roosevelt and "Little						
	White House," Ga.	.08	.08	.50	(4)	3.00	67,255,000
932	3¢ Roosevelt and White House	.10	.08	.55	(4)	3.00	133,870,000
933	5¢ F.D.R., Globe and						
	Four Freedoms, 1946	.12	.08	.75	(4)	3.00	76,455,400
934	3¢ U.S. Army in Paris, Sept. 28	.10	.05	.50	(4)	3.00	128,357,750
935	3¢ U.S. Navy, Oct. 27	.10	.05	.50	(4)	3.00	135,863,000
936	3¢ U.S. Coast Guard, Nov. 10	.10	.05	.50	(4)	3.00	111,616,700
937	3¢ Alfred E. Smith, Nov. 26	.10	.05	.50	(4)	3.00	308,587,700
938	3¢ Texas Statehood, Dec. 29	.10	.05	.50	(4)	3.00	170,640,000
	Issues of 1946						
939	3¢ Merchant Marine, Feb. 26	.10	.05	.50	(4)	3.00	135,927,000

The Merchant Marine

One of the most neglected stories of World War II is that of the Merchant Marine. It demonstrates both the wartime contributions of American civilians and the ability of our country to direct massive resources into a major building program.

Before the war, the U.S. had mostly relied on foreign shipping to carry on international trade. With the onset of a war that had to be fought across two great oceans, it was clear that we needed our own huge fleet. An effort was begun that eventually employed more than a million workers. More than 6,000 ships were built, most of them cargo carriers like the famous Victory ships and the huge Liberty ships (#939). By the end of the war, despite heavy losses to German torpedoes, the U.S. had the largest merchant fleet in the history of the world.

More than 300,000 civilian seamen manned these ships. They and their craft carried 80 percent of the weaponry and supplies used by U.S. forces overseas. In the supremely vital task of keeping the troops armed and fed, over 6,000 of these brave sailors lost their lives. The 1946 "Peace and War" commemorative honored their sacrifice.

24

925

926

27

928

929

30

931

932

33

934

935

940

941

942

943

944

945

946

947

948

949

	1946 continued	Un	U	PB/LP	#	FDC	Q
940	3¢ Veterans of World War II, May 9	.10	.05	.55	(4)	3.00	260,339,100
941	3¢ Tennessee Statehood, June 1	.10	.05	.50	(4)	3.00	132,274,500
942	3¢ Iowa Statehood, Aug.3	.10	.05	.50	(4)	3.00	132,430,000
943	3¢ Smithsonian Institution, Aug. 10	.10	.05	.50	(4)	3.00	139,209,500
944	3¢ Kearny Expedition, Oct. 16	.10	.05	.50	(4)	3.00	114,684,450
	Issues of 1947, Perf. 10½x11						
945	3¢ Thomas A. Edison, Feb. 11	.10	.05	.50	(4)	3.00	156,540,510
	Perf. 11x10½						
946	3¢ Joseph Pulitzer, Apr. 10	.10	.05	.50	(4)	3.00	120,452,600
947	3¢ 100th Anniv. of the						
	Postage Stamp, May 17	.10	.05	.50	(4)	3.00	127,104,300
	Imperf.						
948	Souvenir sheet of two, May 19	1.75	1.00			3.50	10,299,600
948a	5¢ blue, single stamp (1)	.35	.30				
948b	10¢ brn. org., single stamp (2)	.50	.30				

Issued in sheets of two with marginal inscription commemorating the 100th anniversary of U.S. postage stamps and the Centenary International Philatelic Exhibition, held in New York in 1947.

		Un	U	PB/LP	#	FDC	Q
	Perf. 11x10½						
949	3¢ Doctors, June 9	.10	.05	.50	(4)	2.00	132,902,000
950	3¢ Utah, July 24	.10	.05	.50	(4)	2.00	131,968,000
951	3¢ U.S. Frigate Constitution,						
	Oct. 21	.10	.05	.50	(4)	2.00	131,488,000
	Perf. 10½x11						
952	3¢ Everglades Nat'l Park, Dec. 5	.10	.05	.50	(4)	2.00	122,362,000

The House Post Office

The U.S. House of Representatives has its own postal service with 109 permanent employees—this is one of the largest contract stations in the U.S. Postal Service. Once the mail goes to the House, its own postmaster, an elected officer, supervises the distribution of the letters and packages.

Normally, the House of Representatives receives between 200,000 and 250,000 items each day. The most mail received in one day in the House was on May 4, 1981. That was when 1,250,000 letters, approximately 800,000 postal cards, 600,000 Mailgrams and 800,000 "Save the School Lunch Program" paper pie plates were received. This three and one half million pieces of mail set a record which still stands today.

More and more people are writing to their representatives. Back in 1972, a mere 40 million pieces of mail were delivered to the House. During the 1980's, incoming mail averaged 150 million items. The largest amount of mail received by a single Congressman occurred in 1973, when the House Judiciary Committee Chairman received almost three and a half million pieces of mail in one month. Recently, a write-in campaign by bank depositors to influence legislation regarding the withholding of taxes on bank interest also produced a huge volume of mail. It was estimated that the Postal Service sold almost $100 million in postage stamps for this bank protest.

	Issues of 1948	Un	U	PB/LP	#	FDC	Q
953	3¢ Dr. George Washington Carver,						
	Jan. 5	.10	.05	.50	(4)	2.00	121,548,000
	Perf. 11x10½						
954	3¢ Calif. Gold 100th Anniversary,						
	Jan. 24	.10	.05	.50	(4)	2.00	131,109,500
955	3¢ Mississippi Territory, Apr. 7	.10	.05	.50	(4)	2.00	122,650,500
956	3¢ Four Chaplains, May 28	.10	.05	.50	(4)	2.00	121,953,500
957	3¢ Wisconsin Statehood, May 29	.10	.05	.50	(4)	2.00	115,250,000
958	5¢ Swedish Pioneer, June 4	.15	.10	1.00	(4)	2.00	64,198,500
959	3¢ Progress of Women, July 19	.10	.05	.50	(4)	2.00	117,642,500
	Perf. 10½x11						
960	3¢ William Allen White, July 31	.10	.06	.60	(4)	2.00	77,649,600
	Perf. 11x10½						
961	3¢ U.S.-Canada Friendship,						
	Aug. 2	.10	.05	.50	(4)	2.00	113,474,500
962	3¢ Francis Scott Key, Aug. 9	.10	.05	.50	(4)	2.00	120,868,500
963	3¢ Salute to Youth, Aug. 11	.10	.06	.50	(4)	2.00	77,800,500
964	3¢ Oregon Territory, Aug. 14	.10	.10	.90	(4)	2.00	52,214,000
	Perf. 10½x11						
965	3¢ Harlan Fiske Stone, Aug. 25	.10	.08	1.70	(4)	2.00	53,958,100
966	3¢ Palomar Mt. Obs., Aug. 30	.12	.10	2.50	(4)	2.00	61,120,010
	Perf. 11x10½						
967	3¢ Clara Barton, Sept. 7	.10	.08	.60	(4)	1.50	57,823,000
968	3¢ Poultry Industry, Sept. 9	.12	.08	.80	(4)	1.50	52,975,000
	Perf. 10½x11						
969	3¢ Gold Star Mothers, Sept. 21	.12	.08	.65	(4)	2.00	77,149,000
970	3¢ Fort Kearny, Sept. 22	.12	.08	.65	(4)	2.00	58,332,000
971	3¢ Volunteer Firemen, Oct. 4	.12	.08	.75	(4)	2.00	56,228,000

Elizabeth Stanton

In 1840, Elizabeth Cady Stanton (1815-1902), an ardent anti-slavery activist, attended a major abolitionist convention in London, England, only to find that she and other women could not be delegates because they were female. Elizabeth Stanton tirelessly agitated for the cause of the Women's Rights Convention which was held in 1848. It is considered the beginning of a women's rights movement in the United States.

Elizabeth Stanton (#959) persuaded Susan B. Anthony to join the movement. The two worked closely, especially in their efforts to gain voting rights for women. In 1890, Mrs. Stanton became the first president of the National American Woman's Suffrage Association. At times she was even too radical for the women of her age, as when she supported free divorce. A controversial reformer, the ideas she championed were unpopular in her time, but have since found their way into the mainstream of American opinion.

53

954

955

956

57

958

959

960

57

962

963

61

965

966

967

972

973

974

975

976

977

978

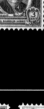

979

980

981

982

983

984

985

986

987

988

990

	1948 continued	Un	U	PB/LP	#	FDC	Q
972	3¢ Five Indian Tribes, Oct. 15	.12	.08	.75	(4)	1.50	57,832,000
973	3¢ Rough Riders, Oct. 27	.12	.10	1.20	(4)	1.50	53,875,000
974	3¢ Juliette Low, Oct. 29	.12	.08	.65	(4)	1.50	63,834,000
	Perf. 10½x11						
975	3¢ Will Rogers, Nov. 4	.12	.08	1.00	(4)	1.50	67,162,200
976	3¢ Fort Bliss 100th Anniv., Nov. 5	.15	.08	2.00	(4)	1.50	64,561,000
	Perf. 11x10½						
977	3¢ Moina Michael, Nov. 9	.12	.08	.65	(4)	1.50	64,079,500
978	3¢ Gettysburg Address, Nov. 19	.12	.08	.70	(4)	1.50	63,388,000
	Perf. 10½x11						
979	3¢ American Turners, Nov. 20	.12	.08	.65	(4)	1.50	62,285,000
980	3¢ Joel Chandler Harris, Dec. 9	.12	.08	.75	(4)	1.50	57,492,610
	Issues of 1949, Perf. 11x10½						
981	3¢ Minnesota Territory, Mar. 3	.10	.05	.50	(4)	1.50	99,190,000
982	3¢ Washington & Lee University,						
	Apr. 12	.10	.05	.50	(4)	1.50	104,790,000
983	3¢ Puerto Rico Election, Apr. 27	.10	.05	.50	(4)	1.50	108,805,000
984	3¢ Annapolis 300th Anniv.,						
	May 23	.10	.05	.50	(4)	1.50	107,340,000
985	3¢ Grand Army of the Republic,						
	Aug. 29	.10	.05	.50	(4)	1.50	117,020,000
	Perf. 10½x11						
986	3¢ Edgar Allan Poe, Oct. 7	.10	.05	.60	(4)	1.50	122,633,000
	Issues of 1950, Perf. 11x10½						
987	3¢ American Bankers Association,						
	Jan. 3	.10	.05	.50	(4)	1.50	130,960,000
	Perf. 10½x11						
988	3¢ Samuel Gompers, Jan. 27	.10	.05	.55	(4)	1.50	128,478,000
	National Capital 150th Anniv. Issue, Perf. 10½x11, 11x10½						
989	3¢ Statue of Freedom	.10	.05	.50	(4)	1.50	132,090,000
990	3¢ Executive Mansion	.11	.05	.50	(4)	1.50	130,050,000

Montgomery Blair

Postmaster General Montgomery Blair was considered to have the best brain in President Abraham Lincoln's cabinet. Blair suspended postal service in the Confederate States and invalidated all existing stamps. Thus southern post offices could not sell their old stamps to raise money for Confederate armies.

Blair inaugurated a wide range of postal reforms. He enforced prepaid postage, devised a new indelible ink for cancellations, took away the franking privilege from individual postmasters, placed them on salaries rather than commission and introduced the concept of the railway mail car.

He is best known for his efforts to bring consistency to international mail delivery, and standardization of rates. His work led to the First International Postal Conference (#C66), the start of the Universal Postal Union.

	1950 continued	Un	U	PB/LP	#	FDC	Q
991	3¢ Supreme Court Building	.10	.05	.50	(4)	1.50	131,350,000
992	3¢ U.S. Capitol Building	.10	.05	.50	(4)	1.50	129,980,000
	Perf. 11x10½						
993	3¢ Railroad Engineers, Apr. 29	.10	.05	.50	(4)	1.50	122,315,000
994	3¢ Kansas City, Mo., June 3	.10	.05	.50	(4)	1.50	122,170,000
995	3¢ Boy Scouts, June 30	.10	.06	.55	(4)	1.50	131,635,000
996	3¢ Indian Territory, July 4	.10	.05	.50	(4)	1.50	121,860,000
997	3¢ California Statehood, Sept. 9	.10	.05	.50	(4)	1.50	121,120,000
	Issues of 1951						
998	3¢ Confederate Veterans, May 30	.10	.05	.50	(4)	1.50	119,120,000
999	3¢ Nevada 100th Anniv., July 14	.10	.05	.50	(4)	1.50	112,125,000
1000	3¢ Landing of Cadillac, July 24	.10	.05	.50	(4)	1.50	114,140,000
1001	3¢ Colorado Statehood, Aug. 1	.10	.05	.50	(4)	1.50	114,490,000
1002	3¢ American Chemical Society,						
	Sept. 4	.10	.05	.50	(4)	1.50	117,200,000
1003	3¢ Battle of Brooklyn, Dec. 10	.10	.05	.50	(4)	1.50	116,130,000
	Issues of 1952						
1004	3¢ Betsy Ross, Jan. 2	.10	.05	.50	(4)	1.50	116,175,000
1005	3¢ 4-H Club, Jan. 15	.10	.05	.50	(4)	1.50	115,945,000
1006	3¢ B&O Railroad, Feb. 28	.10	.05	.50	(4)	2.00	1†2,540,000
1007	3¢ American Auto. Assn., Mar. 4	.10	.05	.60	(4)	.85	117,415,000
1008	3¢ NATO, Apr. 4	.10	.05	.55	(4)	.85	2,899,580,000
1009	3¢ Grand Coulee Dam, May 15	.10	.05	.50	(4)	.85	114,540,000

The Battle of Brooklyn

1003

Independence may never have seemed so far away as on the morning of August 28, 1776. George Washington's army had just suffered a crushing defeat at Brooklyn Heights on Long Island, in its first major Revolutionary War engagement. Out of Washington's force of 9,000 men, close to a thousand had been killed or wounded and another thousand had been taken prisoner. The rest were hemmed in between the East River and the British army. Another British attack would end the American ability to wage war in the north.

General Washington decided to evacuate his troops to American-held Manhattan across the river. It would be a dangerous move, especially if the British attacked during the retreat. Strict secrecy was maintained; no news of the evacuation preparations reached the British. Luckily, the river was extremely calm that evening and night, and a fleet of small craft quietly gathered at the foot of Brooklyn Heights. With muffled oars, sturdy fishermen ferried back and forth through the night. Toward morning, a thick fog settled on the East River, hiding the final boatloads of American troops.

By the time George Washington boarded the last boat, his entire force had landed safely on the Manhattan shore, and American hope had been reborn (#1003).

WASHINGTON 1800-1950 NATIONAL CAPITAL SESQUICENTENNIAL UNITED STATES POSTAGE	WASHINGTON NATIONAL CAPITAL SESQUICENTENNIAL 1800-1950 UNITED STATES OF AMERICA	HONORING RAILROAD ENGINEERS OF AMERICA 3 CENTS 3 UNITED STATES POSTAGE
991	992	993
1950 U.S. POSTAGE KANSAS CITY, MISSOURI CENTENNIAL 1850	ON MY HONOR I WILL DO MY BEST BOY SCOUTS OF AMERICA UNITED STATES POSTAGE	INDIANA TERRITORY SESQUICENTENNIAL 1800-1950 UNITED STATES POSTAGE
994	995	996
CALIFORNIA CENTENNIAL OF STATEHOOD 1850 1950 3¢ UNITED STATES POSTAGE	FINAL REUNION UNITED CONFEDERATE VETERANS UCV 3 CENTS UNITED STATES POSTAGE	NEVADA FIRST SETTLEMENT CENTENNIAL 1850-1950 3 UNITED STATES POSTAGE
997	998	999
U.S. POSTAGE 3¢ THE LANDING OF CADILLAC AT DETROIT 1701-1951	3¢ U.S. POSTAGE 1876 COLORADO 1951 75TH ANNIVERSARY OF STATEHOOD	AMERICAN CHEMICAL SOCIETY DIAMOND JUBILEE 1876 1951 3¢ U.S. POSTAGE 3¢
1000	1001	1002

UNITED STATES POSTAGE WASHINGTON SAVES HIS ARMY AT BROOKLYN 3¢	200TH ANNIVERSARY - THE BIRTH OF BETSY ROSS UNITED STATES POSTAGE 3¢	TO MAKE THE BEST BETTER THE 4-H CLUBS UNITED STATES POSTAGE
1003	1004	1005

UNITED STATES POSTAGE THE BALTIMORE & OHIO RAILROAD CHARTERED FEB. 28, 1827 125 YEARS OF RAIL TRANSPORTATION 3¢	AMERICAN AUTOMOBILE ASSOCIATION 50TH ANNIVERSARY 1902 1952 U.S. POSTAGE 3¢	NORTH ATLANTIC TREATY ORGANIZATION NATO POSTAGE PEACE-STRENGTH-FREEDOM 3¢	3¢ U.S. POSTAGE 1902 RECLAMATION 1952
1006	1007	1008	1009

ARRIVAL OF LAFAYETTE IN AMERICA·1777
U.S. POSTAGE 3¢

1010

U·S·POSTAGE 3¢
SOUTH DAKOTA

1011

CENTENNIAL OF ENGINEERING
1852-1952
AMERICAN SOCIETY OF CIVIL ENGINEERS
3¢ U.S. POSTAGE

1012

WOMEN IN OUR ARMED SERVICES
UNITED STATES OF AMERICA

1013

500th Anniversary of the printing of the first book, The Holy Bible, from movable type, by Johann Gutenberg
U.S. POSTAGE

1014

3¢ U·S·POSTAGE
IN RECOGNITION OF THE IMPORTANT SERVICE RENDERED THEIR COMMUNITIES AND THEIR NATION BY AMERICAS
NEWSPAPERBOYS

1015

INTERNATIONAL RED CROSS
HONORING THE
UNITED STATES POSTAGE 3¢

1016

THE NATIONAL GUARD OF THE U.S.
IN WAR   IN PEACE

1017

OHIO SESQUICENTENNIAL
1803   1953
UNITED STATES POSTAGE 3¢

1018

CENTENNIAL WASHINGTON TERRITORY
ORGANIZED MARCH 2, 1853
UNITED STATES POSTAGE 3¢

1019

U·S·POSTAGE THREE CENTS 3
LOUISIANA PURCHASE SESQUI-CENTENNIAL 1803·1953
MONROE LIVINGSTON MARBOIS

1020

POSTAGE 5¢
CENTENARY OF OPENING OF JAPAN·1853

1021

AMERICAN BAR ASSOCIATION
U·S·POSTAGE
1878·LIBERTY UNDER LAW·1953

1022

3¢ U·S·POSTAGE
SAGAMORE HILL, OYSTER BAY, N.Y.
HOME OF THEODORE ROOSEVELT

1023

U·S POSTAGE 3¢
FUTURE FARMERS OF AMERICA

1024

3¢ U·S·POSTAGE
50TH ANNIVERSARY OF THE TRUCKING INDUSTRY

1025

U·S·POSTAGE 3¢
HONORING GEN. GEORGE S. PATTON, JR.
AND THE ARMORED FORCES OF THE U. S. ARMY

1026

POSTAGE 3¢ U·S·A
300TH ANNIVERSARY OF NEW YORK CITY

1027

1952-1953

	1952 continued	Un	U	PB/LP	#	FDC	Q
1010	3¢ General Lafayette, June 13	.10	.05	.60	(4)	.85	113,135,000
	Perf. 10½x11						
1011	3¢ Mt. Rushmore Mem., Aug. 11	.10	.05	.50	(4)	.85	116,255,000
	Perf. 11x10½						
1012	3¢ Engineering, Sept. 6	.10	.05	.60	(4)	.85	113,860,000
1013	3¢ Service Women, Sept. 11	.10	.05	.50	(4)	.85	124,260,000
1014	3¢ Gutenberg Bible, Sept. 30	.10	.05	.60	(4)	.85	115,735,000
1015	3¢ Newspaper Boys, Oct. 4	.10	.05	.50	(4)	.85	115,430,000
1016	3¢ Red Cross, Nov. 21	.10	.05	.50	(4)	.85	136,220,000
	Issues of 1953						
1017	3¢ National Guard, Feb. 23	.10	.05	.50	(4)	.85	114,894,600
1018	3¢ Ohio Statehood, Mar. 2	.10	.05	.80	(4)	.85	118,706,000
1019	3¢ Washington Territory, Mar. 2	.10	.05	.50	(4)	.85	114,190,000
1020	3¢ Louisiana Purchase, Apr. 30	.10	.05	.50	(4)	.85	113,990,000
1021	5¢ Opening of Japan 100th Anniv.,						
	July 14	.15	.10	2.00	(4)	.85	89,289,600
1022	3¢ American Bar Assn., Aug. 24	.10	.05	.50	(4)	.85	114,865,000
1023	3¢ Sagamore Hill, Sept. 14	.10	.05	.50	(4)	1.00	115,780,000
1024	3¢ Future Farmers, Oct. 13	.10	.05	.50	(4)	.85	115,244,600
1025	3¢ Trucking Industry, Oct. 27	.10	.05	.50	(4)	.85	123,709,600
1026	3¢ General Patton, Nov. 11	.10	.05	.50	(4)	.85	114,798,600
1027	3¢ New York City						
	300th Anniversary, Nov. 20	.10	.05	.50	(4)	.85	115,759,600

The Louisiana Purchase

When the United States purchased the vast Louisiana territory from the French in 1803, it didn't really know what it had bought, or even if it could legally buy new land. This was the first expansion of United States territory since it had become a nation. Because the Constitution made no provision for adding territory, almost everyone seemed to agree that doing so was unconstitutional. President Thomas Jefferson urged Congress to approve the purchase, then pass an amendment justifying it. The purchase was approved; after that, an amendment was considered unnecessary.

At the time, no one really knew that the Louisiana Purchase doubled the size of the United States. The French had bought the territory from Spain only three years earlier and had done no exploration. At first, the Americans thought they had purchased Texas as well and that the western boundary of the new territory was the Pacific Ocean, misconceptions that took decades to clear up. Disagreement with Canada over the northern boundary of the territory also continued for many years. The only real certainties were that the Mississippi was now a United States river and New Orleans a United States city (#1020).

	1953 continued	Un	U	PB/LP	#	FDC	Q
1028	3¢ Gadsden Purchase, Dec. 30	.10	.05	.50	(4)	.85	116,134,600
	Issues of 1954						
1029	3¢ Columbia University 200th						
	Anniv., Jan. 4	.10	.05	.50	(4)	.85	118,540,000
	Liberty Issue, 1954-61, Perf. 11x10½, 10½x11						
1030	½¢ Benjamin Franklin, 1955	.05	.05	.30	(4)	.85	Unlimited
1031	1¢ George Washington, 1954	.05	.05	.25	(4)	.85	Unlimited
1031A	1¼¢ Palace of the Governors,						
	Santa Fe, 1960	.05	.05	1.75	(4)	.85	Unlimited
1032	1½¢ Mount Vernon, 1956	.08	.05	7.50	(4)	.60	Unlimited
1033	2¢ Thomas Jefferson, 1954	.05	.05	.25	(4)	.60	Unlimited
1034	2½¢ Bunker Hill Monument						
	and Massachusetts flag, 1959	.08	.06	2.00	(4)	.60	Unlimited
1035	3¢ Statue of Liberty, 1954	.08	.05	.40	(4)	.60	Unlimited
1035a	Booklet pane of 6	3.00	.50				
1036	4¢ Abraham Lincoln, 1954	.10	.05	.50	(4)	.60	Unlimited
1036a	Booklet pane of 6	2.00	.50				
1037	4½¢ The Hermitage, 1959	.15	.08	1.75	(4)	.60	Unlimited
1038	5¢ James Monroe, 1954	.17	.05	.75	(4)	.60	Unlimited
1039	6¢ Theodore Roosevelt, 1955	.40	.05	2.00	(4)	.65	Unlimited
1040	7¢ Woodrow Wilson, 1956	.25	.05	1.50	(4)	.70	Unlimited
	Perf. 11						
1041	8¢ Statue of Liberty, 1954	.30	.06	5.00	(4)	.80	Unlimited
1042	8¢ Statue of Liberty, redrawn, 1958	.30	.05	1.75	(4)	.60	Unlimited
	Perf. 11x10½, 10½x11						
1042A	8¢ John J. Pershing, 1961	.25	.05	1.50	(4)	.60	Unlimited
1043	9¢ The Alamo, 1956	.30	.05	1.50	(4)	.90	Unlimited
1044	10¢ Independence Hall, 1956	.35	.05	1.65	(4)	.90	Unlimited
	Perf. 11						
1044A	11¢ Statue of Liberty, 1961	.30	.06	1.50	(4)	.90	Unlimited
	Perf. 11x10½, 10½x11						
1045	12¢ Benjamin Harrison, 1959	.55	.05	2.75	(4)	.90	Unlimited
1046	15¢ John Jay, 1958	.85	.03	3.35	(4)	1.00	Unlimited
1047	20¢ Monticello, 1956	.90	.05	4.50	(4)	1.20	Unlimited
1048	25¢ Paul Revere, 1958	3.00	.05	14.00	(4)	1.30	Unlimited
1049	30¢ Robert E. Lee, 1955	2.00	.08	10.00	(4)	1.50	Unlimited
1050	40¢ John Marshall, 1955	4.25	.10	18.00	(4)	1.75	Unlimited
1051	50¢ Susan B. Anthony, 1955	4.00	.04	18.00	(4)	6.00	Unlimited
1052	$1 Patrick Henry, 1955	15.00	.06	65.00	(4)	11.00	Unlimited
	Perf. 11						
1053	$5 Alexander Hamilton, 1956	120.00	8.00	475.00	(4)	65.00	Unlimited
	Coil Stamps, Perf. 10 Vertically						
1054	1¢ dark green Washington						
	(1031), 1954	.35	.12	1.50		.75	Unlimited

1028

1029

1030

1031

1031A

1032

1033

1034

1035

1036

1037

1038

1039

1040

1041

1042

1042A

1043

1044

1044A

1045

1046

1047

1048

1049

1050

1051

1052

1053

060

1061

1062

063

1064

1065

066

1067

1068

069

1070

1071

072

BENJAMIN FRANKLIN
250TH ANNIVERSARY

1074

	1954-65 continued	Un	U	PB/LP	#	FDC	Q
	Perf. 10 Horizontally						
1054A	1¼¢ turquoise, Palace of the						
	Governors, Santa Fe (1031A), 1960	.25	.20	3.00		1.00	Unlimited
	Perf. 10 Vertically						
1055	2¢ rose carmine						
	Jefferson (1033), 1954	.10	.05	.75		.75	Unlimited
1056	2½¢ gray blue, Bunker Hill Monument						
	& Massachusetts flag (1034), 1959	.55	.35	7.00		1.20	Unlimited
1057	3¢ deep violet Statue of Liberty						
	(1035), 1954	.15	.05	1.00		.75	Unlimited
1058	4¢ red violet Lincoln (1036), 1958	.15	.05	1.20		.75	Unlimited
	Perf. 10 Horizontally						
1059	4½¢ bl. grn. Hermitage (1037), 1959	2.75	1.20	17.50		1.75	Unlimited
	Perf. 10 Vertically						
1059A	25¢ green P. Revere (1048), 1965	.70	.30	3.25		1.20	Unlimited
	Issues of 1954, Perf. 11x10½						
1060	3¢ Nebraska Territory, May 7	.10	.05	.50	(4)	.75	115,810,000
1061	3¢ Kansas Territory, May 31	.10	.05	.50	(4)	.75	113,603,700
	Perf. 10½x11						
1062	3¢ George Eastman, July 12	.10	.05	.60	(4)	.75	128,002,000
	Perf. 11x10½						
1063	3¢ Lewis and Clark Expedition,						
	July 28	.10	.05	.50	(4)	.75	116,078,150
	Issues of 1955, Perf. 10½x11						
1064	3¢ Pennsylvania Academy of						
	Fine Arts, Jan. 15	.10	.05	.50	(4)	.75	116,139,800
	Perf. 11x10½						
1065	3¢ Land Grant Colleges, Feb. 12	.10	.05	.50	(4)	.75	120,484,800
1066	8¢ Rotary International, Feb. 23	.20	.12	1.75	(4)	.90	53,854,750
1067	3¢ Armed Forces Reserve, May 21	.10	.05	.50	(4)	.75	176,075,000
	Perf. 10½x11						
1068	3¢ New Hampshire, June 21	.10	.05	.50	(4)	.75	125,944,400
	Perf. 11x10½						
1069	3¢ Soo Locks, June 28	.10	.05	.50	(4)	.75	122,284,600
1070	3¢ Atoms for Peace, July 28	.12	.05	.80	(4)	.75	133,638,850
1071	3¢ Fort Ticonderoga, Sept. 18	.10	.05	.50	(4)	.75	118,664,600
	Perf. 10½x11						
1072	3¢ Andrew W. Mellon, Dec. 20	.10	.05	.60	(4)	.75	112,434,000
	Issues of 1956						
1073	3¢ Benjamin Franklin, Jan. 17	.10	.05	.50	(4)	.75	129,384,550
	Perf. 11x10½						
1074	3¢ Booker T. Washington, Apr. 5	.10	.05	.50	(4)	.75	121,184,600
	Fifth International Philatelic Exhibition, Souvenir Sheet, Imperf.						
1075	Sheet of 2, Apr. 28	5.25	4.50			7.50	2,900,731
1075a	3¢ deep violet (1035)	1.35	1.10				

	1956 continued	Un	U	PB/LP	#	FDC	Q
1075b	8¢ dk. vio. bl. & car. (1041)	1.75	1.50				
	Perf. 11x10½						
1076	3¢ New York Coliseum and						
	Columbus Monument, Apr. 30	.10	.05	.50	(4)	.75	119,784,200
	Wildlife Conservation Issue						
1077	3¢ Wild Turkey, May 5	.12	.05	.65	(4)	1.00	123,159,400
1078	3¢ Pronghorn Antelope, June 22	.12	.05	.65	(4)	1.00	123,138,800
1079	3¢ King Salmon, Nov. 9	.12	.05	.65	(4)	1.00	109,275,000
	Perf. 10½x11						
1080	3¢ Pure Food and Drug Laws,						
	June 27	.10	.05	.50	(4)	.80	112,932,200
	Perf. 11x10½						
1081	3¢ Wheatland, Aug. 5	.10	.05	.50	(4)	.80	125,475,000
	Perf. 10½x11						
1082	3¢ Labor Day, Sept. 3	.10	.05	.50	(4)	.80	117,855,000
	Perf. 11x10½						
1083	3¢ Nassau Hall, Sept. 22	.10	.05	.50	(4)	.80	122,100,000
	Perf. 10½x11						
1084	3¢ Devils Tower, Sept. 24	.10	.05	.50	(4)	.80	118,180,000
	Perf. 11x10½						
1085	3¢ Children's Issue, Dec. 15	.10	.05	.50	(4)	.80	100,975,000
	Issues of 1957						
1086	3¢ Alexander Hamilton, Jan. 11	.10	.05	.50	(4)	.80	115,299,450
	Perf. 10½x11						
1087	3¢ Polio, Jan. 15	.10	.05	.50	(4)	.80	186,949,627
	Perf. 11x10½						
1088	3¢ Coast and Geodetic Survey,						
	Feb. 11	.10	.05	.50	(4)	.80	115,235,000
1089	3¢ Architects, Feb. 23	.10	.05	.50	(4)	.80	106,647,500
	Perf. 10½x11						
1090	3¢ Steel Industry, May 22	.10	.05	.50	(4)	.80	112,010,000
	Perf. 11x10½						
1091	3¢ Int'l. Naval Review, June 10	.10	.05	.50	(4)	.80	118,470,000
1092	3¢ Oklahoma Statehood, June 14	.10	.05	.60	(4)	.80	102,230,000
1093	3¢ School Teachers, July 1	.10	.05	.50	(4)	.80	102,410,000

1076

1077

1078

1079

1080

1081

1082

1083

1084

1085

1086

1087

1088   1089

1090

1091

1092

1093

1957-1958

1094

1095

1096

1097

1098

1099

1100

1104

1105

1106

1107

1108

1109

1110

1111

1112

	1957 continued	Un	U	PB/LP	#	FDC	Q
	Perf. 11						
1094	4¢ Flag Issue, July 4	.10	.05	.60	(4)	.80	84,054,400
	Perf. 10½x11						
1095	3¢ Shipbuilding, Aug. 15	.10	.05	.70	(4)	.80	126,266,000
	Perf. 11						
1096	8¢ Champion of Liberty, Aug. 31,						
	Ramon Magsaysay	.22	.15	1.90	(4)	.80	39,489,600
	Perf. 10½x11						
1097	3¢ Lafayette, Sept. 6	.10	.05	.50	(4)	.80	122,990,000
	Perf. 11						
1098	3¢ Wildlife Conservation, Nov. 22	.10	.05	.65	(4)	1.00	174,372,800
	Perf. 10½x11						
1099	3¢ Religious Freedom, Dec. 27	.10	.05	.50	(4)	.80	114,365,000
	Issues of 1958						
1100	3¢ Gardening-Horticulture, Mar. 15	.10	.05	.50	(4)	.80	122,765,200
	Perf. 11x10½						
1104	3¢ Brussels Fair, Apr. 17	.10	.05	.50	(4)	.80	113,660,200
1105	3¢ James Monroe, Apr. 28	.10	.05	.60	(4)	.80	120,196,580
1106	3¢ Minnesota Statehood, May 11	.10	.05	.50	(4)	.80	120,805,200
	Perf. 11						
1107	3¢ Geophysical Year, May 31	.10	.05	.75	(4)	.80	125,815,200
	Perf. 11x10½						
1108	3¢ Gunston Hall, June 12	.10	.05	.50	(4)	.80	108,415,200
	Perf. 10½x11						
1109	3¢ Mackinac Bridge, June 25	.10	.05	.50	(4)	.80	107,195,200
1110	4¢ Champion of Liberty, July 24,						
	Simon Bolivar	.10	.05	.60	(4)	.80	115,745,280
	Perf. 11						
1111	8¢ Champion of Liberty, July 24,						
	Simon Bolivar	.25	.15	6.00	(4)	.80	39,743,640
	Perf. 11x10½						
1112	4¢ Atlantic Cable 100th Anniversary,						
	Aug. 15	.10	.05	.50	(4)	.80	114,570,200

	1958 continued	Un	U	PB/LP	#	FDC	Q
	Lincoln 150th Anniv. Issue, 1958-59, Perf. 10½x11, 11x10½						
1113	1¢ Portrait by George Healy,						
	Feb. 12, 1959	.05	.05	.40	(4)	.80	120,400,200
1114	3¢ Sculptured Head						
	by Gutzon Borglum, Feb. 27, 1959	.10	.06	.60	(4)	.80	91,160,200
1115	4¢ Lincoln and Stephen Douglas						
	Debating, Aug. 27, 1958	.10	.05	.55	(4)	.80	114,860,200
1116	4¢ Statue in Lincoln Memorial						
	by Daniel Chester French,						
	May 30, 1959	.10	.05	.65	(4)	.80	126,500,000
	Issues of 1958, Perf. 10½x11						
1117	4¢ Champion of Liberty, Sept. 19,						
	Lajos Kossuth	.10	.05	.60	(4)	.80	120,561,280
	Perf. 11						
1118	8¢ Champion of Liberty, Sept, 19,						
	Lajos Kossuth	.22	.12	4.25	(4)	.80	44,064,576
	Perf. 10½x11						
1119	4¢ Freedom of Press, Sept. 22	.10	.05	.50	(4)	.80	118,390,200
	Perf. 11x10½						
1120	4¢ Overland Mail, Oct. 10	.10	.05	.50	(4)	.80	125,770,200
	Perf. 10½x11						
1121	4¢ Noah Webster, Oct. 16	.10	.05	.50	(4)	.80	114,114,280
	Perf. 11						
1122	4¢ Forest Conservation, Oct. 27	.10	.05	.60	(4)	.80	156,600,200
	Perf. 11x10½						
1123	4¢ Fort Duquesne, Nov. 25	.10	.05	.50	(4)	.80	124,200,200
	Issues of 1959						
1124	4¢ Oregon Statehood, Feb. 14	.10	.05	.50	(4)	.80	120,740,200
	Perf. 10½x11						
1125	4¢ Champion of Liberty, Feb. 25,						
	Josè de San Martin	.10	.05	.55	(4)	.80	133,623,280
	Perf. 11						
1126	8¢ Champion of Liberty, Feb. 25,						
	Josè de San Martin	.20	.12	2.25	(4)	.80	45,569,088
	Perf. 10½x11						
1127	4¢ NATO, Apr. 1	.10	.05	.50	(4)	.80	122,493,280
	Perf. 11x10½						
1128	4¢ Arctic Explorations, Apr. 6	.13	.05	.85	(4)	.80	131,260,200
1129	8¢ World Peace through World						
	Trade, Apr. 20	.20	.12	1.50	(4)	.80	47,125,200
1130	4¢ Nevada Silver, June 8	.10	.05	.50	(4)	.80	123,105,000
	Perf. 11						
1131	4¢ St. Lawrence Seaway, June 26	.10	.05	.50	(4)	.80	126,105,050

1113

1114

1115

1116

1117

1118

1119

1120

1121

1122

1123

1124

1125

1126

1127

1128

1129

1130

1131

1132

1133

1134

1135

1136

1137

1138

1139

1140

1141

1142

1143

1144

1145

1146

1147

1148

	1959 continued	Un	U	PB/LP	#	FDC	Q
1132	4¢ 49-Star Flag, July 4	.10	.05	.50	(4)	.80	209,170,000
1133	4¢ Soil Conservation, Aug. 26	.10	.05	.65	(4)	.80	120,835,000
	Perf. 10½x11						
1134	4¢ Petroleum Industry, Aug. 27	.10	.05	.50	(4)	.80	115,715,000
	Perf. 11x10½						
1135	4¢ Dental Health, Sept. 14	.10	.05	.50	(4)	.80	118,445,000
	Perf. 10½x11						
1136	4¢ Champion of Liberty, Sept. 29,						
	Ernst Reuter	.10	.05	.60	(4)	.80	111,685,000
	Perf. 11						
1137	8¢ Champion of Liberty, Sept. 29,						
	Ernst Reuter	.20	.12	2.25	(4)	.80	43,099,200
	Perf. 10½x11						
1138	4¢ Dr. Ephraim McDowell, Dec. 3	.10	.05	.50	(4)	.80	115,444,000
	Issues of 1960, Perf. 11, American Credo						
1139	4¢ Quotation from Washington's						
	Farewell Address, 1960	.18	.05	1.00	(4)	.80	126,470,000
1140	4¢ B. Franklin Quotation, 1960	.18	.05	1.00	(4)	.80 ·	124,560,000
1141	4¢ T. Jefferson Quotation, 1960	.18	.05	1.00	(4)	.80	115,455,000
1142	4¢ Francis Scott Key Quotation, 1960	.18	.05	1.00	(4)	.80	122,060,000
1143	4¢ Lincoln Quotation, 1960	.18	.05	1.00	(4)	.80	120,540,000
1144	4¢ Patrick Henry Quotation, 1961	.18	.05	1.00	(4)	.80	113,075,000
1145	4¢ Boy Scout Jubilee, Feb. 8	.10	.05	.50	(4)	.80	139,325,000
	Perf. 10½x11						
1146	4¢ Olympic Winter Games, Feb. 18	.10	.05	.50	(4)	.80	124,445,000
1147	4¢ Champion of Liberty, Mar. 7,						
	Masaryk	.10	.05	.60	(4)	.80	113,792,000
	Perf. 11						
1148	8¢ Champion of Liberty, Masaryk	.20	.12	2.50	(4)	.80	44,215,200

	1960 continued	Un	U	PB/LP	#	FDC	Q
	Perf. 11x10½						
1149	4¢ World Refugee Year, Apr. 7	.10	.05	.50	(4)	.80	113,195,000
	Perf. 11						
1150	4¢ Water Conservation, Apr. 18	.10	.05	.65	(4)	.80	121,805,000
	Perf. 10½x11						
1151	4¢ SEATO, May 31	.10	.05	.50	(4)	.80	115,353,000
	Perf. 11x10½						
1152	4¢ American Woman, June 2	.10	.05	.50	(4)	.80	111,080,000
	Perf. 11						
1153	4¢ 50-Star Flag, July 4	.10	.05	.50	(4)	.80	153,025,000
	Perf. 11x10½						
1154	4¢ Pony Express 100th Anniv., July 19	.10	.05	.50	(4)	.80	119,665,000
	Perf. 10½x11						
1155	4¢ Employ the Handicapped, Aug. 28	.10	.05	.50	(4)	.80	117,855,000
1156	4¢ World Forestry Congress, Aug. 29	.10	.05	.50	(4)	.80	118,185,000
	Perf. 11						
1157	4¢ Mexican Independence, Sept. 16	.10	.05	.50	(4)	.80	112,260,000
1158	4¢ U.S.-Japan Treaty, Sept. 28	.10	.05	.50	(4)	.80	125,010,000
	Perf. 10½x11						
1159	4¢ Champion of Liberty, Oct. 8, I.J. Paderewski	.10	.05	.55	(4)	.80	119,798,000
	Perf. 11						
1160	8¢ Champion of Liberty, I.J. Paderewski	.20	.12	2.00	(4)	.80	42,696,000
	Perf. 10½x11						
1161	4¢ Sen. Taft Memorial, Oct. 10	.10	.05	.50	(4)	.80	106,610,000
	Perf. 11x10½						
1162	4¢ Wheels of Freedom, Oct. 15	.10	.05	.50	(4)	.80	109,695,000
	Perf. 11						
1163	4¢ Boy's Clubs of America, Oct. 18	.10	.05	.50	(4)	.80	123,690,000
1164	4¢ Automated P.O., Oct. 20	.10	.05	.50	(4)	.80	123,970,000
	Perf. 10½ x 11						
1165	4¢ Champion of Liberty, Oct. 26, Baron Gustaf Mannerheim	.10	.05	.55	(4)	.80	124,796,000
	Perf. 11						
1166	8¢ Champion of Liberty, Baron Gustaf Mannerheim	.20	.12	2.25	(4)	.80	42,076,800

1960

 1149

 1150

 1151

 1152

 1153

 1154

1155

 1156

 1157

 1158

 1159

 1160

 1161

 1162

  1163

 1164

 1165

 1166

1960-1965

1167

1168

1169

1170

1171

1172

1173

1174

1175

1176

1177

1178

1179

1180

1181

1182

1183

1184

	1960-61 continued	Un	U	PB/LP	#	FDC	Q
1167	4¢ Camp Fire Girls, Nov. 4	.10	.05	.50	(4)	.80	116,210,000
	Perf. 10½x11						
1168	4¢ Champion of Liberty, Nov. 2,						
	Giuseppe Garibaldi	.10	.05	.55	(4)	.80	126,252,000
	Perf. 11						
1169	8¢ Champion of Liberty,						
	Giuseppe Garibaldi	.20	.12	2.25	(4)	.80	42,746,400
	Perf. 10½x11						
1170	4¢ Sen. George Memorial, Nov. 5	.10	.05	.50	(4)	.80	124,117,000
1171	4¢ Andrew Carnegie, Nov. 25	.10	.05	.50	(4)	.80	119,840,000
1172	4¢ John Foster Dulles Memorial,						
	Dec. 6	.10	.05	.55	(4)	.80	117,187,000
	Perf. 11x10½						
1173	4¢ Echo I—Communications for						
	Peace, Dec. 15	.35	.12	2.25	(4)	1.40	124,390,000
	Issues of 1961, Perf. 10½x11						
1174	4¢ Champion of Liberty, Jan. 26,						
	Mahatma Gandhi	.10	.05	.55	(4)	.80	112,966,000
	Perf. 11						
1175	8¢ Champion of Liberty,						
	Mahatma Gandhi	.20	.12	2.25	(4)	.80	41,644,200
1176	4¢ Range Conservation, Feb. 2	.10	.05	.65	(4)	.75	110,850,000
	Perf. 10½x11						
1177	4¢ Horace Greeley, Feb. 3	.10	.05	.55	(4)	.75	98,616,000
	Civil War 100th Anniv. Issue, 1961-1965, Perf. 11x10½						
1178	4¢ Fort Sumter Centenary, 1961	.18	.05	1.10	(4)	1.25	101,125,000
1179	4¢ Shiloh Centenary, 1962	.15	.05	1.00	(4)	1.25	124,865,000
	Perf. 11						
1180	5¢ Gettysburg Centenary, 1963	.15	.05	1.00	(4)	1.25	79,905,000
1181	5¢ Wilderness Centenary, 1964	.15	.05	1.00	(4)	1.25	125,410,000
1182	5¢ Appomattox Centenary, 1965	.15	.05	1.10	(4)	1.25	112,845,000
	Issues of 1961						
1183	4¢ Kansas Statehood, May 10	.10	.05	.55	(4)	.75	106,210,000
	Perf. 11x10½						
1184	4¢ Sen. George W. Norris, July 11	.10	.05	.55	(4)	.75	110,810,000

	1961 continued	Un	U	PB/LP	#	FDC	Q
1185	4¢ Naval Aviation, Aug. 20	.10	.05	.55	(4)	.90	116,995,000
	Perf. 10½x11						
1186	4¢ Workmen's Comp., Sept. 4	.10	.05	.55	(4)	.75	121,015,000
	Perf. 11						
1187	4¢ Frederic Remington, Oct. 4	.12	.05	1.00	(4)	.75	111,600,000
	Perf. 10½x11						
1188	4¢ Republic of China, Oct. 10	.10	.05	.55	(4)	.75	110,620,000
1189	4¢ Naismith-Basketball, Nov. 6	.10	.05	.55	(4)	.90	109,110,000
	Perf. 11						
1190	4¢ Nursing, Dec. 28	.10	.05	.70	(4)	.75	145,350,000
	Issues of 1962						
1191	4¢ New Mexico Statehood, Jan. 6	.10	.05	.55	(4)	.75	112,870,000
1192	4¢ Arizona Statehood, Feb. 14	.10	.05	.75	(4)	.75	121,820,000
1193	4¢ Project Mercury, Feb. 20	.10	.10	.75	(4)	1.50	289,240,000
1194	4¢ Malaria Eradication, Mar. 30	.10	.05	.55	(4)	.75	120,155,000
	Perf. 10½x11						
1195	4¢ Charles Evans Hughes, Apr. 11	.10	.05	.55	(4)	.75	124,595,000
	Perf. 11						
1196	4¢ Seattle World's Fair, Apr. 25	.10	.05	.70	(4)	.75	147,310,000
1197	4¢ Louisiana Statehood, Apr. 30	.10	.05	.55	(4)	.75	118,690,000
	Perf. 11x10½						
1198	4¢ Homestead Act, May 20	.10	.05	.55	(4)	.75	122,730,000
1199	4¢ Girl Scout Jubilee, July 24	.10	.05	.55	(4)	.75	126,515,000
1200	4¢ Sen. Brien McMahon, July 28	.10	.05	.75	(4)	.75	130,960,000
1201	4¢ Apprenticeship, Aug. 31	.10	.05	.55	(4)	.75	120,055,000

IGY

The International Geophysical Year (IGY) took place from July 1, 1957 to December 31, 1958 (#1107). The background of this postage stamp is a fascinating story.

There was no government money for the costly experiments needed for scientific study. In 1950, a group of scientists came up with an ingenious solution. They suggested that another Polar Year be established. The first Polar Year, 1882, had set a precedent for international scientists' cooperation. The normal interval for Polar Years was every 50 years; the last one had been in 1932. The group decided to change the time span to 25 years, making the next Polar Year 1957 —a time of maximum solar activity.

Since the project was to include 67 nations, the name was changed to International Geophysical Year. On July 29, 1955, President Eisenhower announced that "small Earth-circling satellites" would be launched as part of America's participation. One day later, the USSR announced it would place a satellite in orbit. America won the press relations race by one day, but Russia launched Sputnik I on October 4, 1957, four months ahead of the U.S. Explorer I. The "Space Race" was on, and the IGY stamp documents the beginning of this dramatic era.

1911·NAVAL AVIATION·1961
UNITED STATES POSTAGE
4c
185

1911 1961
WISCONSIN
WORKMENS COMPENSATION LAW
UNITED STATES POSTAGE
4c
1186

FREDERIC REMINGTON
ARTIST OF THE WEST
1861   1961
4c U.S. POSTAGE
1187

1911 ANNIVERSARY REPUBLIC OF CHINA 1961
SUN YAT-SEN
4c
1188

NAISMITH 1861-1961
4c U.S.POSTAGE
189

U.S.POSTAGE
4c
NURSING
1190

4c
NEW MEXICO STATEHOOD
1912   U.S. POSTAGE   1962
1191

1912 ARIZONA 1962
U.S.POSTAGE 4c
1192

4c U.S. IN SPACE
PROJECT MERCURY
193

WORLD UNITED AGAINST MALARIA
4c
UNITED STATES POSTAGE
1194

CHARLES EVANS HUGHES
1862   1962
4c U.S.POSTAGE
1195

SEATTLE WORLD'S FAIR 1962
1196

1812·1962
U.S. POSTAGE
4c
LOUISIANA
197

4c U.S.POSTAGE
THE HOMESTEAD ACT
1862   1962
1198

4c
U.S POSTAGE
GIRL SCOUTS·U.S.A.
1199

ATOMIC ENERGY ACT
Peaceful Uses
4c U.S. POSTAGE
BRIEN McMAHON

APPRENTICESHIP
NATIONAL
PROGRAM
UNITED STATES 4c

4¢
U.S. POSTAGE

RAYBURN

DAG HAMMARSKJOLD
SECRETARY-GENERAL
OF THE
UNITED NATIONS
4¢

1203

DAG HAMMARSKJOLD
SECRETARY-GENERAL
OF THE
UNITED NATIONS
4¢

1204

istmas 1962

EDUCATION
HIGHER
UNITED STATES POSTAGE
4¢

1206

4¢ U.S. POSTAGE   WINSLOW HOMER

1207

5¢

1208

ANDREW JACKSON
POSTAGE

5¢ U.S. POSTAGE

1213

Carolina
Charter
1663-1963
5 cents   U S postage

1230

FOOD FOR PEACE
5¢
UNITED STATES
FREEDOM FROM HUNGER

1231

ST VIRGINIA
1863-1963

1232

1863-1963 UNITED STATES 5 CENTS
EMANCIPATION PROCLAMATION

1233

ALLIANCE FOR
PROGRESS
5¢ U.S. POSTAGE

1234

5¢

CORDELL HULL

1235

ELEANOR
ROOSEVELT
5¢ U.S.
POSTAGE

U.S. POSTAGE   THE SCIENCES
5¢

	1962 continued	Un	U	PB/LP	#	FDC	Q
	Perf. 11						
1202	4¢ Sam Rayburn, Sept. 16	.10	.05	.55	(4)	.75	120,715,000
1203	4¢ Dag Hammarskjöld, Oct. 23	.10	.05	.70	(4)	.75	121,440,000
1204	4¢ Dag Hammarskjöld Special						
	Printing: black, brown and yellow						
	(yellow inverted), Nov. 16	.12	.08	5.00	(4)	6.00	40,270,000
1205	4¢ Christmas Issue, Nov. 1	.10	.05	.50	(4)	.75	861,970,000
1206	4¢ Higher Education, Nov. 14	.10	.05	.55	(4)	.75	120,035,000
1207	4¢ Winslow Homer, Dec. 15	.15	.05	1.50	(4)	.75	117,870,000
	Flag Issue of 1963						
1208	5¢ Flag over White House, Jan. 9	.12	.05	.55	(4)	.75	
	Regular Issue of 1962-66, Perf. 11x10½						
1209	1¢ Andrew Jackson, March 22	.05	.05	.25	(4)	.75	
1213	5¢ George Washington, Nov. 23	.12	.05	.65	(4)	.75	
1213a	Booklet pane of 5 (Your Mailman)	2.00	.75				
	Coil Stamps, Perf. 10 Vertically						
1225	1¢ green Jackson (1209), May 31	.20	.05	.85		.75	
1229	5¢ dk. blue gray Washington (1213),						
	Nov. 23	1.75	.05	3.75		.75	
	Issues of 1963, Perf. 11						
1230	5¢ Carolina Charter, Apr. 6	.12	.05	.60	(4)	.75	129,945,000
1231	5¢ Food for Peace—Freedom from						
	Hunger, June 4	.12	.05	.60	(4)	.75	135,620,000
1232	5¢ W. Virginia Statehood, June 20	.12	.05	.60	(4)	.75	137,540,000
1233	5¢ Emancipation Proclamation,						
	Aug. 16	.12	.05	.60	(4)	.75	132,435,000
1234	5¢ Alliance for Progress, Aug. 17	.12	.05	.60	(4)	.75	135,520,000
	Perf. 10½x11						
1235	5¢ Cordell Hull, Oct. 5	.12	.05	.60	(4)	.75	131,420,000
	Perf. 11x10½						
1236	5¢ Eleanor Roosevelt, Oct. 11	.12	.05	.60	(4)	.75	133,170,000
	Perf. 11						
1237	5¢ Science, Oct. 14	.12	.05	1.35	(4)	.75	130,195,000

	1963 continued	Un	U	PB/LP	#	FDC	Q
1238	5¢ City Mail Delivery, Oct. 26	.12	.05	.60	(4)	.75	128,450,000
1239	5¢ Red Cross 100th Anniv., Oct. 29	.12	.05	.60	(4)	.75	118,665,000
1240	5¢ Christmas Issue, Nov. 1	.12	.05	.60	(4)	75	1,291,250,000
1241	5¢ John James Audubon, Dec. 7	.12	.05	1.25	(4)	.75	175,175,000
	Issues of 1964, Perf. 10½x11						
1242	5¢ Sam Houston, Jan. 10	.12	.05	.60	(4)	.75	125,995,000
	Perf. 11						
1243	5¢ Charles M. Russell, Mar. 9	.15	.05	1.20	(4)	.75	128,925,000
	Perf. 11x10½						
1244	5¢ New York World's Fair, Apr. 22	.12	.05	1.00	(4)	.75	145,700,000
	Perf. 11						
1245	5¢ John Muir, Apr. 29	.12	.05	.60	(4)	.75	120,310,000
	Perf. 11x10½						
1246	5¢ Kennedy Memorial, May 29	.12	.05	.60	(4)	.75	511,750,000
	Perf. 10½x11						
1247	5¢ New Jersey 300th Anniv., June 15	.12	.05	.60	(4)	.75	123,845,000
	Perf. 11						
1248	5¢ Nevada Statehood, July 22	.12	.05	.60	(4)	.75	122,825,000
1249	5¢ Register and Vote, Aug. 1	.12	.05	.60	(4)	.75	453,090,000
	Perf. 10½x11						
1250	5¢ Shakespeare, Aug. 14	.12	.05	.60	(4)	.75	123,245,000
1251	5¢ Doctors Mayo, Sept. 11	.12	.05	.60	(4)	.75	123,355,000
	Perf. 11						
1252	5¢ American Music, Oct. 15,	.12	.05	.60	(4)	.75	126,970,000
1253	5¢ Homemakers, Oct. 26, Perf. 11	.12	.05	.60	(4)	.75	121,250,000

Sam Houston

Virginia-born Sam Houston (#1242) was one of the most unconventional and colorful Americans who ever lived. Unhappy working in his family's general store, Houston ran off at the age of 16 to become an adopted Cherokee Indian, living with them for three years. It's been reported that when his white brothers tried to bring him home, he claimed that only among the Cherokee was it quiet enough to read classical literature.

He eventually returned, ran his own school (even though he couldn't spell), became a hero in the War of 1812, served as a Congressman and governor of Tennessee. While in office, Houston married, divorced, quit the governorship and went to live with the Cherokee again. He became an advocate of Indian rights, often representing the Cherokee in Washington. When Houston became president of the Republic of Texas, his honest and understanding relations with the Indians kept the young country at peace.

After Texas's annexation to the United States, which Houston engineered, he was one of the few major Southern statesmen to oppose secession. Most Texans were for it, but despite his Unionist stand, Houston was elected governor of the state in 1859. He didn't finish this term either. When Texas did secede against his wishes, Houston was forced to retire.

1238

1239

1240

1241

1242

1243

1244

1245

1246

1247

1248

1249

250

1251

1252

1253

1259

1254   1255
1256   1257

1258

1260

1261

1262   1263   1264

1265   1266

1267   1268

1269

1270

1271

1272

	1964 continued	Un	U	PB/LP	#	FDC	Q
	Christmas Issue, Nov. 9						
1254	5¢ Holly, Perf. 11	.75	.05	5.50	(4)	.75	351,940,000
1255	5¢ Mistletoe, Perf. 11	.75	.05	5.50	(4)	.75	351,940,000
1256	5¢ Poinsettia, Perf. 11	.75	.05	5.50	(4)	.75	351,940,000
1257	5¢ Sprig of Conifer, Perf. 11	.75	.05	5.50	(4)	.75	351,940,000
	Block of four, #1254-1257	3.50	1.25			3.00	
	Perf. 10½x11						
1258	5¢ Verrazano-Narrows Bridge,						
	Nov. 21	.12	.05	.60	(4)	.75	120,005,000
	Perf. 11						
1259	5¢ Fine Arts, Dec. 2	.12	.05	.75	(4)	.75	125,800,000
	Perf. 10½x11						
1260	5¢ Amateur Radio, Dec. 15	.12	.05	.75	(4)	.75	122,230,000
	Issues of 1965, Perf. 11						
1261	5¢ Battle of New Orleans, Jan. 8	.12	.05	.75	(4)	.75	115,695,000
1262	5¢ Physical Fitness-Sokol, Feb. 15	.12	.05	.75	(4)	.75	115,095,000
1263	5¢ Crusade Against Cancer, Apr. 1	.12	.05	.75	(4)	.75	119,560,000
	Perf. 10½x11						
1264	5¢ Churchill Memorial, May 13	.12	.05	.75	(4)	.75	125,180,000
	Perf. 11						
1265	5¢ Magna Carta, June 15	.12	.05	.75	(4)	.75	120,135,000
1266	5¢ Intl. Cooperation Year, June 26	.12	.05	.75	(4)	.75	115,405,000
1267	5¢ Salvation Army, July 2	.12	.05	.75	(4)	.75	115,855,000
	Perf. 10½x11						
1268	5¢ Dante Alighieri, July 17	.12	.05	.75	(4)	.75	115,340,000
1269	5¢ Herbert Hoover, Aug. 10	.12	.05	.75	(4)	.75	114,840,000
	Perf. 11						
1270	5¢ Robert Fulton, Aug. 19	.12	.05	.75	(4)	.75	116,140,000
1271	5¢ Settlement of Florida, Aug. 28	.12	.05	1.00	(4)	.75	116,900,000
1272	5¢ Traffic Safety, Sept. 3	.12	.05	1.00	(4)	.75	114,085,000

World Wide Communications

On October 28, 1959, the National Aeronautics and Space Administration launched a plastic balloon from Wallops Island, Virginia, to an altitude of 250 miles. There the balloon was inflated to a 100-foot diameter; a series of successful tests followed. On August 12, 1960, the world's first operational communication satellite was placed in orbit around the world, and this satellite is pictured on the Echo postage stamp (#1173).

This 1960 stamp included the inscription "World Wide Communications Through Space." This proved prophetic, since Echo was followed in short order by Telstar, Relay, and Tiros communications satellites. The effort to bring communications to all peoples continues as new space vehicles are launched to bring television signals to the remotest parts of every country.

	1965 continued	Un	U	PB/LP	#	FDC	Q
1273	5¢ John Singleton Copley, Sept. 17	.15	.05	1.25	(4)	.75	114,880,000
1274	11¢ International Telecommunication Union,						
	Oct. 6	.50	.25	15.00	(4)	.75	26,995,000
1275	5¢ Adlai E. Stevenson, Oct. 23	.12	.05	.75	(4)	.75	128,495,000
1276	5¢ Christmas Issue, Nov. 2	.12	.05	.60	(4)	.75	1,139,930,000
	Issues of 1965-78, Prominent Americans, Perf. 11x10, 10½x11						
1278	1¢ Thomas Jefferson, 1968	.05	.05	.20	(4)	.35	
1278a	Booklet pane of 8, 1968	1.00	.25				
1278b	Booklet pane of 4, 1971	.75	.20				
1279	1¼¢ Albert Gallatin, 1967	.10	.05	22.50	(4)	.35	
1280	2¢ Frank Lloyd Wright, 1966	.05	.05	.30	(4)	.35	
1280a	Booklet pane of 5 + label, 1968	1.20	.40				
1280c	Booklet pane of 6, 1971	1.00	.35				
1281	3¢ Francis Parkman, 1967	.06	.05	.70	(4)	.35	
1282	4¢ Abraham Lincoln, 1965	.12	.05	.40	(4)	.35	
1283	5¢ George Washington, 1966	.18	.05	.50	(4)	.45	
1283B	5¢ Washington redrawn, 1967	.12	.05	1.00	(4)	.45	
1284	6¢ Franklin D. Roosevelt, 1966	.18	.05	.65	(4)	.45	
1284b	Booklet pane of 8, 1967	1.50	.50				
1284c	Booklet pane of 5 + label, 1968	1.25	.50				
1285	8¢ Albert Einstein, 1966	.25	.05	1.25	(4)	.50	
1286	10¢ Andrew Jackson, 1967	.25	.05	1.30	(4)	.60	
1286A	12¢ Henry Ford, 1968	.30	.05	1.75	(4)	.50	
1287	13¢ John F. Kennedy, 1967	.30	.05	1.65	(4)	.65	
1288	15¢ Oliver Wendell Holmes, 1968	.30	.06	1.50	(4)	.60	
	Perf. 10, 1978						
1288B	15¢ dk. rose claret Holmes (1288),						
	Booklet pane of 8	.30	.05			.65	
1288c	Booklet pane of 8, 1978	2.40	1.25				
1289	20¢ George C. Marshall, 1967	.55	.06	2.00	(4)	.80	
1290	25¢ Frederick Douglass, 1967	.60	.05	2.50	(4)	1.00	
1291	30¢ John Dewey, 1968	.75	.08	3.00	(4)	1.20	
1292	40¢ Thomas Paine, 1968	.95	.10	4.00	(4)	1.60	
1293	50¢ Lucy Stone, 1968	1.10	.05	5.00	(4)	3.25	
1294	$1 Eugene O'Neill, 1967	2.40	.08	10.00	(4)	7.50	
1295	$5 John Bassett Moore, 1966	12.50	2.00	50.00	(4)	60.00	
	Coil Stamps, Issues of 1966-78, Perf. 10 Horizontally						
1297	3¢ violet Parkman (1281), 1975	.12	.05	.60		.75	
1298	6¢ gray brown F.D.R. (1284), 1967	.30	.05	2.75		.75	
	Perf. 10 Vertically						
1299	1¢ green Jefferson (1278), 1968	.06	.05	.35		.75	
1303	4¢ black Lincoln (1282), 1966	.15	.05	1.85		.75	
1304	5¢ blue Washington (1283), 1966	.15	.05	.90		.75	
1305	6¢ Franklin D. Roosevelt, 1968	.20	.05	1.25		.75	

146

1273

1274

1275

1276

1278

1279

1280

1281

1282

1283

1283B

1284

1285

1286

1286A

1287

1288

1289

1290

1291

1292

1293

1294

1295

1305

147

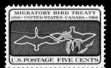

1306

1307

1308

1309

1310

1312

1313

1314

1311

1315

1316

1317

1318

1319

		Un	U	PB/LP	#	FDC	Q
	Coil Stamps, Issues of 1966-78, continued						
1305E	15¢ rose claret Holmes (1288), 1978	.30	.05	1.20		.75	
1305C	$1 dull purple Eugene O'Neill						
	(1294), 1973	2.25	.20	6.50		3.00	
	Issues of 1966, Perf. 11						
1306	5¢ Migratory Bird Treaty, Mar. 16	.12	.05	1.00	(4)	.75	116,835,000
1307	5¢ Humane Treatment of Animals,						
	Apr. 9	.12	.05	.90	(4)	.75	117,470,000
1308	5¢ Indiana Statehood, Apr. 16	.12	.05	.75	(4)	.75	123,770,000
1309	5¢ American Circus, May 2	.12	.05	.90	(4)	.75	131,270,000
	Sixth International Philatelic Exhibition Issues						
1310	5¢ Stamped Cover, May 21	.12	.05	.90	(4)	.75	122,285,000
	Imperf.						
1311	5¢ Souvenir Sheet, May 23	.30	.15			.75	14,680,000
	Issued in sheets of one stamp with marginal inscription commemorating the Sixth International Philatelic Exhibition (SIPEX), held in Washington, D.C. from May 21-30.						
	Perf. 11						
1312	5¢ Bill of Rights, July 1	.12	.05	.75	(4)	.75	114,160,000
	Perf. 10½x11						
1313	5¢ Polish Millennium, July 30	.12	.05	.90	(4)	.75	128,475,000
	Perf. 11						
1314	5¢ National Park Service, Aug. 25	.12	.05	.75	(4)	.75	119,535,000
1315	5¢ Marine Corps Reserve, Aug. 29	.12	.05	1.00	(4)	.75	125,110,000
1316	5¢ General Federation of Women's						
	Clubs, Sept. 12	.12	.05	1.00	(4)	.75	114,853,200
1317	5¢ Johnny Appleseed, Sept. 24	.12	.05	1.00	(4)	.75	124,290,000
1318	5¢ Beautification of America, Oct. 5	.12	.05	1.25	(4)	.75	128,460,000
1319	5¢ Great River Road, Oct. 21	.12	.05	1.00	(4)	.75	127,585,000

The Bill of Rights

Americans point proudly to the freedoms and rights they enjoy as citizens of the United States. Some of the most important are spelled out in the Bill of Rights—the first ten amendments to the Constitution. These rights cannot be taken away by the government. Among them are freedom of speech, freedom of religion, freedom against unreasonable searches and seizures and the right to due process of law.

Interestingly enough, many framers of the Constitution were against including a bill of rights. They argued that U.S. citizens were already free—so cataloguing certain rights might tempt later governments to remove other rights not actually mentioned in the bill.

However, eight state constitutions already had bills of rights, and the state conventions that finally ratified the U.S. Constitution wanted a similar bill in the federal document. Congress was directed to prepare amendments listing citizens' inalienable rights. Congress did so; the Bill of Rights was ratified by the states on December 15, 1791 (#1312).

	1966 continued	Un	U	PB/LP	#	FDC	Q
1320	5¢ Savings Bond—Servicemen,						
	Oct. 26	.12	.05	1.00	(4)	.75	115,875,000
1321	5¢ Christmas Issue, Nov. 1	.12	.05	.75	(4)	.75	1,173,547,420
1322	5¢ Mary Cassatt, Nov. 17	.20	.05	2.75	(4)	.75	114,015,000
	Issues of 1967						
1323	5¢ National Grange, Apr. 17	.12	.05	.90	(4)	.75	121,105,000
1324	5¢ Canada 100th Anniv., May 25	.12	.05	.90	(4)	.90	132,045,000
1325	5¢ Erie Canal, July 4	.12	.05	.90	(4)	.75	118,780,000
1326	5¢ "Peace"—Lions, July 5	.12	.05	.90	(4)	.75	121,985,000
1327	5¢ Henry David Thoreau, July 12	.12	.05	.90	(4)	.75	111,850,000
1328	5¢ Nebraska Statehood, July 29	.12	.05	.90	(4)	.75	117,225,000
1329	5¢ Voice of America, Aug. 1	.12	.05	1.00	(4)	.75	111,515,000
1330	5¢ Davy Crockett, Aug. 17	.12	.05	1.00	(4)	.75	114,270,000
	Space Accomplishments Issue, Sept. 29						
1331	5¢ Space-Walking Astronaut	.90	.25				60,432,500
1332	5¢ Gemini 4 Capsule and Earth	.90	.25				60,432,500
	Block of 4, 2 #1331 & 2 #1332	7.00	5.00	7.00		10.00	
1333	5¢ Urban Planning, Oct. 2	.15	.05	2.00	(4)	.75	110,675,000
1334	5¢ Finnish Independence, Oct. 6	.15	.05	2.00	(4)	.75	110,670,000
	Perf. 12						
1335	5¢ Thomas Eakins, Nov. 2	.18	.05	2.50	(4)	.75	113,825,000
	Perf. 11						
1336	5¢ Christmas Issue, Nov. 6	.12	.05	.60	(4)	.75	1,208,700,000
1337	5¢ Mississippi Statehood, Dec. 11	.15	.05	2.00	(4)	.75	113,330,000
	Issues of 1968-71						
1338	6¢ Flag and White House, 1968	.15	.05	.60	(4)	.75	

Finnish Independence

On December 6, 1917, Finland declared its independence from Russia, and 700 years of foreign rule came to an end. For centuries, Finland had been dominated so completely by Sweden that the Finnish language was no longer spoken. When Czarist Russia gained control of Finland in 1809, it granted Finland a high degree of self-government.

Throughout the 19th century a Finnish nationalist movement developed and grew. It sparked a revival of the Finnish language and a renewed interest in the roots of Finnish culture. Russia, meanwhile, began to think of incorporating Finland into its empire and began a program of Russification.

With the Russian Revolution, Finns saw their chance for freedom. But independence was not won easily. Russian troops had to be driven out by force; then civil war ensued between those who wanted a republican Finland and those who wanted a socialist state. The republican forces were victorious, and in 1919 Finland ratified a constitution. Stamp #1334 paid tribute to the 50th anniversary of the Republic of Finland.

1321

1322

1320

1323

1324

1325

1326

1328

1330

1327

1329

1331

1332

1333

1334

1335

1337

1338

1336

1339

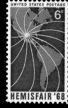

1340

1341

1342

1343

1344

1345

1346

1347

1348

1349

1350

1351

1352

1353

1354

1355

152

	1968-71 continued	Un	U	PB/LP #	FDC	Q
	Perf. 11x10½					
1338D	6¢ dark blue, red & green					
	(1338), 1970	.15	.05	3.25 (20)	.75	
1338F	8¢ multicolored (1338), 1971	.16	.05	3.50 (20)	.75	
	Coil Stamps of 1969-71, Perf. 10 Vertically					
1338A	6¢ dark blue, red & green					
	(1338), 1969	.20	.05			
1338G	8¢ multicolored (1338), 1971	.20	.05			
	Issues of 1968, Perf. 11					
1339	6¢ Illinois Statehood, Feb. 12	.18	.05	1.00 (4)	.75	141,350,000
1340	6¢ HemisFair '68, Mar. 30	.18	.05	1.00 (4)	.75	144,345,000
1341	$1 Airlift, Apr. 4	6.00	3.00	32.50 (4)	6.50	
1342	6¢ "Youth"—Elks, May 1	.18	.05	1.00 (4)	.75	147,120,000
1343	6¢ Law and Order, May 17	.18	.05	1.00 (4)	.75	130,125,000
1344	6¢ Register and Vote, June 27	.18	.05	1.00 (4)	.75	158,700,000
	Historic Flag Series, July 4					
1345	6¢ Ft. Moultrie Flag (1776)	1.00	.50		4.00	23,153,000
1346	6¢ Ft. McHenry Flag (1795-1818)	1.00	.50		4.00	23,153,000
1347	6¢ Washington's Cruisers Flag					
	(1775)	.60	.50		4.00	23,153,000
1348	6¢ Bennington Flag (1777)	.60	.40		4.00	23,153,000
1349	6¢ Rhode Island Flag (1775)	.60	.45		4.00	23,153,000
1350	6¢ First Stars and Stripes Flag					
	(1777)	.60	.35		4.00	23,153,000
1351	6¢ Bunker Hill Flag (1775)	.60	.35		4.00	23,153,000
1352	6¢ Grand Union Flag (1776)	.60	.35		4.00	23,153,000
1353	6¢ Phila. Light Horse Flag (1775)	.80	.35		4.00	23,153,000
1354	6¢ First Navy Jack (1775)	.80	.40		4.00	23,153,000
	Plate Block, (1345-1354)			18.00 (20)		
	#1345-1354 printed se-tenant in vertical rows of 10.					
	Perf. 12					
1355	6¢ Walt Disney, Sept. 11	.20	.05	1.75 (4)	1.00	153,015,000

	1968 continued	Un	U	PB/LP	#	FDC	Q
	Perf. 11						
1356	6¢ Father Marquette, Sept. 20	.20	.05	1.10	(4)	.75	132,560,000
1357	6¢ Daniel Boone, Sept. 26	.20	.05	1.10	(4)	.75	130,385,000
1358	6¢ Arkansas River, Oct. 1	.20	.05	1.10	(4)	.75	132,265,000
1359	6¢ Leif Erikson, Oct. 9	.20	.05	1.20	(4)	.75	128,710,000
	Perf. 11x10½						
1360	6¢ Cherokee Strip, Oct. 15	.20	.05	1.65	(4)	.75	124,775,000
	Perf. 11						
1361	6¢ John Trumbull, Oct. 18	.25	.05	2.25	(4)	.75	128,295,000
1362	6¢ Waterfowl Conservation, Oct. 24	.30	.05	3.00	(4)	.75	142,245,000
1363	6¢ Christmas Issue, Nov. 1	.20	.05	2.75	(10)	.75	1,410,580,000
1364	6¢ American Indian, Nov. 4	.40	.05	3.00	(4)	.75	125,100,000
	Issues of 1969, Beautification of America, Jan. 16						
1365	6¢ Capitol, Azaleas and Tulips	1.10	.15	10.00	(4)	2.00	48,142,500
1366	6¢ Washington Monument,						
	Potomac River and Daffodils	1.10	.15	10.00	(4)	2.00	48,142,500
1367	6¢ Poppies and Lupines						
	along Highway	1.10	.15	10.00	(4)	2.00	48,142,500
1368	6¢ Blooming Crabapples						
	along Street	1.10	.15	10.00	(4)	2.00	48,142,500
	Block of four, #1365-1368	5.50	3.50			5.00	
1369	6¢ American Legion, Mar. 15	.20	.05	1.10	(4)	.75	148,770,000
1370	6¢ Grandma Moses, May 1	.25	.05	1.35	(4)	.75	139,475,000
1371	6¢ Apollo 8, May 5	.30	.06	3.00	(4)	2.00	187,165,000
1372	6¢ W. C. Handy, May 17	.20	.05	1.00	(4)	.75	125,555,000

The Secret Stamp

The manned space program reached epic proportions for the United States when John Glenn orbited the earth on February 20, 1962. Before the event, the Postal Service prepared a commemorative stamp, but they couldn't predict the success of the mission. In the late fall of 1961, the stamps were distributed to 305 post offices with strict instructions that the sealed pouch not be unlocked until permission came from postal headquarters. The 305 postmasters did not know what was in the packet.

1193

John Glenn safely completed his journey into space, and at 3:30 pm, orders were sent to the field to open the pouch and to immediately place on sale the stamps inside. Project Mercury (#1193) commemorative stamps, a press release and a poster for the post office lobbies were in each container. The demand for the stamp was so great that many post offices sold out that first day, even though they closed at 5 pm.

1356

1357

1358

1359

1360

1361

1362

1363

1364

1365
1367

1366
1368

1369

1370

1371

1372

1374

1375

1373

1376
1378

1377
1379

1380

1381

1382

1384

1383

1384a

1385

1386

	1969 continued	Un	U	PB/LP	#	FDC	Q
1373	6¢ California Settlement, July 16	.20	.05	1.00	(4)	.75	144,425,000
1374	6¢ John Wesley Powell, Aug. 1	.20	.05	1.00	(4)	.75	135,875,000
1375	6¢ Alabama Statehood, Aug. 2	.20	.05	1.00	(4)	.75	151,110,000
	Botanical Congress Issue						
1376	6¢ Douglas Fir (Northwest)	1.50	.15	12.00	(4)	2.00	39,798,750
1377	6¢ Lady's Slipper (Northeast)	1.50	.15	12.00	(4)	2.00	39,798,750
1378	6¢ Ocotillo (Southwest)	1.50	.15	12.00	(4)	2.00	39,798,750
1379	6¢ Franklinia (Southeast)	1.50	.15	12.00	(4)	2.00	39,798,750
	Block of four, #1376-1379	8.00	5.00			7.00	
	Perf. 10½x11						
1380	6¢ Dartmouth College Case, Sept. 22	.20	.05	1.35	(4)	.75	129,540,000
	Perf. 11						
1381	6¢ Professional Baseball, Sept. 24	.25	.05	1.75	(4)	.75	130,925,000
1382	6¢ Intercollegiate Football, Sept. 26	.25	.05	1.85	(4)	.75	139,055,000
1383	6¢ Dwight D. Eisenhower, Oct. 14	.20	.05	1.00	(4)	.75	150,611,200
	Perf. 11x10½						
1384	6¢ Christmas Issue, Nov. 3	.18	.05	2.25	(10)	.75	1,709,795,000
1384a	Precanceled	.60	.06				
1385	6¢ Hope for Crippled, Nov. 20	.18	.05	1.00	(4)	.75	127,545,000
1386	6¢ William M. Harnett, Dec. 3	.18	.05	1.20	(4)	.75	145,788,800

Errors, Freaks and Oddities

The most famous error in U.S. stamps is the 24 cents air mail invert (#C3a). The stamp went on sale May 14, 1918 in Philadelphia and New York. W. T. Robey, a stamp collector, bought a full sheet at the post office for his collection. He noticed that the centers were inverted, showed the sheet to the window postal clerk, and kept the lucky purchase. Postal inspectors tried to obtain the sheet, but Robey kept it. The sheet was reportedly sold to a Philadelphia stamp dealer for $15,000. The dealer immediately resold the stamps to a famous collector for $20,000. The collector kept several blocks for himself, and sold the balance. In 1979, a block of four was sold for $500,000.

Errors, Freaks and Oddities are usually mistakes that have resulted in the stamp (or postal card, souvenir card, etc.) production process. The term EFO also includes errors in stamp usage, inverted cancels, experimental perforations, plate varieties, almost anything that deviates from the normal.

An Error can be a total absence of one color on a multi-color issue, or a sheet with no perforations, or paper with no watermark when there should be one. Minor production problems can result in Freaks—for example, a line through a stamp caused by a hair on the plate, a smear or white space caused by a fold in the stamps during the printing process, or perforations not where they should be. Oddities can be anything that fits or doesn't fit into these categories—depending on the imagination of the collector.

		Un	U	PB/LP	#	FDC	Q
	Issues of 1970, Natural History, May 6						
1387	6¢ American Bald Eagle	.22	.12	2.75	(4)	2.00	50,448,550
1388	6¢ African Elephant Herd	.22	.12	2.75	(4)	2.00	50,448,550
1389	6¢ Tlingit Chief in						
	Haida Ceremonial Canoe	.22	.12	2.75	(4)	2.00	50,448,550
1390	6¢ Brontosaurus, Stegosaurus						
	and Allosaurus from Jurassic						
	Period	.22	.12	2.75	(4)	2.00	50,448,550
	Block of four, #1387-1390	1.00	1.00			3.00	
1391	6¢ Maine Statehood, July 9	.18	.05	1.10	(4)	.75	171,850,000
	Perf. 10½x11						
1392	6¢ Wildlife Conservation, July 20	.18	.05	1.10	(4)	.75	142,205,000
	Issues of 1970-74, Perf. 11x10½, 10½x11, 11						
1393	6¢ Dwight D. Eisenhower, 1970	.12	.05	.60	(4)	.75	
	Booklet pane of 8	1.00	.50				
	Booklet pane of 5 + label	.85	.35				
1393D	7¢ Benjamin Franklin, 1972	.14	.05	1.35	(4)	.75	
1394	8¢ Eisenhower, 1971	.16	.05	1.00	(4)	.75	
1395	8¢ Eisenhower (1393), 1971	.16	.05			.75	
	Booklet pane of 8, 1971	1.50	1.25				
	Booklet pane of 6, 1971	1.00	.75				
	Booklet pane of 4 + 2 labels, 1972	1.00	.50				
	Booklet pane of 7 + label, 1972	1.25	1.00				
1396	8¢ U.S. Postal Service, 1971	.25	.05	7.50	(12)	.75	
1397	14¢ Fiorello H. LaGuardia, 1972	.32	.05	2.35	(4)	.85	
1398	16¢ Ernie Pyle, 1971	.35	.05	2.35	(4)	.75	
1399	18¢ Dr. Elizabeth Blackwell, 1974	.40	.06	1.80	(4)	1.25	
1400	21¢ Amadeo P. Giannini, 1973	.45	.06	2.10	(4)	1.00	
	Coil Stamps, Perf. 10 Vertically						
1401	6¢ dark blue gray Eisenhower						
	(1393), 1970	.20	.05	1.00		.75	
1402	8¢ deep claret Eisenhower						
	(1395), 1971	.22	.05	1.00		.75	
	Issues of 1970, Perf. 11						
1405	6¢ Edgar Lee Masters, Aug. 22	.18	.05	1.00	(4)	.75	137,660,000
1406	6¢ Woman Suffrage, Aug. 26	.18	.05	1.00	(4)	.75	135,125,000
1407	6¢ South Carolina, Sept. 12	.18	.05	1.00	(4)	.75	135,895,000
1408	6¢ Stone Mountain Mem., Sept. 19	.18	.05	1.00	(4)	.75	132,675,000
1409	6¢ Fort Snelling, Oct. 17	.18	.05	1.00	(4)	.75	134,795,000

AMERICAN BALD EAGLE : AFRICAN ELEPHANT HERD

1391

HAIDA CEREMONIAL CANOE : THE AGE OF REPTILES

1392

1387
1389

1388
1390

1393

1393D

1394

1396

1397

1398

1399

1400

1406

1405

1407

1408

1409

SAVE OUR SOIL · UNITED STATES · SIX CENTS
SAVE OUR CITIES · UNITED STATES · SIX CENTS

Christmas 6 u.s.
1414

Christmas 6 u.s.
1414a

SAVE OUR WATER · UNITED STATES · SIX CENTS
SAVE OUR AIR · UNITED STATES · SIX CENTS

1410
1412
1411
1413

Christmas 6 u.s.
Christmas 6 u.s.

UNITED STATES POSTAGE 6 CENTS
UN
United Nations 25ᵗʰ Anniversary
1419

1829 THE LANDING OF THE PILGRIMS
U.S. POSTAGE 6 CENTS
1420

Christmas 6 u.s.
Christmas 6 u.s.

1415
1417
1416
1418

50 years of service
DISABLED AMERICAN VETERAN
UNITED 6 STATES

HONORING U.S. SERVICEMEN
PRISONERS OF WAR
MISSING AND KILLED IN ACTION
UNITED 6 STATES

UNITED STATES 6
AMERICA'S WOOL

DOUGLAS MacARTHUR
6 US

giving BLOOD saves lives
United States Postage 6
1425

1421
1422
1423
1424

Missouri 1821-1971 United States
1426

TROUT 8¢ UNITED STATES
WILDLIFE CONSERVATION

ALLIGATOR 8¢ UNITED STATES
WILDLIFE CONSERVATION

WILDLIFE CONSERVATION
8¢ UNITED STATES
POLAR BEAR

WILDLIFE CONSERVATION
UNITED STATES
CALIFORNIA CONDOR

1427
1429
1428
1430

1970-1971

		Un	U	PB/LP	#	FDC	Q
	Perf. 11x10½, Anti-Pollution Issue, Oct. 28						
1410	6¢ Save Our Soil	.45	.13	2.75	(4)	1.40	40,400,000
1411	6¢ Save Our Cities	.45	.13	2.75	(4)	1.40	40,400,000
1412	6¢ Save Our Water	.45	.13	2.75	(4)	1.40	40,400,000
1413	6¢ Save Our Air	.45	.13	2.75	(4)	1.40	40,400,000
	Block of four, #1410-1413	2.50	2.00			4.25	
	Christmas Issue, Nov. 5, Perf. 10½x11						
1414	6¢ Nativity, by Lorenzo Lotto	.20	.05	3.00	(8)	1.40	638,730,000
1414a	Precanceled	.35	.08				358,245,000
	Perf. 11x10½						
1415	6¢ Tin and Cast-Iron Locomotive	.85	.10	4.50	(4)	1.40	122,313,750
1415a	Precanceled	2.00	.15				109,912,500
1416	6¢ Toy Horse on Wheels	.85	.10	4.50	(4)	1.40	122,313,750
1416a	Precanceled	2.00	.15				109,912,500
1417	6¢ Mechanical Tricycle	.85	.10	4.50	(4)	1.40	122,313,750
1417a	Precanceled	2.00	.15				109,912,500
1418	6¢ Doll Carriage	.85	.10	4.50	(4)	1.40	122,313,750
1418a	Precanceled	2.00	.15				109,912,500
	Block of 4, #1415-1418	4.50		3.50			
	Block of 4, #1415a-1418a	9.00		6.00			
	Perf. 11						
1419	6¢ United Nations, Nov. 20	.18	.05	1.25	(4)	.75	127,610,000
1420	6¢ Landing of the Pilgrims, Nov. 21	.18	.05	1.25	(4)	.75	129,785,000
	Disabled Veterans and Servicemen Issue, Nov. 24						
1421	6¢ Disabled American Veterans						
	Emblem	.20	.10	7.00	(4)	.75	67,190,000
1422	6¢ U.S. Servicemen	.20	.10	7.00	(4)	.75	67,190,000
	Pair #1421-1422	.50	.65			1.20	
	Issues of 1971						
1423	6¢ American Wool Industry, Jan. 19	.18	.05	1.00	(4)	.75	135,305,000
1424	6¢ Gen. Douglas MacArthur,						
	Jan. 26	.18	.05	1.00	(4)	.75	134,840,000
1425	6¢ Blood Donor, Mar. 12	.18	.05	1.00	(4)	.75	130,975,000
	Perf. 11x10½						
1426	8¢ Missouri 150th Anniv., May 8	.20	.05	3.50	(12)	.75	161,235,000
	Perf. 11, Wildlife Conservation Issue, June 12						
1427	8¢ Trout	.30	.10	2.25	(4)	1.75	43,920,000
1428	8¢ Alligator	.30	.10	2.25	(4)	1.75	43,920,000
1429	8¢ Polar Bear and Cubs	.30	.10	2.25	(4)	1.75	43,920,000
1430	8¢ California Condor	.30	.10	2.25	(4)	1.75	43,920,000
	Block of four #1427-1430	1.30	1.00			3.00	

	1971 continued	Un	U	PB/LP #	FDC	Q
1431	8¢ Antarctic Treaty, June 23	.25	.05	1.65 (4)	.75	138,700,000
1432	8¢ American Revolution					
	200th Anniversary, July 4	.50	.05	4.00 (4)	.75	138,165,000
1433	8¢ John Sloan, Aug. 2	.20	.05	1.65 (4)	.75	152,125,000
	Decade of Space Achievements Issue, Aug. 2					
1434	8¢ Earth, Sun, Landing Craft					
	on Moon	.20	.10	1.75 (4)		88,147,500
1435	8¢ Lunar Rover and Astronauts	.20	.10	1.75 (4)		88,147,500
	Pair # (1434/1435)	.50	.65		1.75	
1436	8¢ Emily Dickinson, Aug. 28	.18	.05	1.25 (4)	.75	142,845,000
1437	8¢ San Juan, Sept 12	.18	.05	1.25 (4)	.75	148,755,000
	Perf. 10½x11					
1438	8¢ Prevent Drug Abuse, Oct. 5	.18	.05	1.85 (6)	.75	139,080,000
1439	8¢ CARE, Oct. 27	.18	.05	2.10 (8)	.75	130,755,000
	Perf. 11, Historic Preservation Issue, Oct. 29					
1440	8¢ Decatur House,					
	Washington, D.C.	.25	.12	1.85 (4)	1.20	42,552,000
1441	8¢ Whaling Ship					
	Charles W. Morgan	.25	.12	1.85 (4)	1.20	42,552,000
1442	8¢ Cable Car, San Francisco, Calif.	.25	.12	1.85 (4)	1.20	42,552,000
1443	8¢ San Xavier del Bac Mission, Ariz.	.25	.12	1.85 (4)	1.20	42,552,000
	Block of four, # 1440-1443	1.20	1.20		3.00	
	Perf. 10½x11, Christmas Issue, Nov. 10					
1444	8¢ Adoration of the Shepherds,					
	by Giorgione	.18	.05	2.50 (12)	.75	1,074,350,000
1445	8¢ Partridge in a Pear Tree,					
	by Jamie Wyeth	.18	.05	2.50 (12)	.75	979,540,000
	Issues of 1972, Perf. 11					
1446	8¢ Sidney Lanier, Feb. 3	.18	.05	1.00 (4)	.75	137,355,000
	Perf. 10½x11					
1447	8¢ Peace Corps. Feb. 11	.18	.05	1.50 (6)	.75	150,400,000

1971-1972

1431

1432

1433

1434   1435

1436   1437

1438   1439

1440   1441
1442   1443

1444   1445   1446   1447

1452

1453

1448   1449
1450   1451

1454

1455

1456   1457
1458   1459

1460   1461   1462

1463

1464   1465
1466   1467

164

	1972 continued	Un	U	PB/LP	#	FDC	Q
	National Parks 100th Anniversary Issue, Perf. 11						
1448	2¢ Hulk of Ship, Apr. 5	.06	.06	1.60	(4)		172,730,000
1449	2¢ Cape Hatteras Lighthouse,						
	Apr. 5	.06	.06	1.60	(4)		172,730,000
1450	2¢ Laughing Gulls on Driftwood,						
	Apr. 5	.06	.06	1.60	(4)		172,730,000
1451	2¢ Laughing Gulls and Dune,						
	Apr. 5	.06	.06	1.60	(4)		172,730,000
	Block of four, # 1448-1451	.25	.30			1.25	
1452	6¢ Wolf Trap Farm, June 26	.16	.08	1.25	(4)	.75	104,090,000
1453	8¢ Yellowstone, Mar. 1	.18	.05	1.00	(4)	.75	164,096,000
1454	15¢ Mt. McKinley, July 28	.35	.22	2.50	(4)	.75	53,920,000

Note: Beginning with this issue, the U.S.P.S. began to offer stamp collectors first day cancellations affixed to 8x10½ inch souvenir pages. The pages are similar to the stamp announcements that have appeared on post office bulletin boards since Scott No. 1132.

		Un	U	PB/LP	#	FDC	Q
1455	8¢ Family Planning, Mar. 18	.16	.05	1.00	(4)	.75	153,025,000
	Perf. 11x10½, American Revolution Bicentennial Issue, Jul. 4,						
	Craftsmen in Colonial America						
1456	8¢ Glassmaker	.30	.08	2.25	(4)	1.00	50,472,500
1457	8¢ Silversmith	.30	.08	2.25	(4)	1.00	50,472,500
1458	8¢ Wigmaker	.30	.08	2.25	(4)	1.00	50,472,500
1459	8¢ Hatter	.30	.08	2.25	(4)	1.00	50,472,500
	Block of four, # 1456-1459	1.25	1.25			2.50	
	Olympic Games Issue, Aug. 17						
1460	6¢ Bicycling and Olympic Rings	.16	.12	2.00	(10)	.75	67,335,000
1461	8¢ Bobsledding	.16	.05	2.25	(10)	.85	179,675,000
1462	15¢ Running	.35	.18	4.00	(10)	1.00	46,340,000
1463	8¢ P.T.A. 75th Anniv., Sept. 15	.16	.05	1.00	(4)	.75	180,155,000
	Perf. 11, Wildlife Conservation Issue, Sep. 20						
1464	8¢ Fur Seals	.25	.08	1.40	(4)	2.00	49,591,200
1465	8¢ Cardinal	.25	.08	1.40	(4)	2.00	49,591,200
1466	8¢ Brown Pelican	.25	.08	1.40	(4)	2.00	49,591,200
1467	8¢ Bighorn Sheep	.25	.08	1.40	(4)	2.00	49,591,200
	Block of 4, # 1464-1467	1.10	.85			3.00	

Note: With this issue the U.S.P.S. introduced the "American Commemorative Series" Stamp Panels. Each panel contains a block of four mint stamps, mounted with text, and background illustrations.

	1972 continued	Un	U	PB/LP #	FDC	Q
	Perf. 11x10½					
1468	8¢ Mail Order 100th Anniv.,					
	Sept. 27	.16	.05	2.75 (12)	.75	185,490,000
	Perf. 10½x11					
1469	8¢ Osteopathic Medicine, Oct. 9	.16	.05	1.35 (6)	.75	162,335,000
	Perf. 11					
1470	8¢ American Folklore Issue,					
	Oct. 13	.16	.05	1.00 (4)	.75	162,789,950
	Perf. 10½x11, Christmas Issue, Nov. 9					
1471	8¢ Angel form "Mary,					
	Queen of Heaven"	.16	.05	2.75 (12)	.75	1,003,475,000
1472	8¢ Santa Claus	.16	.05	2.75 (12)	.75	1,017,025,000
	Perf. 11					
1473	8¢ Pharmacy, Nov. 11	.16	.05	1.00 (4)	.75	165,895,000.
1474	8¢ Stamp Collecting, Nov. 17	.16	.05	1.00 (4)	.75	166,508,000
	Issues of 1973, Perf. 11x10½					
1475	8¢ Love, Jan. 26	.16	.05	1.35 (6)	.75	330,055,000
	This "special stamp for someone special" depicts "Love" by contemporary artist Robert Indiana.					
	Perf. 11					
	American Revolution Bicentennial Issues, Communications in Colonial America					
1476	8¢ Printer and Patriots Examining					
	Pamphlet, Feb. 16	.20	.05	1.35 (4)	.75	166,005,000
1477	8¢ Posting a Broadside, Apr. 13	.20	.05	1.35 (4)	.75	163,050,000
1478	8¢ Postrider, June 22	.20	.05	1.35 (4)	.75	159,005,000
1479	8¢ Drummer, Sept. 28	.20	.05	1.35 (4)	.75	147,295,000
	Boston Tea Party, July 4					
1480	8¢ British Merchantman	.20	.10	1.35 (4)	1.75	49,068,750
1481	8¢ British Three-master	.20	.10	1.35 (4)	1.75	49,068,750
1482	8¢ Boats and Ship's Hull	.20	.10	1.35 (4)	1.75	49,068,750
1483	8¢ Boat and Dock	.20	.10	1.35 (4)	1.75	49,068,750
	Block of four, #1480-1483	.85	.80		3.75	
	American Arts Issue					
1484	8¢ George Gershwin, Feb. 28	.16	.05	2.75 (12)	.75	139,152,000

100th Anniversary of Mail Order

1468

OSTEOPATHIC MEDICINE

1469

Tom Sawyer
United States 8c

1470

Christmas

1471

Twas the Night before Christmas

U.S. POSTAGE 8c

1472

PHARMACY
UNITED STATES POSTAGE 8c

1473

Stamp Collecting U.S. 8c

1474

1475

Rise of the Spirit of Independence

1476

1477

Rise of the Spirit of Independence

1478

1479

THE BOSTON TEA PARTY

1480
1482

1481
1483

GEORGE GERSHWIN

1484

ROBINSON JEFFERS

1485

HENRY O. TANNER

1486

WILLA CATHER

1487

Copernicus
1473-1973

8¢US

1488

U.S. POSTAL SERVICE 8¢ · U.S. POSTAL SERVICE 8¢ · U.S. POSTAL SERVICE 8¢ · U.S. POSTAL SERVICE 8¢ · U.S. POSTAL SERVICE 8¢

| Nearly 27 billion U.S. stamps are sold yearly to carry your letters to every corner of the world. | Mail is picked up from nearly a third of a million local collection boxes, as well as your mailbox. | More than 87 billion letters and packages are handled yearly—almost 300 million every delivery day. | The People in your Postal Service handle and deliver more than 500 million packages yearly. | Thousands of machines, buildings, and vehicles must be operated and maintained to keep your mail moving. |

People Serving You · People Serving You · People Serving You · People Serving You · People Serving You

1489   1490   1491   1492   1493

U.S. POSTAL SERVICE 8¢ · U.S. POSTAL SERVICE 8¢ · U.S. POSTAL SERVICE 8¢ · U.S. POSTAL SERVICE 8¢ · U.S. POSTAL SERVICE 8¢

| The skill of sorting mail manually is still vital to delivery of your mail. | Employees use modern, high-speed equipment to sort and process huge volumes of mail in central locations. | Thirteen billion pounds of mail are handled yearly by postal employees as they speed your letters and packages. | Our customers include 54 million urban and 12 million rural families, plus 9 million businesses. | Employees cover 4 million miles each delivery day to bring mail to your home or business. |

People Serving You · People Serving You · People Serving You · People Serving You · People Serving You

1494   1495   1496   1497   1498

	1973 continued	Un	U	PB/LP #	FDC	Q
1485	8¢ Robinson Jeffers, Aug. 13	.16	.05	2.75 (12)	.75	128,048,000
1486	8¢ Henry Ossawa Tanner, Sept. 10	.16	.05	2.75 (12)	.75	146,008,000
1487	8¢ Willa Cather, Sept. 20	.16	.05	2.75 (12)	.75	139,608,000
1488	8¢ Nicolaus Copernicus, Apr. 23	.16	.05	.80 (4)	.75	159,475,000
	Perf. 10½x11, Postal Service Employees Issue, Apr. 30					
1489	8¢ Stamp Counter	.20	.12	2.25 (10)	1.10	48,602,000
1490	8¢ Mail Collection	.20	.12	2.25 (10)	1.10	48,602,000
1491	8¢ Letter Facing Conveyor	.20	.12	2.25 (10)	1.10	48,602,000
1492	8¢ Parcel Post Sorting	.20	.12	2.25 (10)	1.10	48,602,000
1493	8¢ Mail Cancelling	.20	.12	2.25 (10)	1.10	48,602,000
1494	8¢ Manual Letter Routing	.20	.12	2.25 (10)	1.10	48,602,000
1495	8¢ Electronic Letter Routing	.20	.12	2.25 (10)	1.10	48,602,000
1496	8¢ Loading Mail on Truck	.20	.12	2.25 (10)	1.10	48,602,000
1497	8¢ Mailman	.20	.12	2.25 (10)	1.10	48,602,000
1498	8¢ Rural Mail Delivery	.20	.12	2.25 (10)	1.10	48,602,000
	Plate Block of 20, #1489-1498			4.50 (20)	6.00	

Cats

The Guinness Book reported that cats were used for a mail service in Liege, Belgium in 1879. Bundles of letters were tied to approximately 37 cats to carry the mail to villages within an 18 mile radius of the Liege city center. The cats proved to be thoroughly undisciplined, and the experiment was short-lived. In spite of this, cats are a very popular subject for topical collectors who collect stamps based on the subjects' designs.

When Charles Lindbergh made a flight around the country in 1927, he was said to have been accompanied by a black cat. Since the famous pilot was very conscious of weight aboard his plane, it is unlikely that he ever took a cat on board. However, this did not stop Spain, which issued a stamp commemorating the first solo crossing of the Atlantic Ocean with a stamp picturing Lindbergh, the Statue of Liberty, "The Spirit of St. Louis" plane, and a black cat looking on.

There is a United States issue with a cat in the scene of the 100th anniversary of mail order commemorative stamp (#1468). The scene depicts an event in the life of a rural family, going to the post office to pick up mail order merchandise. A close look at the stamp reveals a black cat atop a bag of flour staring at a nearby dog.

	1973 continued	Un	U	PB/LP	#	FDC	Q
	Perf. 11						
1499	8¢ Harry S. Truman, May 8	.16	.05	1.00	(4)	.75	157,052,800
	Electronics Progress Issue, July 10						
1500	6¢ Marconi's Spark Coil and Gap	.12	.10	1.25	(4)	.75	53,005,000
1501	8¢ Transistor and						
	Printed Circuit Board	.16	.05	1.00	(4)	.75	159,775,000
1502	15¢ Microphone, Speaker,						
	Vacuum Tube, TV Camera	.30	.20	2.25	(4)	.80	39,005,000
1503	8¢ Lyndon B. Johnson, Aug. 27	.16	.05	2.50	(12)	.75	152,624,000
	Issues of 1973-74, Rural America Issue						
1504	8¢ Angus and Longhorn Cattle,						
	by F.C. Murphy, Oct. 5, 1973	.16	.05	1.00	(4)	.75	145,840,000
1505	10¢ Chautauqua centenary,						
	Aug. 6, 1974	.20	.05	1.00	(4)	.75	151,335,000
1506	10¢ Kansas hard winter wheat						
	centenary, Aug. 16, 1974	.20	.05	1.00	(4)	.75	141,085,000
	Perf. 10½x11, Christmas Issue, Nov. 7, 1973						
1507	8¢ Madonna and Child by Raphael	.16	.05	2.10	(12)	.75	885,160,000
1508	8¢ Christmas Tree in Needlepoint	.16	.05	2.10	(12)	.75	939,835,000
	Issue of 1973-74, Perf. 11x10½						
1509	10¢ 50-Star and 13-Star Flags, 1973	.20	.05	4.50	(20)	.75	
1510	10¢ Jefferson Memorial						
	and Signature, 1973	.20	.05	1.00	(4)	.75	
1510b	Booklet pane of 5 + label, 1973	1.00	.30				
1510c	Booklet pane of 8, 1973	1.60	.30				
1510d	Booklet pane of 6, 1974	1.20	.30				
1511	10¢ Mail Transport; "ZIP", 1974	.20	.05	1.80	(8)	.75	
	Coil Stamps, Perf. 10 Vertically						
1518	6.3¢ Bells, Oct. 1, 1974	.13	.07	.35		.75	
1519	10¢ red & blue Flags (1509), 1973	.25	.05	—		.75	
1520	10¢ blue Jefferson Memorial						
	(1510),-73	.20	.05	.50		.75	

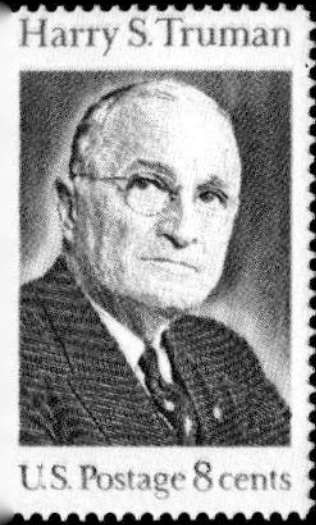

Harry S. Truman
U.S. Postage 8 cents

499

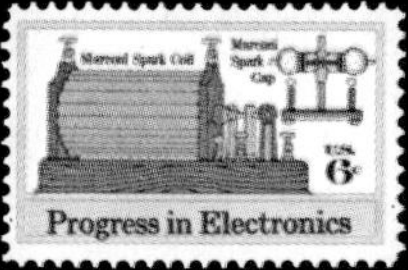

U.S. 6¢
Progress in Electronics

1500

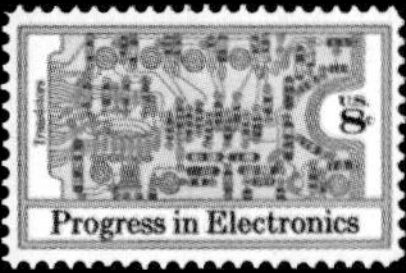

U.S. 8¢
Progress in Electronics

1501

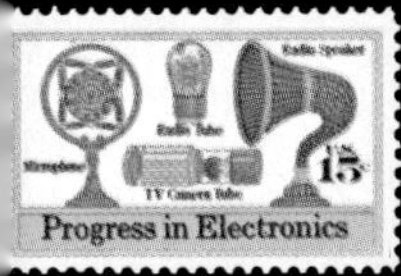

U.S. 15¢
Progress in Electronics

502

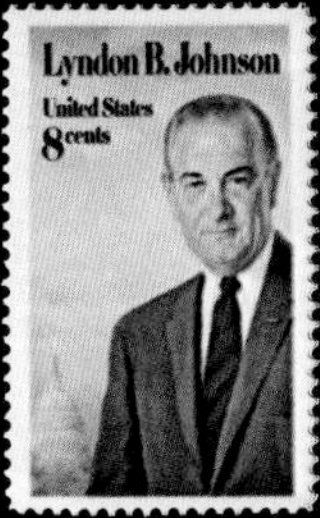

Lyndon B. Johnson
United States
8 cents

1503

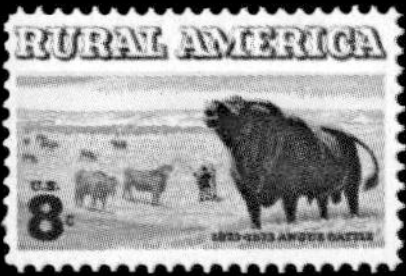

RURAL AMERICA
U.S. 8¢

1504

RURAL AMERICA
U.S. 10¢

505

RURAL AMERICA
U.S. 10¢

1506

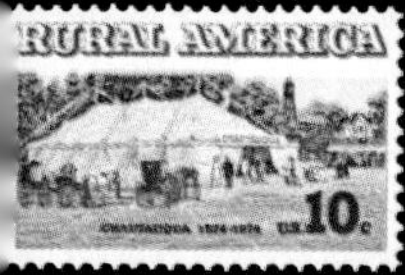

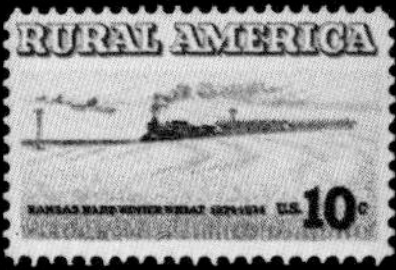

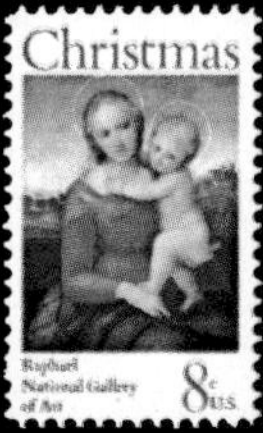

Christmas
Raphael
National Gallery
of Art
8¢ U.S.

1507

U.S. 8¢
CHRISTMAS

1508

UNITED 10¢ STATES

We hold these Truths...
UNITED STATES 10¢

IT ALL DEPENDS ON
ZIP
CODE

6.3¢
U.S. Postage

UNITED 10¢ STATES

We hold these Truths...
UNITED STATES 10¢

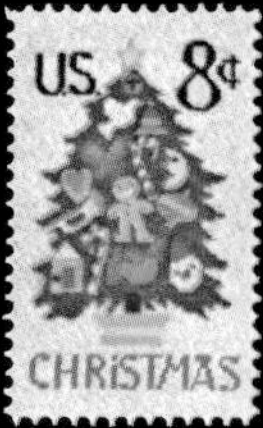

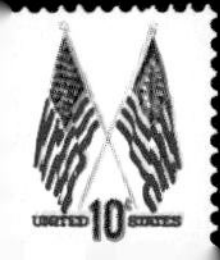

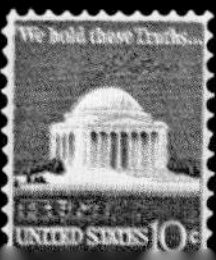

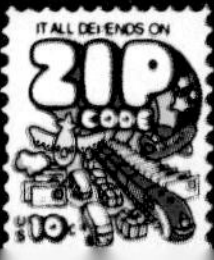

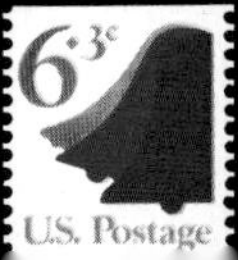

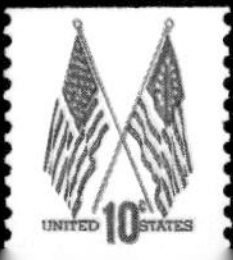

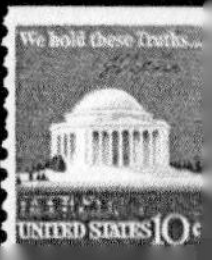

525

1526

1527

528

1529

	Issues of 1974, Perf. 11	Un	U	PB/LP	#	FDC	Q
1525	10¢ V.F.W. Emblem, Mar. 11	.20	.05	1.25	(4)	.75	143,930,000
	Perf. 10½x11						
1526	10¢ Robert Frost, Mar. 26	.20	.05	1.00	(4)	.75	145,235,000
	Perf. 11						
1527	10¢ Cosmic Jumper and Smiling						
	Sage, by Peter Max, Apr. 18	.20	.05	2.60	(12)	.75	135,052,000
	Perf. 11x10½						
1528	10¢ Horses Rounding Turn, May 4	.20	.05	2.60	(12)	.75	156,750,000
	Perf. 11						
1529	10¢ Skylab II, May 14	.20	.05	1.00	(4)	1.25	164,670,000
	Centenary of UPU Issue, June 6						
1530	10¢ Michelangelo, by Raphael	.20	.18	3.40	(16)	1.10	23,769,600
1531	10¢ "Five Feminine Virtues,"						
	by Hokusai	.20	.18	3.40	(16)	1.10	23,769,600
1532	10¢ Old Scraps,						
	by John Frederick Peto	.20	.18	3.40	(16)	1.10	23,769,600
1533	10¢ The Lovely Reader,						
	by Jean Liotard	.20	.18	3.40	(16)	1.10	23,769,600
1534	10¢ Lady Writing Letter, by Terborch	.20	.18	3.40	(16)	1.10	23,769,600
1535	10¢ Inkwell and Quill,						
	by Jean Chardin	.20	.18	3.40	(16)	1.10	23,769,600
1536	10¢ Mrs. John Douglas,						
	by Thomas Gainsborough	.20	.18	3.40	(16)	1.10	23,769,600
1537	10¢ Don Antonio Noriega, by Goya	.20	.18	3.40	(16)	1.10	23,769,600
	Block or strip of 8, #1530-37	1.60	2.00			4.25	

Pop Art

Take a look at the Expo 74 commemorative stamp (#1527). It is one of the most brightly colored, energetic stamps ever printed. It was designed by artist Peter Max, whose bold, merging colors and smiling, friendly sense of motion represented an extremely popular art style in the 1960s and 1970s. His bright, fanciful creations appeared on everything from stationery to furniture, bringing a rainbow of colors and an eclectic sense of decoration into people's lives.

Max's art was an offshoot of a larger movement in modern art called "pop art." Pop art began in the 1950s when painters and sculptors broadened the range of subjects in their artwork to include objects from popular culture. It became common to see everyday objects blown up bigger than life, like Andy Warhol's huge silk screen print of a soup can, or Claes Oldenberg's giant plastic sculptures of hamburgers. Pop artists also constructed their work out of modern man-made materials such as neon tubing, plastic and vinyl. By widening the resources of their art, these artists left a legacy of imaginative freedom that is still being felt today.

	1974 continued	Un	U	PB/LP	#	FDC	Q
	Mineral Heritage Issue, June 13						
1538	10¢ Petrified Wood	.20	.10	1.25	(4)	1.50	41,803,200
1539	10¢ Tourmaline	.20	.10	1.25	(4)	1.50	41,803,200
1540	10¢ Amethyst	.20	.10	1.25	(4)	1.50	41,803,200
1541	10¢ Rhodochrosite	.20	.10	1.25	(4)	1.50	41,803,200
	Block of 4, #1538-1541	.80	.80			3.00	
1542	10¢ Fort Harrod, June 15	.20	.05	1.00	(4)	.75	156,265,000
	American Revolution Bicentennial, First Continental Congress, July 4						
1543	10¢ Carpenter's Hall	.20	.10	1.20	(4)	1.10	48,896,250
1544	10¢ "We ask but for Peace, Liberty and Safety"	.20	.10	1.20	(4)	1.10	48,896,250
1545	10¢ "Deriving their Just Powers"	.20	.10	1.20	(4)	1.10	48,896,250
1546	10¢ Independence Hall	.20	.10	1.20	(4)	1.10	48,896,250
	Block of four, #1543-1546	.80	.80			3.00	
1547	10¢ Molecules and Drops of Gasoline and Oil, Sept. 22	.20	.05	1.00	(4)	.75	148,850,000
1548	10¢ The Headless Horsemen, Oct. 10	.20	.05	1.00	(4)	.75	157,270,000
1549	10¢ Little Girl, Oct. 12	.20	.05	1.00	(4)	.75	150,245,000
	Christmas Issues, 1974						
1550	10¢ Angel, Oct. 23	.20	.05	2.20 (10)		.75	835,180,000
1551	10¢ Sleigh Ride, by Currier and Ives, Oct. 23	.20	.05	2.60 (12)		.75	882,520,000
1552	10¢ Weather Vane; precanceled, Nov. 15, Imperf. Self-adhesive	.20	.08	5.50 (20)		.75	213,155,000

America's Revolutionary Congress

The 1974 se-tenant issue of a block of four stamps (#1543-#1546) commemorates the 200th anniversary of the Continental Congress, the first full assembly of representatives from the 13 American colonies. It first met as an emergency assembly in 1774 to consider responses to the Coercive Acts passed by the British Parliament. But as disagreement between Britain and America turned into armed conflict, the Congress assumed the duties of a temporary government.

Its accomplishments were little short of miraculous. It declared America's independence and found, to its surprise, that most Americans went along with that declaration. It had no power to make either the new states or their citizens comply with its decisions, yet it managed to raise an army, wage a victorious war and guide a new nation in the troubled years following the war.

In 1789, the new Constitution of the United States of America was ratified. As the new two-house Congress began its first session, the old Continental Congress was quietly dissolved, having brought a new form of government into being.

1538

1539

1540

1541

1542

1547

1548

1543
1545

1544
1546

1549

1550

1551

1552

Benjamin West

American artist
10 cents U.S. postage

1553

Paul Laurence **Dunbar**

American poet

10 cents U.S. postage

1554

MOVIEMAKER   US 10 ¢

D.W. GRIFFITH

1555

PIONEER ★ JUPITER

US 10 c

1556

MARINER 10 ★ VENUS/MERCURY

US 10 c

1557

UNITED STATES

collective bargaining
out of conflict...accord

10 c

1558

Contributors To The Cause...

U.S. 8 c

Sybil Ludington   *Youthful Heroine*

1559

YOUTHFUL HEROINE
On the dark night of April 26, 1777,
16-year-old Sybil Ludington rode
her horse "Star" alone through the
Connecticut countryside rallying
her father's militia to repel a
raid by the British on Danbury.

1559

Contributors To The Cause...

U.S. 10 c

Salem Poor   *Gallant Soldier*

GALLANT SOLDIER
The conspicuously courageous
actions of black foot soldier
Salem Poor at the Battle of
Bunker Hill on June 17, 1775,
earned him citations for his
bravery and leadership ability.

1560

Contributors To The Cause...

U.S. 10 c

Haym Salomon   *Financial Hero*

FINANCIAL HERO
Businessman and broker Haym
Salomon was responsible for
raising most of the money
needed to finance the American
Revolution and later to save
the new nation from collapse.

1561

Contributors To The Cause...

U.S. 18 c

Peter Francisco   *Fighter Extraordinary*

FIGHTER EXTRAORDINARY
Peter Francisco's strength
and bravery made him a
legend around campfires.
He fought with distinction
at Brandywine, Yorktown
and Guilford Court House.

1562

Lexington & Concord 1775 by Sandham

US Bicentennial 10 cents

1563

Bunker Hill 1775 by Trumbull

US Bicentennial 10c

1564

	Un	U	PB/LP #	FDC	Q
Issues of 1975					
American Art Issue, Perf. 10½x11, 11					
1553 10¢ Benjamin West, Self-portrait,					
Feb. 10	.20	.05	2.20 (10)	.75	156,995,000
1554 10¢ Paul Laurence Dunbar, May 1	.20	.05	2.20 (10)	.75	146,365,000
1555 10¢ D. W. Griffith, May 27	.20	.05	1.00 (4)	.75	148,805,000
Space Issue, Perf. 11					
1556 10¢ Pioneer 10, Feb. 28	.20	.05	1.00 (4)	1.10	173,685,000
1557 10¢ Mariner 10, Apr. 4	.20	.05	1.00 (4)	1.10	158,600,000
1558 10¢ "Labor and Management",					
Mar. 13	.20	.05	1.80 (8)	.75	153,355,000
American Bicentennial Issues, Contributors to the Cause, Mar. 25, Perf. 11x10½					
1559 8¢ Sybil Ludington	.16	.13	1.75 (10)	.75	63,205,000
1560 10¢ Salem Poor	.20	.05	2.20 (10)	.75	157,865,000
1561 10¢ Haym Salomon	.20	.05	2.20 (10)	.75	166,810,000
1562 18¢ Peter Francisco	.36	.20	4.00 (10)	.75	44,825,000
Perf. 11					
1563 10¢ "Birth of Liberty",					
by Henry Sandham, April 19	.20	.05	2.60 (12)	.75	144,028,000
Perf. 11x10½					
1564 10¢ Battle of Bunker Hill,					
by John Trumbull, June 17	.20	.05	2.60 (12)	.75	139,928,000

Benjamin West

Benjamin West (#1553), born in Pennsylvania in 1738, was the first American painter to gain international recognition. His portraits so impressed some merchants in his home town that they raised funds to send West to Italy, where he could study the masters. By 1763 he was in London, where he would remain for the rest of his life. His rise to prominence was swift. At 30 he was one of the founding members of the Royal Academy of Arts; at 34 he became King George III's historical painter. Upon Sir Joshua Reynold's death, West became the president of the Royal Academy, holding that revered post for 27 years.

A master of technique, West was the first to paint a recent historical event with figures in contemporary clothing rather than classical dress. Although he was known primarily as a neo-classical artist, his Death on a Pale Horse *anticipates the romantic excitement of a younger generation of artists. His influence on American painters was great, and his London studio became a gathering place for young artists from his native country seeking advice and instruction.*

1975

	1975 continued	Un	U	PB/LP #	FDC	Q
	Military Uniforms, July 4, Perf. 11					
1565	10¢ Soldier with Flintlock Musket,					
	Uniform Button	.20	.08	2.60 (12)	.90	44,963,750
1566	10¢ Sailor with Grappling Hook,					
	First Navy Jack, 1775	.20	.08		.90	44,963,750
1567	10¢ Marine with Musket,					
	Full-rigged Ship	.20	.08	2.60 (12)	.90	44,963,750
1568	10¢ Militiaman with Musket,					
	Powder Horn	.20	.08		.90	44,963,750
	Block of 4, #1565-1568	.80	.70		2.40	
	Apollo-Soyuz Space Issue, July 15, Perf. 11x10½					
1569	10¢ Apollo and Soyuz after					
	Docking, and Earth	.20	.10	2.60 (12)	1.00	80,931,600
1570	10¢ Spacecraft before Docking,					
	Earth and Project Emblem	.20	.10	3.40 (16)	1.00	80,931,600
	Pair, #1569-1570	.40	.25		2.75	
1571	10¢ Worldwide Equality for Women,					
	Aug. 26	.20	.05	1.40 (6)	.75	145,640,000
	Postal Service Bicentennial Issue, Sep. 3					
1572	10¢ Stagecoach and Trailer Truck	.20	.08	2.60 (12)	.75	42,163,750
1573	10¢ Old and New Locomotives	.20	.08	2.60 (12)	.75	42,163,750
1574	10¢ Early Mail Plane and Jet	.20	.08		.75	42,163,750
1575	10¢ Satellite for Transmission					
	of Mailgrams	.20	.08		.75	42,163,750
	Block of 4, #1572-1575	.80	.80		2.40	
	Perf. 11					
1576	10¢ World Peace, Sept. 29	.20	.05	1.00 (4)	.75	146,615,000
	Banking and Commerce Issue, Oct. 6					
1577	10¢ Engine Turning, Indian Head					
	Penny and Morgan Silver Dollar	.20	.08	1.00 (4)	.75	73,098,000
1578	10¢ Seated Liberty, Quarter,					
	$20 Gold (Double Eagle),					
	Engine Turning	.20	.08	1.00 (4)	.75	73,098,000
	Pair, #1577-1578	.40	.20		1.00	

1569
1570

1565   1566
1567   1568

1571

1572   1573
1574   1575

1576

1577   1578

1582b

1579

1580

1581
1584

1582
1585

1591
1593

1592
1594

1596
1597

1618
1599

1595a

1603
1605

1604
1606

1608
1611

1610
1612

1975 continued	Un	U	PB/LP	#	FDC	Q
Christmas Issue, Oct. 14, Perf. 11						
1579 (10¢) Madonna by						
Domenico Ghirlandaio	.20	.05	2.60 (12)		.75	739,430,000
1580 (10¢) Christmas Card,						
by Louis Prang, 1878	.20	.05	2.60 (12)		.75	878,690,000
Issues of 1975-81, Americana, Perf. 11x10½						
1581 1¢ Inkwell & Quill, 1977	.05	.05	.15 (4)		.40	
1582 2¢ Speaker's Stand, 1977	.05	.05	.20 (4)		.40	
1584 3¢ Early Ballot Box, 1977	.06	.05	.30 (4)		.40	
1585 4¢ Books, Bookmark, Eyeglasses,	.08	.05	.40 (4)		.40	
Size: 17½x20½mm., 1977						
1590 9¢ Capitol Dome (1591), 1977	.75	.20			1.00	
1590a Perf. 10	25.00	6.00			1.00	.
Size: 18½x22½mm.						
1591 9¢ Capitol Dome, 1975	.18	.05	.90 (4)		.60	
1592 10¢ Contemplation of Justice, 1977	.20	.05	1.00 (4)		.60	
1593 11¢ Printing Press, 1975	.22	.05	1.10 (4)		.60	
1594 12¢ Torch, 1981	.24	.05	1.15 (4)		.60	
1595 13¢ Liberty Bell, 1975	.26	.05			.60	
1595a Booklet pane of 6	1.60	.50			.60	
1595b Booklet pane of 7 + label	1.80	.50			.60	
1595c Booklet pane of 8	2.10	.50			.60	
1595d Booklet pane of 5 + label, 1976	1.30	.50			.60	
1596 13¢ Eagle and Shield, 1975	.26	.05	3.38 (12)		.60	
Perf. 11						
1597 15¢ Fort McHenry Flag, 1978	.30	.05	2.10 (6)		.65	
Perf. 11x10½						
1598 15¢ Fort McHenry Flag (1597), 1978	.30	.05			.65	
1598a Booklet pane of 8	2.40	.60				
1599 16¢ Head of Liberty, 1978	.32	.05	1.60 (4)		.65	
1603 24¢ Old North Church, 1975	.48	.09	2.40 (4)		.75	
1604 28¢ Fort Nisqually, 1978	.56	.08	2.80 (4)		1.20	
1605 29¢ Sandy Hook Lighthouse, 1978	.58	.08	2.90 (4)		1.10	
1606 30¢ One-room Schoolhouse, 1979	.60	.08	3.00 (4)		1.10	

No. 1590 is on white paper. No. 1591 on gray paper. Nos. 1590 and 1590a, 1595, 1598 issued only in booklets. Additional American Series, see No. 1813.

1608 50¢ Whale Oil Lamp, 1979	1.00	.25	5.00 (4)		1.25	
1610 $1 Candle and Rushlight Holder,						
1979	2.00	.25	10.00 (4)		3.00	
1611 $2 Kerosene Table Lamp, 1978	4.00	.50	20.00 (4)		4.75	
1612 $5 Railroad Lantern, 1979	10.00	2.00	50.00 (4)		10.00	

	1975-1981 continued	Un	U	PB/LP #	FDC	Q
	Coil Stamps, Perf. 10 Vertically					
1613	3.1¢ Guitar, 1979	.11	.05	.55	.40	
1614	7.7¢ Saxhorns, 1976	.20	.08	.60	.60	
1615	7.9¢ Drum, 1976	.20	.08	.60	.60	
1615C	8.4¢ Piano, 1978	.20	.08	.68	.40	
1616	9¢ Capitol Dome (1591), 1976	.18	.05	.68	.60	
1617	10¢ Contemplation of Justice					
	(1592), 1977	.20	.05	.75	.60	
1618	13¢ Liberty Bell (1595), 1975	.26	.05	1.00	.65	
1618C	15¢ Fort McHenry Flag (1597),					
	1978	.40	.03	—	.65	
1619	16¢ Head of Liberty (1599), 1978	.32	.05	.90	.60	
	Perf. 11x10½					
1622	13¢ Flag over Independence					
	Hall, 1975	.26	.05		.65	
1623	13¢ Flag over Capitol, 1977	.26	.05		1.00	
1623a	Booklet pane of 8	2.50	.60			
1623b	Perf. 10	1.00	.50			
1623c	Booklet pane of 8, Perf. 10	32.50	—			
	Nos. 1623, 1623b issued only in booklets					
	Coil Stamp. Perf. 10 Vertically					
1625	13¢ Flag over Independence Hall					
	(1622), 1975	.30	.05		.65	
	Issues of 1976					
1629	13¢ Drummer Boy	.26	.08		.65	
1630	13¢ Old Drummer	.26	.08		.65	
1631	13¢ Fifer	.26	.08		.65	
	Strip of 3, # 1629/1631	.78	.60	3.40 (12)	1.75	218,585,000
1632	13¢ Interphil	.26	.05	1.30 (4)	.65	157,825,000
	American Bicentennial, State Flags Issue, Feb. 23, 1976					
1633	13¢ Delaware	.45	.30		1.75	8,720,100
1634	13¢ Pennsylvania	.45	.30		1.75	8,720,100
1635	13¢ New Jersey	.45	.30		1.75	8,720,100
1636	13¢ Georgia	.45	.30		1.75	8,720,100
1637	13¢ Connecticut	.45	.30		1.75	8,720,100
1638	13¢ Massachusetts	.45	.30		1.75	8,720,100

1613

1614

1615

1615c

1616

1622

1623a

1629   1630   1631

1632

1633

1634

1635

639

1640

1641

642

1643

1644

645

1646

1647

648

1649

1650

651

1652

1653

	1976 continued	Un	U	PB/LP	#	FDC	Q
1639	13¢ Maryland	.45	.30			1.75	8,720,100
1640	13¢ South Carolina	.45	.30			1.75	8,720,100
1641	13¢ New Hampshire	.45	.30			1.75	8,720,100
1642	13¢ Virginia	.45	.30			1.75	8,720,100
1643	13¢ New York	.45	.30			1.75	8,720,100
1644	13¢ North Carolina	.45	.30			1.75	8,720,100
1645	13¢ Rhode Island	.45	.30			1.75	8,720,100
1646	13¢ Vermont	.45	.30			1.75	8,720,100
1647	13¢ Kentucky	.45	.30			1.75	8,720,100
1648	13¢ Tennessee	.45	.30			1.75	8,720,100
1649	13¢ Ohio	.45	.30			1.75	8,720,100
1650	13¢ Louisiana	.45	.30			1.75	8,720,100
1651	13¢ Indiana	.45	.30			1.75	8,720,100
1652	13¢ Mississippi	.45	.30			1.75	8,720,100
1653	13¢ Illinois	.45	.30			1.75	8,720,100
1654	13¢ Alabama	.45	.30			1.75	8,720,100
1655	13¢ Maine	.45	.30			1.75	8,720,100
1656	13¢ Missouri	.45	.30			1.75	8,720,100

The New USPS Hall of Stamps

There's something new for visitors to the U.S. Postal Service Headquarters at L'Enfant Plaza in Washington, D.C. The USPS has opened a public philatelic exhibit area, a permanent display space in an area adjoining its Philatelic Center. This new Hall of Stamps will house a variety of U.S. postal materials, including unique items like the famous "moon letter" and a first day cover from the August, 1983, Challenger space shuttle mission that bears a canceled marginal imperforate single from a press proof.

The majority of the exhibits are on permanent display, but the USPS also offers temporary exhibits that are changed every three to six months. Topics displayed in the Hall include postal history and progress, airmail service, outer space-related philatelic items and postal devices. A special focus of the Hall of Stamps is on stamp design and production. Original stamp design artwork, imperforate press proofs and die proofs, uncut full stamp sheets and exhibits on the development of stamp design are among the existing or planned displays.

Opening day ceremonies were held on May 17, 1984, and were also used to unveil a new set of stamp designs, the block of 4 Duck Decoys, scheduled for 1985 issue. Nationally known artist Stephan Dohanos' design for this issue is the latest of 29 U.S. stamps he has executed.

The Hall of Stamps should fascinate anyone interested in stamps and the U.S. Postal Service. It is free to the public, and can be visited Mondays through Saturdays from 9:00 a.m. to 5:00 p.m.

	1976 continued	Un	U	PB/LP	#	FDC	Q
1657	13¢ Arkansas	.45	.30			1.75	8,720,100
1658	13¢ Michigan	.45	.30			1.75	8,720,100
1659	13¢ Florida	.45	.30			1.75	8,720,100
1660	13¢ Texas	.45	.30			1.75	8,720,100
1661	13¢ Iowa	.45	.30			1.75	8,720,100
1662	13¢ Wisconsin	.45	.30			1.75	8,720,100
1663	13¢ California	.45	.30			1.75	8,720,100
1664	13¢ Minnesota	.45	.30			1.75	8,720,100
1665	13¢ Oregon	.45	.30			1.75	8,720,100
1666	13¢ Kansas	.45	.30			1.75	8,720,100
1667	13¢ West Virginia	.45	.30			1.75	8,720,100
1668	13¢ Nevada	.45	.30			1.75	8,720,100
1669	13¢ Nebraska	.45	.30			1.75	8,720,100
1670	13¢ Colorado	.45	.30			1.75	8,720,100
1671	13¢ North Dakota	.45	.30			1.75	8,720,100
1672	13¢ South Dakota	.45	.30			1.75	8,720,100
1673	13¢ Montana	.45	.30			1.75	8,720,100
1674	13¢ Washington	.45	.30			1.75	8,720,100

Presidential Widows' Franks

Certain officials of the U.S. Government have the privilege of sending their mail for free. Your U.S. Representative to Congress, for example, merely signs his or her envelope or card and mails it. This signature, whether signed by hand or reproduced mechanically, is called a "frank."

It has been customary on the death of a president or former president to allow lifetime free use of the mails to his widow. It isn't a law, however. Each time this franking privilege is extended, it requires a special act of Congress. In 1800, Congress set the precedent by allowing Martha Washington the franking privilege. Since then, it has been extended to every other presidential widow, with two exceptions.

Mrs. Andrew Johnson only outlived her husband by six months. Congress hadn't gotten around to voting on her frank before she died, but would undoubtedly have granted it to her. The case of President John Tyler's widow was different, however. When the Civil War broke out, her husband, a Virginian, was elected to the Confederate Congress. Although he died before he could take office in the rebel government, his allegiance to it was well-known. Whether Congress, caught up in the turmoil of war, merely neglected Mrs. Tyler's frank, or whether it was felt improper to vote on the matter is not known. But a vote was never taken, and the privilege was never extended to this former First Lady.

1976

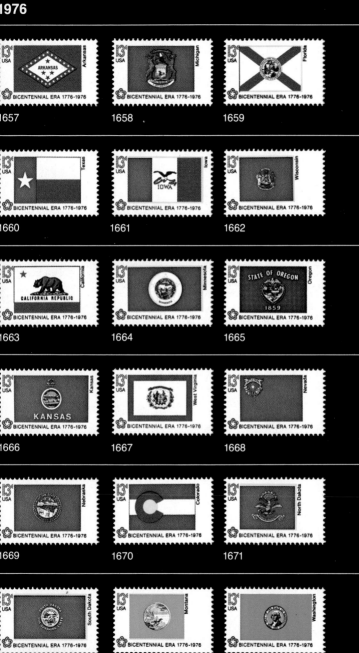

BICENTENNIAL ERA 1776-1976 — Arkansas — 1657

BICENTENNIAL ERA 1776-1976 — Michigan — 1658

BICENTENNIAL ERA 1776-1976 — Florida — 1659

BICENTENNIAL ERA 1776-1976 — Texas — 1660

BICENTENNIAL ERA 1776-1976 — Iowa — 1661

BICENTENNIAL ERA 1776-1976 — Wisconsin — 1662

BICENTENNIAL ERA 1776-1976 — California — 1663

BICENTENNIAL ERA 1776-1976 — Minnesota — 1664

BICENTENNIAL ERA 1776-1976 — Oregon — 1665

BICENTENNIAL ERA 1776-1976 — Kansas — 1666

BICENTENNIAL ERA 1776-1976 — West Virginia — 1667

BICENTENNIAL ERA 1776-1976 — Nevada — 1668

BICENTENNIAL ERA 1776-1976 — Nebraska — 1669

BICENTENNIAL ERA 1776-1976 — Colorado — 1670

BICENTENNIAL ERA 1776-1976 — North Dakota — 1671

BICENTENNIAL ERA 1776-1976 — South Dakota — 1672

BICENTENNIAL ERA 1776-1976 — Montana — 1673

BICENTENNIAL ERA 1776-1976 — Washington — 1674

1675

1676

1677

1678

1679

1680

1681

1682

1683

1684

1685

The Surrender of Lord Cornwallis at Yorktown
From a Painting by John Trumbull

1686

	1976 continued	Un	U	PB/LP	#	FDC	Q
1675	13¢ Idaho	.45	.30			1.75	8,720,100
1676	13¢ Wyoming	.45	.30			1.75	8,720,100
1677	13¢ Utah	.45	.30			1.75	8,720,100
1678	13¢ Oklahoma	.45	.30			1.75	8,720,100
1679	13¢ New Mexico	.45	.30			1.75	8,720,100
1680	13¢ Arizona	.45	.30			1.75	8,720,100
1681	13¢ Alaska	.45	.30			1.75	8,720,100
1682	13¢ Hawaii	.45	.30			1.75	8,720,100
	Pane of 50, #1633-1682		—	25.00 (50)		32.50	
1683	13¢ Bell's Telephone Patent						
	Application, Mar. 10	.26	.05	1.30	(4)	.65	159,915,000
1684	13¢ Ford-Pullman Monoplane						
	and Laird Swallow Biplane, Mar. 19	.26	.05	2.90 (10)		.65	156,960,000
1685	13¢ Various Flasks, Separatory						
	Funnel, Computer Tape, Apr. 6	.26	.05	3.40 (12)		.65	158,470,000
	American Bicentennial Issues, Souvenir Sheets, May 29						
	Sheets of 5 Stamps Each						
1686	13¢ Surrender of Cornwallis at						
	Yorktown, by John Trumbull	4.50	—			6.00	1,990,000
	a. 13¢ Two American Officers	.65	.40				1,990,000
	b. 13¢ Gen. Benjamin Lincoln	.65	.40				1,990,000
	c. 13¢ George Washington	.65	.40				1,990,000
	d. 13¢ John Trumbull, Col. Cobb,						
	von Steuben,						
	Lafayette, Thomas Nelson	.65	.40				1,990,000
	e. 13¢ Alexander Hamilton, John						
	Laurens, Walter Stewart	.65	.40				1,990,000

Bulk Mail Centers

There are 21 Bulk Mail Centers (BMC) located throughout the United States. A typical BMC handles 250,000 packages and 125,000 sacks of mail every day, seven days a week, 52 weeks a year. The centers handle all second, third and fourth class mail, not-for-profit mail and mass mailings. Ninety percent of all parcels sent household to household are handled through the Postal Service. Basically, everything that isn't first class mail goes into and out of a BMC.

A BMC may have as many as 120 truck docks. At each opening, a 40-foot long trailer can receive mail. Long conveyor belts snake into the semi-trailer, unloading parcels and sacks, slowly moving back as the truck fills up. The trucks are sent on regular schedules to post offices within their BMCs area, or to other BMCs for distribution in other sections of the country.

Although a BMC may handle everything from automobile tires to deer antlers, a large portion of its volume is generated by books. The Chicago BMC handles fifty to sixty thousand books every day. The Postal Service Employees Issue (#1489 to 1498) picture some of the workers at the job in BMCs.

1976

	1976 continued	Un	U	PB/LP	#	FDC	Q
1687	18¢ Declaration of Independence,						
	by John Trumbull	6.00	—			7.50	1,983,000
	a. 18¢ John Adams, Roger Sherman,						
	Robert R. Livingston	.80	.55				1,983,000
	b. 18¢ Thomas Jefferson, Benjamin						
	Franklin	.80	.55				1,983,000
	c. 18¢ Thomas Nelson, Jr., Francis						
	Lewis, John Witherspoon,						
	Samuel Huntington	.80	.55				1,983,000
	d. 18¢ John Hancock,						
	Charles Thomson	.80	.55				1,983,000
	e. 18¢ George Read, John						
	Dickinson, Edward Rutledge	.80	.55				1,983,000
1688	24¢ Washington Crossing the						
	Delaware, by Emanuel Leutze/						
	Eastman Johnson	7.50	—			8.50	1,953,000
	a. 24¢ Boatsman	1.00	.75				1,953,000
	b. 24¢ George Washington	1.00	.75				1,953,000
	c. 24¢ Flagbearer	1.00	.75				1,953,000
	d. 24¢ Men in Boat	1.00	.75				1,953,000
	e. 24¢ Men on Shore	1.00	.75				1,953,000
1689	31¢ Washington Reviewing Army						
	at Valley Forge, by William T. Trego	9.00	—			9.50	1,903,000
	a. 31¢ Two Officers	1.25	.90				1,903,000
	b. 31¢ George Washington	1.25	.90				1,903,000
	c. 31¢ Officer and Black Horse	1.25	.90				1,903,000
	d. 31¢ Officer and White Horse	1.25	.90				1,903,000
	e. 31¢ Three Soldiers	1.25	.90				1,903,000

The Declaration of Independence, 4 July 1776 at Philadelphia
From a Painting by John Trumbull

Washington Crossing the Delaware
From a Painting by Emanuel Leutze / Eastman Johnson

Washington Reviewing His Ragged Army at Valley Forge
From a Painting by William T. Trego

1690

JULY 4,1776 · JULY 4,1776 · JULY 4,1776 · JULY 4,1776

1691   1692   1693   1694

1699

1700

1695   1696
1697   1698

1701

1702

1703

1705

1704

192

	1976 continued	Un	U	PB/LP #	FDC	Q
1690	13¢ Franklin and Map					
	of North America, 1776, June 1	.26	.05	1.30 (4)	.65	164,890,000
	American Bicentennial Issue, Declaration of Independence, by Trumbull, July 4					
1691	13¢	.26	.08	5.50 (20)	.65	51,008,750
1692	13¢	.26	.08		.65	51,008,750
1693	13¢	.26	.08		.65	51,008,750
1694	13¢	.26	.08	5.00 (20)	.65	51,008,750
	Strip of 4, #1691-1694	1.10	.75		2.00	
	Olympic Games Issue, July 16					
1695	13¢ Diving	.26	.08	3.40 (12)	.70	46,428,750
1696	13¢ Skiing	.26	.08		.70	46,428,750
1697	13¢ Running	.26	.08	3.40 (12)	.70	46,428,750
1698	13¢ Skating	.26	.08		.70	46,428,750
	Block of 4, #1695-1698	1.10	1.00		2.00	
1699	13¢ Clara Maass, Aug. 18	.26	.06	3.40 (12)	.65	130,592,000
1700	13¢ Adolph S. Ochs, Sept. 18	.26	.05	1.30 (4)	.65	158,332,800
	Christmas Issue, Oct. 27					
1701	13¢ Nativity,					
	by John Singleton Copley	.26	.05	3.40 (12)	.65	809,955,000
	Christmas Issue, Oct. 27, 1976 continued					
1702	13¢ "Winter Pastime",					
	by Nathaniel Currier	.26	.05	2.86 (10)	.65	481,685,000
1703	13¢ as 1702	.26	.05	5.70 (20)	.65	481,685,000

No. 1702 has overall tagging. Lettering at base is black and usually ½mm. below design. As a rule, no "snowflaking" in sky or pond. Pane of 50 has margins on 4 sides with slogans. No. 1703 has block tagging the size of the printed area. Lettering at base is gray black and usually ¾mm. below design. "Snowflaking" generally in sky and pond. Pane of 50 has margin only at right or left, and no slogans.

	Issues of 1977 American Bicentennial, Perf. 11					
1704	13¢ Washington,					
	by Charles Wilson Peale, Jan. 3	.26	.05	2.90 (10)	.65	150,328,000
1705	13¢ Tin Foil Phonograph, Mar. 23	.26	.05	1.30 (4)	.65	176,830,000

	1977 continued	Un	U	PB/LP #	FDC	Q
	Pueblo Indian Art Issue, Apr. 13, Perf. 11					
1706	13¢ Zia Pot	.26	.08	3.00 (10)	.65	48,994,000
1707	13¢ San Ildefonso Pot	.26	.08		.65	48,994,000
1708	13¢ Hopi Pot	.26	.08	5.00 (16)	.65	48,994,000
1709	13¢ Acoma Pot	.26	.08		.65	48,994,000
	Block or strip of 4, #1706-1709	1.05	1.00		1.75	
1710	13¢ Spirit of St. Louis, May 20	.26	.05	3.65 (12)	.65	208,820,000
1711	13¢ Columbine and Rocky					
	Mountains, May 21	.26	.05	3.65 (12)	.65	192,250,000
	Butterfly Issue, June 6					
1712	13¢ Swallowtail	.26	.08	3.65 (12)	.65	54,957,500
1713	13¢ Checkerspot	.26	.08	3.65 (12)	.65	54,957,500
1714	13¢ Dogface	.26	.08		.65	54,957,500
1715	13¢ Orange Tip	.26	.08		.65	54,957,500
	Block of 4, #1712-1715	1.05	.90		1.75	
	American Bicentennial Issues					
1716	13¢ Marquis de Lafayette, June 13	.26	.05	1.30 (4)	.65	159,852,000
	Skilled Hands for Independence, July 4					
1717	13¢ Seamstress	.26	.08	3.65 (12)	.65	47,077,500
1718	13¢ Blacksmith	.26	.08	3.65 (12)	.65	47,077,500
1719	13¢ Wheelwright	.26	.08		.65	47,077,500
1720	13¢ Leatherworker	.26	.08		.65	47,077,500
	Block of 4, #1717-1720	1.05	.90		1.75	
	Perf. 11x10½					
1721	13¢ Peace Bridge and Dove,					
	Aug. 4	.26	.05	1.30 (4)	.65	163,625,000

The Shilling Green Forgery

Occasionally a forgery is so well done that it isn't detected for years. This happened with the British one shilling green stamp. A large number of forgeries of this stamp were circulated in 1872 and 1873, but they weren't detected until 25 years later, when a young British collector noticed a number of them didn't have the proper watermark.

The one shilling green itself had become a stamp of interest to collectors by then, and a check of dealers showed that many of their copies were actually this well-executed forgery. Subsequent investigation by British authorities established that the British post had probably been defrauded of thousands of dollars.

Of course, after 25 years, it was much too late to solve the crime. It is believed that a postal clerk had been in league with a counterfeiting ring and had sold the forged stamps over the counter, keeping the shillings for himself and his cronies.

The forgery continues to be a success. It is difficult to obtain, and is now more highly prized than the real shilling green.

1977

Zia. Museum of New Mexico
Pueblo Art USA 13c

San Ildefonso. Denver Art Museum
Pueblo Art USA 13c

Hopi. Heard Museum Phoenix
Pueblo Art USA 13c

Acoma. School of American Research
Pueblo Art USA 13c

1706
1708

1707
1709

USA·13c

50th Anniversary Solo Transatlantic Flight

1710

COLORADO

13c
USA
THE CENTENNIAL STATE

1711

Swallowtail
USA13c *Papilio oregonius*

Checkerspot
USA13c *Euphydryas phaeton*

Dogface
USA13c *Colias eurydice*

Orange-Tip
USA13c *Anthocaris midea*

1712
1714

1713
1715

Lafayette

US Bicentennial 13c

1716

the SEAMSTRESS
for INDEPENDENCE USA 13c

the BLACKSMITH
for INDEPENDENCE USA 13c

the WHEELWRIGHT
for INDEPENDENCE USA 13c

the LEATHERWORKER
for INDEPENDENCE USA 13c

1717
1719

1718
1720

United States of Canada
Peace Bridge 1927-77
USA 13

1721

195

Herkimer at Oriskany 1777 by Yohn
US Bicentennial 13 cents
722

ENERGY CONSERVATION
USA 13c
1723
1724

First Civil Settlement·Alta California·1777
1725

ENERGY DEVELOPMENT
USA 13c

Drafting the Articles of Confederation
York Town, Pennsylvania 1777
USA 13c
726

13c USA
50TH ANNIVERSARY YEAR OF TALKING PICTURES
1727

Surrender at Saratoga 1777 by Trumbull
US Bicentennial 13 cents
1728

Christmas 13c USA
730

Carl Sandburg
USA 13c
1731

Alaska 1778 Capt. JAMES Cook 13c USA
Capt. JAMES COOK Hawaii 1778 13c USA
1732
1733

USA 13c
1734

K A U
17

15c
USA
737

USA 15c Virginia 1720
USA 15c Rhode Island 1790
USA 15c Massachusetts 1793
USA 15c Illinois 1860
USA 15c Texas 1890

1977-1980

	1977 continued	Un	U	PB/LP	#	FDC	Q
	American Bicentennial Issue, Perf. 11						
1722	13¢ Herkimer at Oriskany,						
	by Frederick Yohn, Aug. 6	.26	.05	3.10	(10)	.65	156,296,000
	Energy Issue, Oct. 20						
1723	13 ¢ Energy Conservation	.26	.08	3.65	(12)	.65	79,338,000
1724	13¢ Energy Development	.26	.08			.65	79,338,000
	Pair, #1723-1724	.52	.35			1.00	
	American Bicentennial Issues						
1725	13¢ Farm House, Sept. 9	.26	.05	1.30	(4)	.65	154,495,000
	First civil settlement in Alta, California, 200th anniversary.						
1726	13¢ Articles of Confederation,						
	Sept. 30	.26	.05	1.30	(4)	.65	168,050,000
	200th anniversary of the Drafting of the Articles of Confederation, York Town, Pa.						
1727	13¢ Movie Projector and						
	Phonograph, Oct. 6	.26	.05	1.30	(4)	.65	156,810,000
	American Bicentennial Issue						
1728	13¢ Surrender of Saratoga,						
	by John Trumbull, Oct. 7	.26	.05	3.10	(10)	.65	153,736,000
	Christmas Issue, Oct. 21						
1729	13¢ Washington at Valley Forge	.26	.05	5.70	(20)	.65	882,260,000
1730	13¢ Rural Mailbox	.26	.05	3.10	(10)	.65	921,530,000
	Issues of 1978, Perf. 11						
1731	13¢ Carl Sandburg, Jan. 6	.26	.05	1.30	(4)	.65	156,580,000
	Capt. Cook Issue, Jan. 20						
1732	13¢ Capt. Cook	.26	.08	1.30	(4)	.75	101,095,000
1733	13¢ "Resolution" and "Discovery"	.26	.08	1.30	(4)	.75	101,095,000
	Pair, #1732-1733	.55	.30			1.50	
1734	13¢ Indian Head Penny, 1877,						
	Jan. 11	.26	.10	1.30	(4)	.90	
1735	(15¢) Eagle (A), May 22	.30	.03	1.50	(4)	.65	
	Perf. 11x10½						
1736	(15¢) orange Eagle (1735), May 22	.30	.05			.65	
1736a	Booklet pane of 8	2.40	.60				
	Perf. 10						
1737	15¢ Roses, July 11	.30	.06			.65	
1737a	Booklet pane of 8	2.40	.60				
	Nos. 1736 and 1737 issued only in booklets.						
	1980 Windmills, Feb. 7, Perf. 11						
1738	15¢ Virginia, 1720	.30	.05			.65	
1739	15¢ Rhode Island, 1790	.30	.05			.65	
1740	15¢ Massachusetts, 1793	.30	.05			.65	
1741	15¢ Illinois, 1860	.30	.05			.65	
1742	15¢ Texas, 1890	.30	.05			.65	
	Booklet pane of 10	3.25	.60			6.50	

	1978 continued	Un	U	PB/LP	#	FDC	Q
	Coil Stamp, Perf. 10 Vertically						
1743	(15¢) orange Eagle (1735), May 22	.30	.05	1.00		.65	
	Perf. 11						
1744	13¢ Harriet Tubman, Feb. 1	.26	.05	3.65	(12)	.65	156,555,000
	American Folk Art Issue, American Quilts, Mar. 8, 1978						
1745	13¢ Basket design, red & orange	.26	.08	3.65	(12)	.65	41,295,600
1746	13¢ Basket design, red	.26	.08	3.65	(12)	.65	41,295,600
1747	13¢ Basket design, orange	.26	.08			.65	41,295,600
1748	13¢ Basket design, black	.26	.08			.65	41,295,600
	Block of 4, #1745-1748	1.05	.75			2.00	
	American Dance Issue, Apr. 26						
1749	13¢ Ballet	.26	.08	3.65	(12)	.65	39,399,600
1750	13¢ Theater	.26	.08	3.65	(12)	.65	39,399,600
1751	13¢ Folk Dance	.26	.08			.65	39,399,600
1752	13¢ Modern Dance	.26	.08			.65	39,399,600
	Block of 4, #1749-1752	1.05	.75			1.75	
1753	13¢ French Alliance, May 4	.26	.05	1.30	(4)	.65	102,920,000
	Perf. 10½x11						
1754	13¢ Dr. Papanicolaou with						
	Microscope, May 13	.26	.05	1.30	(4)	.65	152,355,000
	Performing Arts Issue, Perf. 11						
1755	13¢ Jimmie Rodgers, May 24	.26	.05	3.65	(12)	.65	94,625,000
1756	15¢ George M. Cohan, July 3	.30	.05	4.20	(12)	.65	151,570,000

Jimmie Rodgers

Some people gather nicknames just as a matter of course. When you hear of the "Blue Yodeler," or the "Singing Brakeman," or the "Father of Country Music," you're hearing one of the names an affectionate public gave to Jimmie Rodgers, one of the first distinctive country music stylists.

Variety came naturally to Rodgers, who combined a number of musical styles to create his original songs. His music brought together the vocal techniques of the blues with the twangy sound of the Hawaiian steel guitar, and he added yodels just for the fun of it. From 1927 to 1933 he recorded more than 100 songs that sold altogether over 20 million copies—yet he remained virtually unknown outside of the South. Today, country and western music is enjoyed everywhere, and Jimmie Rodgers has taken his place as one of the great innovators of American pop music (#1755).

1744

1745 1746
1747 1748

1749

1750

1752

1751

1753

1754

1755

1756

199

1757a,b,c,d

1757e,f,g,h

1757

Viking missions to Mars

1759

1758

1760   1761
1762   1763

1768   1769

1764   1765
1766   1767
200

	1978 continued	Un	U	PB/LP	#	FDC	Q
1757	13¢ Souvenir sheet of 8, June 10	2.10	2.50	2.75	(8)	3.50	15,170,400
1757a	13¢ Cardinal	.26	.10				
1757b	13¢ Mallard	.26	.10				
1757c	13¢ Canada Goose	.26	.10				
1757d	13¢ Blue Jay	.26	.10				
1757e	13¢ Moose	.26	.10				
1757f	13¢ Chipmunk	.26	.10				
1757g	13¢ Red Fox	.26	.10				
1757h	13¢ Raccoon	.26	.10				
1758	15¢ Photographic Equipment,						
	June 26	.30	.05	4.20	(12)	.65	163,200,000
1759	15¢ Viking I Landing on Mars,						
	July 20	.30	.05	1.50	(4)	.80	158,880,000
	American Owls, Aug. 26						
1760	15¢ Great Gray Owl	.30	.08	1.50	(4)	.65	46,637,500
1761	15¢ Saw-whet Owl	.30	.08	1.50	(4)	.65	46,637,500
1762	15¢ Barred Owl	.30	.08	1.50	(4)	.65	46,637,500
1763	15¢ Great Horned Owl	.30	.08	1.50	(4)	.65	46,637,500
	Block of 4, #1760-1763	1.25	.85			2.00	
	American Trees, Oct. 9						
1764	15¢ Giant Sequoia	.30	.08	4.20	(12)	.65	42,034,000
1765	15¢ White Pine	.30	.08	4.20	(12)	.65	42,034,000
1766	15¢ White Oak	.30	.08			.65	42,034,000
1767	15¢ Gray Birch	.30	.08			.65	42,034,000
	Block of 4, #1764-1767	1.25	.85			2.00	
	Christmas Issue, Oct. 18						
1768	15¢ Madonna and Child	.30	.05	4.20	(12)	.65	963,370,000
1769	15¢ Hobby Horse	.30	.05	4.20	(12)	.65	916,800,000

1979

	Issues of 1979, Perf. 11	Un	U	PB/LP	#	FDC	Q
1770	15¢ Robert F. Kennedy, Jan. 12	.30	.05	1.50	(4)	.65	159,297,600
1771	15¢ Martin Luther King, Jr., Jan. 13	.30	.05	4.20	(12)	.65	166,435,000
1772	15¢ Internt'l Year of the Child,						
	Feb. 15	.30	.05	1.50	(4)	.65	162,535,000
	Perf. 10½x11						
1773	15¢ John Steinbeck, Feb. 27	.30	.05	1.50	(4)	.65	155,000,000
1774	15¢ Albert Einstein, Mar. 4	.30	.05	1.50	(4)	.65	157,310,000
	American Folk Art Issue, Apr. 19, Pennsylvania Toleware, Perf. 11						
1775	15¢ Coffeepot	.30	.08	3.50	(10)	.65	43,524,000
1776	15¢ Tea Caddy	.30	.08			.65	43,524,000
1777	15¢ Sugar Bowl	.30	.08	5.40	(16)	.65	43,524,000
1778	15¢ Coffeepot	.30	.08			.65	43,524,000
	Block or strip of 4, #1775-1778	1.20	.85			2.00	174,096,000
	American Architecture Issue, June 4						
1779	15¢ Virginia Rotunda	.30	.08	1.50	(4)	.65	41,198,400
1780	15¢ Baltimore Cathedral	.30	.08	1.50	(4)	.65	41,198,400
1781	15¢ Boston State House	.30	.08	1.50	(4)	.65	41,198,400
1782	15¢ Philadelphia Exchange	.30	.08	1.50	(4)	.65	41,198,400
	Block of 4, #1779-1782	1.20	.85			2.00	164,793,600
	Endangered Flora Issue, June 7						
1783	15¢ Persistent Trillium	.30	.06	4.20	(12)	.65	40,763,750
1784	15¢ Hawaiian Wild Broadbean	.30	.08			.65	40,763,750
1785	15¢ Contra Costa Wallflower	.30	.08	4.20	(12)	.65	40,763,750
1786	15¢ Antioch Evening Primrose	.30	.08			.65	40,763,750
	Block of 4, #1783-1786	1.25	.85			2.00	163,055,000
1787	15¢ Seeing Eye Dogs, June 15	.30	.05	6.50	(20)	.65	161,860,000

Robert Kennedy on Mt. Kennedy

Robert F. Kennedy, the subject of stamp #1770, was well-known for his belief in physical fitness. Sometimes that belief got him involved in some grueling feats of endurance, like a 50-mile, 20-hour hike with the Marines.

His real test came when he scaled a 14,000 foot mountain that had been named after his brother, the late President John F. Kennedy. At the time, Mt. Kennedy, located near the western border of the Canadian Yukon, was the highest unclimbed mountain in North America. Accompanied by two seasoned mountain climbers, Kennedy successfully completed the two-day climb over glaciers and bare rock faces. Kennedy had also braved something besides the physical hardships of the climb—his lifelong terror of heights—to become the first man to set foot on Mt. Kennedy's summit.

Robert F Kennedy
USA 15c

770

Martin Luther King Jr.

Black Heritage USA 15c

1771

International Year of the Child

1772

John Steinbeck

USA 15c

1773

Einstein
USA 15c

774

Pennsylvania Toleware
Folk Art USA 15c
Pennsylvania Toleware
Folk Art USA 15c

Pennsylvania Toleware
Folk Art USA 15c
Pennsylvania Toleware
Folk Art USA 15c

1775   1776
1777   1778

Jefferson 1743-1826 Virginia Rotunda
Architecture USA 15c
Latrobe 1764-1820 Baltimore Cathedral
Architecture USA 15c

Bulfinch 1763-1844 Boston State House
Architecture USA 15c
Strickland 1788-1854 Philadelphia Exchange
Architecture USA 15c

779   1780
781   1782

Endangered Flora
PERSISTENT TRILLIUM
15c USA
Endangered Flora
HAWAIIAN WILD BROADBEAN
15c USA

Endangered Flora
15c
Endangered Flora
15c

USA 15c

Seeing For Me

1787

Special Olympics

Sharing·Joy
USA 15c

I have not yet begun to fight

John Paul Jones
US Bicentennial 15c

1789

1790

1792
1794

1796
1798

Gerard David National Gallery
Christmas USA 15c

1799

Christmas
15c USA

1800

L ROGERS

USA·15c
HONORING VIETNAM VETERANS
NOV·11·1979

W.C. FIELDS

Benjamin Banneker

	1979 continued	Un	U	PB/LP	#	FDC	Q
1788	15¢ Special Olympics, Aug. 9	.30	.05	3.50	(10)	.65	165,775,000
	Perf. 11x12						
1789	15¢ John Paul Jones,						
	by Charles Wilson Peale, Sept. 23	.30	.05	3.50	(10)	.65	160,000,000
	Olympic Games Issue, Perf. 11						
1790	10¢ Javelin, Sept. 5	.25	.22	3.75	(12)	.60	67,195,000
1791	15¢ Running, Sept. 28	.35	.08	5.25	(12)	.65	46,726,250
1792	15¢ Swimming, Sept. 28	.35	.08	5.25	(12)	.65	46,726,250
1793	15¢ Canoeing, Sept. 28	.35	.08			.65	46,726,250
1794	15¢ Equestrian, Sept. 28	.35	.08			.65	46,726,250
	Block of 4, #1791-1794	1.50	.85			2.00	187,650,000
	Issues of 1980						
	Winter Olympic Games Issue, Feb. 1, Perf. 11x10½						
1795	15¢ Speed Skating	.45	.08	4.25	(12)	.65	
1796	15¢ Downhill Skiing	.45	.08	4.25	(12)	.65	
1797	15¢ Ski Jump	.45	.08			.65	
1798	15¢ Hockey Goaltender	.45	.08			.65	
	Block of 4, #1795-1798	1.90	.85			2.00	208,295,000
	Christmas Issue, Oct. 18, 1979, Perf. 11						
1799	15¢ Virgin and Child,						
	by Gerard David	.30	.05	4.25	(12)	.65	873,710,000
1800	15¢ Santa Claus	.30	.05	4.25	(12)	.65	931,880,000
1801	15¢ Will Rogers, Nov. 4	.30	.05	4.25	(12)	.65	161,290,000
1802	15¢ Vietnam Veterans, Nov. 11	.30	.05	3.50	(10)	.65	172,740,000
	Perf. 11½x11½						
1803	15¢ W.C. Fields, Jan. 29	.30	.05	4.25	(12)	.65	168,995,000
	Perf. 11						
1804	15¢ Benjamin Banneker, Feb. 15	.30	.05	4.25	(12)	.65	160,000,000

RFD

Rural Free Delivery had a hard time getting started. Postmaster General John Wanamaker finally got Congress to appropriate $10,000, and RFD began in 1896 with routes in West Virginia. Later that year, RFD was expanded to 80 routes in 29 states, each served by a horsedrawn wagon.

There were objections to RFD. A congressman claimed that delivering mail to farms would destroy the American way of life. A farmer claimed RFD would take away his excuse for a daily drink in town. By contrast, a Missouri farmer calculated that in 15 years before RFD, he'd had to travel 12,000 miles to and from the post office.

Today, 34,000 carriers and almost 10,000 substitutes travel a total of 2.4 million miles daily to deliver mail and packages to 15.7 rural homes. Rural America is commemorated on three postage stamps (#1504-1506).

1980

	1980 continued	Un	U	PB/LP	#	FDC	Q
	Letter Writing Issue, Feb. 25						
1805	15¢ Letter Preserve Memories	.30	.08	11.00	(36)	.65	
1806	15¢ P.S. Write Soon	.30	.08			.65	
1807	15¢ Letters Lift Spirits	.30	.08			.65	
1808	15¢ P.S. Write Soon	.30	.08			.65	
1809	15¢ Letters Shape Opinions	.30	.08			.65	
1810	15¢ P.S. Write Soon	.30	.08	11.00	(36)	.65	
	Vertical Strip of 6, #1805-1810	1.80	1.25			3.00	233,598,000
	Perf. 10, Vertical Coil						
1811	1¢ Americana Type Coil, March 6	.05	.05	.10		.40	
1813	3.5¢ Coil, June 23	.08	.05	.30		.50	
1816	12¢ Freedom of Conscience,						
	Apr. 8	.24	.05	.75		.60	
	Perf. 11x10½						
1818	(18¢) "B" Mar. 15	.36	.05	1.80	(4)	.75	
	Perf. 10						
1819	(18¢) "B" Booklet, Mar. 15	.36	.05			.75	
	Perf. 10 Vert.						
1820	(18¢) "B" Coil, Mar. 15	.36	.05	1.00		.75	
	Perf. 10½x11						
1821	15¢ Frances Perkins, April 10	.30	.05	1.50	(4)	.65	163,510,000
	Perf. 11						
1822	15¢ Dolley Madison, May 20	.30	.05	1.50	(4)	.65	256,620,000
1823	15¢ Emily Bissell, May 31	.30	.05	1.50	(4)	.65	95,695,000
1824	15¢ Helen Keller/Anne Sullivan,						
	June 27	.30	.05	1.50	(4)	.65	153,975,000
1825	15¢ Veterans Administration,						
	July 21	.30	.05	1.50	(4)	.65	160,000,000
1826	15¢ General Bernardo de Galvez,						
	July 23	.30	.05	1.50	(4)	.65	103,855,000
	Coral Reefs Issue, Aug. 26						
1827	15¢ Brain Coral	.30	.08	4.50	(12)	.65	
1828	15¢ Elkhorn Coral	.30	.08			.65	
1829	15¢ Chalice Coral	.30	.08	4.50	(12)	.65	
1830	15¢ Finger Coral	.30	.08			.65	
	Block of 4, #1827-1830	1.20	.85			2.00	205,165,000

1811   1813

1805
1806

1807
1808

1809
1810

1816

1818

Frances Perkins
USA 15c

1822

Emily Bissell
Crusader Against Tuberculosis
USA 15c

1821

1823

HELEN KELLER
ANNE SULLIVAN

1824

1825

1826

1827
1829

1828
1830

Organized Labor
Proud and Free
USA 15c

1831

Edith Wharton

USA 15c

1832

Clou by Josef Albers **USA** 15c

Learning
never ends

1833

Heiltsuk, Bella Bella
Indian Art USA 15c

Chilkat Tlingit
Indian Art USA 15c

Tlingit
Indian Art USA 15c

Bella Coola
Indian Art USA 15c

1834   1835
1836   1837

Renwick 1818-1895 Smithsonian Washington
Architecture USA 15c

Richardson 1838-1886 Trinity Church Boston
Architecture USA 15c

Furness 1839-1912 Penn Academy Philadelphia
Architecture USA 15c

AJ Davis 1803-1892 Lyndhurst Tarrytown NY
Architecture USA 15c

1838   1839
1840   1841

Christmas USA 15c

1842

USA 15c
Season's Greetings

1843

	1980 continued	Un	U	PB/LP #	FDC	Q
1831	15¢ Organized Labor, Sept. 1	.30	.05	4.50 (12)	.65	166,590,000
	Perf. 10½x11					
1832	15¢ Edith Wharton, Sept. 5	.30	.05	1.50 (4)	.65	163,275,000
	Perf. 11					
1833	15¢ American Education, Sept. 12	.30	.05	2.25 (6)	.65	160,000,000
	Indian Art—Masks Issue, Sept. 25					
1834	15¢ Bella Bella	.30	.08		.65	
1835	15¢ Chilkat	.30	.08		.65	
1836	15¢ Tlingit	.30	.08		.65	
1837	15¢ Bella Coola	.30	.08		.65	
	Block of 4, #1834-1837	1.20	.85		2.00	152,404,000
	American Architecture Issue, Oct. 9					
1838	15¢ Smithsonian	.30	.08		.65	
1839	15¢ Trinity Church	.30	.08		.65	
1840	15¢ Pennsylvania Academy of					
	Fine Arts	.30	.08		.65	
1841	15¢ Lyndhurst	.30	.08		.65	
	Block of 4, #1838-1841	1.20	.85	1.50 (4)	2.00	155,024,000
1842	15¢ Christmas Stained Glass					
	Windows, Oct. 31	.30	.05	4.25 (12)	.65	693,250,000
1843	15¢ Christmas Antique Toys,					
	Oct. 31	.30	.05	6.50 (20)	.65	718,715,000

USPS Services

The local post offices in America handle a variety of activities for their customers. These include servicing passport applications, IRS tax forms, Gold Medallion orders and food stamps; selling packaging products such as cartons and padded envelopes; registering for Selective Service; serving as depositories of flags for veteran burials; displaying Federal job notices and FBI wanted posters; registering aliens; selling money orders; and selling duck stamps for the Interior Department.

For example, through the Carrier Alert program, elderly or handicapped residents can register with a local service organization such as the United Way or Red Cross. If the letter carrier sees the mail accumulate in a mail box, the carrier notifies the service group and they investigate. This program has really paid off in the number of lives saved.

These are among the valuable services, above and beyond the normal line of duty, that our postal employees handle for all residents. Stories such as these rarely make the newspapers and are not seen on television —indeed, they happen so frequently that even the Postal Service takes them in stride.

1980-1983

Great Americans Issue, 1980-1983, Perf. 11x10½

		Un	U	PB/LP	#	FDC	Q
1843A	1¢ Dorothea Dix, Sept. 23, 1983	.05	.05				
1844	2¢ Igor Stravinsky, Nov. 18, 1982	.05	.05	.20	(4)	.60	
1844A	3¢ Henry Clay, July 13, 1983	.06	.05	.30	(4)		
1845	4¢ Carl Schurz, June 3, 1983	.08	.05	.40	(4)		
1846	5¢ Pearl Buck, June 25, 1983	.10	.05	.50	(4)		
1847	13¢ Crazy Horse, Jan. 15, 1982	.26	.05	1.30	(4)	.60	
1849	17¢ Rachel Carson, May 28, 1981	.34	.05	1.75	(4)	.75	
1850	18¢ George Mason, May 7, 1981	.36	.05	1.75	(4)	.75	
1851	19¢ Sequoyah, Dec. 27, 1980	.38	.07	2.00	(4)	.80	
1852	20¢ Ralph Bunche, Jan. 12, 1982	.40	.05	2.00	(4)	.75	
1853	20¢ Thomas Gallaudet, June 10, 1983	.40	.05	2.00	(4)		
1859	35¢ Dr. Charles Drew, June 3, 1981	.70	.08	3.50	(4)	1.00	
1860	37¢ Robert Millikan, Jan. 26, 1982	.75	.06	3.75	(4)	1.00	
	Issues of 1981, Perf. 11						
1874	15¢ Everett Dirksen, Jan. 4	.30	.05	1.50	(4)	.65	160,155,000
1875	15¢ Whitney Moore Young, Jr.,						
	Jan. 30	.30	.05	1.50	(4)	.65	159,505,000
	Flower Issue, April 23						
1876	18¢ Rose	.36	.08			.75	52,658,250
1877	18¢ Camellia	.36	.08			.75	52,658,250
1878	18¢ Dahlia	.36	.08			.75	52,658,250
1879	18¢ Lily	.36	.08			.75	52,658,250
	Block of 4, #1876-1879	1.50	.85	1.75	(4)	2.50	
	Wildlife Issue, May 14						
1880	18¢ Bighorned Sheep	.36	.05			.75	
1881	18¢ Puma	.36	.05			.75	
1882	18¢ Harbor Seal	.36	.05			.75	
1883	18¢ Bison	.36	.05			.75	
1884	18¢ Brown Bear	.36	.05			.75	
1885	18¢ Polar Bear	.36	.05			.75	
1886	18¢ Elk (wapiti)	.36	.05			.75	
1887	18¢ Moose	.36	.05			.75	
1888	18¢ White Tailed Deer	.36	.05			.75	
1889	18¢ Prong Horned Antelope	.36	.05			.75	
	Booklet Pane of 10, #1880-1889	3.60				7.00	
	Flag Issue, April 24						
1890	18¢ Flag and Anthem, for amber						
	waves of grain	.36	.05	7.50	(20)	.75	
	Perf. 10 Vert.						
1891	18¢ Flag and Anthem, from sea, coil	.36	.05			.75	

Dorothea Dix USA 1c — 1843A

Igor Stravinsky USA 2c — 1844

Henry Clay USA 3c — 1844A

Carl Schurz 4c USA — 1845

Pearl Buck USA 5c — 1846

USA 13c Crazy Horse — 1847

Rachel Carson USA 17c — 1849

George Mason USA 18c — 1850

USA 19c Sequoyah — 1851

Ralph Bunche USA 20c — 1852

Thomas H. Gallaudet USA 20c — 1853

Charles R Drew MD USA 35c — 1859

Robert Millikan 37c USA — 1860

USA 15c Everett Dirksen — 1874

Whitney Moore Young Black Heritage USA 15c — 1875

Rose USA 18c — 1876
Dahlia USA 18c — 1878

Camellia USA 18c — 1877
Lily USA 18c — 1879

1889a

USA 18c ...for amber waves of grain — 1890

USA 18c ...from sea to shining sea — 1891

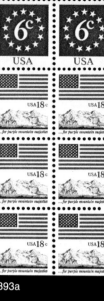

1894

1895

1896C

1897

1897A

1897B

1893a

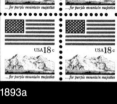

1897C

1897D

1898

1900

1901

1905

1906

1907

1909

1910

1911

1981-1983

	1981 continued, Perf. 11	Un	U	PB/LP	#	FDC	Q
1892	6¢ USA Circle of Stars, booklet	.12	.10			.75	
1893	18¢ Flag and Anthem, for purple						
	mountains majesties, booklet	.36	.05			.75	
1893a	Booklet Pane of 8,						
	2 #1892, 6 #1893	2.40	—				
1894	20¢ Flag over Supreme Court,						
	Dec. 17	.40	.05	8.50 (20)		.75	
	Perf. 10 Vert. Coil						
1895	20¢ Flag over Supreme Court,						
	Dec. 17	.40	.05	—		.75	
	Perf. 11 x 10½						
1896	20¢ Flag over Supreme Court	.40	.05	—		.75	
1896a	Booklet Pane of 6, Dec. 17	2.50					
1896c	1¢ Omnibus, Aug. 19, 1983	.05	.05	.15			
	Transportation Issues, 1982-1983 Perf. 10 Vert.						
1897	2¢ Locomotive 1870's,						
	May 20, 1982	.05	.05	.15		.60	
1897A	4¢ Stagecoach 1890's,						
	Aug. 19, 1982	.08	.05	.35		.60	
1897B	3¢ Railroad Handcar,						
	Mar. 25, 1983	.06	.05	.18			
1897C	5¢ Motorcycle, Oct. 10, 1983	.10	.05	.30			
1897D	5.2¢ Antique Sleigh,						
	Mar. 21, 1983	.12	.05	.35			
1898	5.9¢ Bicycle 1870's, Feb. 17, 1982	.12	.05	.50		.60	
1900	9.3¢ Mail Wagon, Dec. 15, 1982	.20	.08	.60		.65	
1901	10.9¢ Hansom Cab 1890's,						
	Mar. 26, 1982	.22	.05	.70		.65	
1905	17¢ Electric Auto, June 25, 1982	.34	.05	1.00		.75	
1906	18¢ Surrey, May 15, 1982	.36	.05	1.00		.75	
1907	20¢ Fire Pumper, Dec. 10, 1982	.40	.05	1.20		.75	
1909	$9.35 Express Mail, Aug. 12, 1983	19.00	—	—			
	Booklet Pane of 3	60.00	—				
	Perf. 11x10½						
1910	18¢ American Red Cross, May 1	.36	.05	1.75	(4)	.75	165,175,000
	Perf. 11						
1911	18¢ Savings and Loan, May 8	.36	.05	1.75	(4)	.75	107,240,000

1981 continued	Un	U	PB/LP	#	FDC	Q
Space Achievement Issue, May 21						
1912 18¢ Exploring the Moon	.36	.10			.75	42,227,375
1913 18¢ Benefitting Mankind	.36	.10			.75	42,227,375
1914 18¢ Benefitting Mankind	.36	.10			.75	42,227,375
1915 18¢ Understanding the Sun	.36	.10			.75	42,227,375
1916 18¢ Probing the Planets	.36	.10			.75	42,227,375
1917 18¢ Benefitting Mankind	.36	.10			.75	42,227,375
1918 18¢ Benefitting Mankind	.36	.10			.75	42,227,375
1919 18¢ Comprehending the Universe	.36	.10			.75	42,227,375
Block of 8, #1912-1919	3.00	2.25	3.50	(8)	5.00	
1920 18¢ Professional Management, June 18	.36	.05	1.75	(4)	.75	99,420,000
Wildlife Habitat Issue, June 26						
1921 18¢ Wetland Habitats	.36	.08			.75	46,732,500
1922 18¢ Grassland Habitats	.36	.08			.75	46,732,500
1923 18¢ Mountain Habitats	.36	.08			.75	46,732,500
1924 18¢ Woodland Habitats	.36	.08			.75	46,732,500
Block of 4, #1921-1924	1.50	.85	1.75	(4)	2.50	
1925 18¢ International Year of the Disabled, June 29	.36	.05	1.75	(4)	.75	100,265,000
1926 18¢ Edna St. Vincent Millay, July 10	.36	.05	1.75	(4)	.75	99,615,000
1927 18¢ Alcoholism, Aug. 19	.36	.05	8.00	(20)	.75	97,535,000

The Beginning of Modern Astronomy

The stamp commemorating the 500th birthday of Polish astronomer Nicolaus Copernicus (#1488) shows him holding a sceptre that depicts the earth in its orbit around the sun. Copernicus was the first astronomer to gather a large body of convincing evidence that the earth moved. In his era, the 15th century, most people believed the earth was the stationary center of the universe. By tirelessly reviewing ancient records of the movement of heavenly bodies and by adding his own observations of the sun and the planets, Copernicus demonstrated that what happened in the sky would be easier to explain if we assumed the earth were a planet moving through space.

1488

The theory that the earth moved around the sun had to wait the evidence of later astronomers before it was widely accepted. But Copernicus started the process by which men seriously began to consider their solid, stable earth as a traveler in the skies.

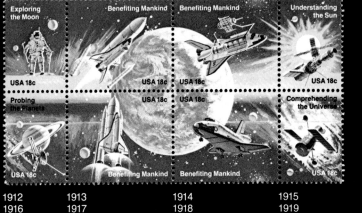

| 1912 | 1913 | 1914 | 1915 |
| 1916 | 1917 | 1918 | 1919 |

1920

1925

| 1921 | 1922 |
| 1923 | 1924 |

Stanford White 1853-1906 NYU Library New York
Architecture USA 18c

Richard Morris Hunt 1828-1895 Biltmore Asheville NC
Architecture USA 18c

Bernard Maybeck 1862-1957 Palace of Arts San Francisco
Architecture USA 18c

Louis Sullivan 1856-1924 Bank Owatonna Minn
Architecture USA 18c

928
930

1929
1931

Babe Zaharias
USA 18c

Bobby Jones
USA 18c

1932

1933

FREDERIC REMINGTON
American
Sculptor
18c
USA

934

USA 18c
James Hoban White House Architect

1935

USA 20c
James Hoban White House Architect

1936

WILLIAMSBURG
YORKTOWN
18c USA
Yorktown 1781

937

18c USA
Cape Charles
Cape Henry
Virginia Capes 1781

1938

Christmas USA 1981
Botticelli Art Institute of Chicago

1939

Season's Greetings
USA
1981

	1981 continued	Un	U	PB/LP	#	FDC	Q
	American Architecture Issue, Aug. 28						
1928	18¢ NYU Library	.36	.08			.75	41,827,000
1929	18¢ Biltmore House	.36	.08			.75	41,827,000
1930	18¢ Palace of the Arts	.36	.08			.75	41,827,000
1931	18¢ National Farmer's Bank	.36	.08			.75	41,827,000
	Block of 4, #1928-1931	1.50	.85	1.75	(4)	2.50	
	Perf. 10½x11						
1932	18¢ Babe Zaharias, Sept. 22	.36	.05	1.75	(4)	.75	101,625,000
1933	18¢ Bobby Jones, Sept. 22	.36	.05	1.75	(4)	.75	99,170,000
	Perf. 11						
1934	18¢ Remington Sculpture, Oct. 9	.36	.05	1.75	(4)	.75	101,155,000
1935	18¢ James Hoban, Oct. 13	.50	.25	1.75	(4)	.75	101,200,000
1936	20¢ James Hoban, Oct. 13	.40	.05	2.00	(4)	.75	167,360,000
1937	18¢ Yorktown 1781, Oct. 16	.36	.06			.75	81,210,000
1938	18¢ Virginia Capes 1781, Oct. 16	.36	.06			.75	81,210,000
	Pair, #1937-1938	.72	.15	1.75	(4)	1.00	
1939	(20¢) Christmas Madonna, Oct. 28	.40	.05	2.00	(4)	.75	597,720,000
1940	(20¢) Christmas Child Art, Oct. 28	.40	.05	2.00	(4)	.75	792,600,000
1941	20¢ John Hanson, Nov. 5	.40	.05	2.00	(4)	.75	167,130,000

Louis Sullivan

The word "skyscraper" was first used by a Chicago newspaper in 1889. It was not simply a description of buildings that were tall for the day (the New York Tribune building, for example, with its spire at 285 feet). Rather, "skyscraper" meant the new buildings constructed on iron and steel frames —an engineering breakthrough that marked the dawn of modern architecture.

Louis Henri Sullivan, 1856-1924, was a pioneer of skyscraper design. Widely regarded as the Father of Modernism, Sullivan was the first to see how tall, steel-framed buildings could break from the classical styles.

"Form follows function"—this was the kernel of Sullivan's philosophy. He meant that a building's design should reflect its purpose.

It was a radical concept in the last decades of the 19th century, but Sullivan was hardly a slave to convention. He'd dropped out of MIT after his freshman year because he was bored with their "theology of architecture." He went to France and miraculously won entrance to Paris' prestigous Ecole des Beaux Arts—only to drop out, again after one year of study.

The city of Chicago fascinated Sullivan, and it was there he went to find his fortune. The Auditorium Theater, Carson, Pirie, Scott & Co. and Chicago's Stock Exchange (now preserved in the Art Institute) are among the treasures he left behind. Of the dozens of buildings Sullivan created, many still serve the purpose for which they were originally designed—a testimony to the idea that form follows function.

1981-1982	Un	U	PB/LP	#	FDC	Q
U.S. Desert Plants Issue, December 11						
1942 20¢ Barrel Cactus	.40	.06			.75	47,890,000
1943 20¢ Agave	.40	.06			.75	47,890,000
1944 20¢ Beavertail Cactus	.40	.06			.75	47,890,000
1945 20¢ Saguaro	.40	.06			.75	47,890,000
Block of 4, #1942-1945	1.60	.85	2.00	(4)	2.50	
Perf. 11x10½						
1946 (20¢) "C" Eagle, Oct. 11	.40	.05	2.00	(4)	.75	
Perf. 10 Vert.						
1947 (20¢) "C" Eagle, coil, Oct. 11	.40	.05	1.00		.75	
1948 (20¢) "C" Eagle, booklet, Oct. 11	.40	.05			.75	
Perf. 11x10½						
1948a Booklet Pane of 10	4.25	—				
Issues of 1982, Perf. 11						
1949 20¢ Bighorn, booklet, Jan. 8	.40	.05			.75	
1949a Booklet Pane of 10	4.00	—			8.00	
1950 20¢ Franklin D. Roosevelt, Jan. 3	.40	.05	2.00	(4)	.75	163,939,200
1951 20¢ Love, Feb. 1	.40	.05	2.00	(4)	.75	
1952 20¢ George Washington, Feb. 22	.40	.05	2.00	(4)	.75	180,700,000

Desert Plants

Arizona policeman Richard Countryman has a prickly problem on his hands every day: cactus rustling. As head of a small division of "cactus cops," Countryman stalks the desperados who steal and mutilate hundreds of cacti every year.

1942

It's a new problem in the Southwest—the result of a booming world market for cactus. With prices for certain species up over $1,000, amateur diggers and professional smugglers have taken an uncommon interest in desert horticulture.

And state legislators are striking back. Arizona passed the first anti-cactus rustling laws in 1980, making it illegal to remove any of the 212 varieties of cacti without written permission from the Agriculture and Horticulture Commission. California, New Mexico and Nevada have followed with similar regulations.

Officer Countryman admits he and his seven-man team have a big job patrolling 90,000 square miles of desert. One time, though, they got some unexpected help. It was in 1982. An out-of-state troublemaker was blasting a 23-foot saguaro with his shotgun and two rifles when suddenly the ton-and-a-half cactus collapsed, crushing its assailant as it fell.

"That time," Countryman told the press, "a native plant struck back" (#1942-1945).

USA 20ᶜ

Agave deserti

Agave

USA 20ᶜ

Ferocactus wislizenii

Barrel Cactus

Opuntia basilaris

Beavertail Cactus

USA 20ᶜ

USA 20ᶜ

Cereus giganteus

Saguaro

Domestic Mail

C US Postage

1946

942

1943
1944

1945

USA 20ᶜ

1882 1982 USA 20ᶜ

Franklin D. Roosevelt

1950

949

USA 20c

1951

George Washington

1732-1982

USA 20c

Alabama USA 20c	Alaska USA 20c	Arizona USA 20c	Arkansas USA 20c	California USA 20c
Yellowhammer & Camellia	*Willow Ptarmigan & Forget-Me-Not*	*Cactus Wren & Saguaro Cactus Blossom*	*Mockingbird & Apple Blossom*	*California Quail & California Poppy*
953	1954	1955	1956	1957

Colorado USA 20c	Connecticut USA 20c	Delaware USA 20c	Florida USA 20c	Georgia USA 20c
Lark Bunting & Rocky Mountain Columbine	*Robin & Mountain Laurel*	*Blue Hen Chicken & Peach Blossom*	*Mockingbird & Orange Blossom*	*Brown Thrasher & Cherokee Rose*
958	1959	1960	1961	1962

Hawaii USA 20c	Idaho USA 20c	Illinois USA 20c	Indiana USA 20c	Iowa USA 20c
Hawaiian Goose & Hibiscus	*Mountain Bluebird & Syringa*	*Cardinal & Violet*	*Cardinal & Peony*	*Eastern Goldfinch & Wild Rose*
963	1964	1965	1966	1967

Kansas USA 20c	Kentucky USA 20c	Louisiana USA 20c	Maine USA 20c	Maryland USA 20c
Western Meadowlark & Sunflower	*Cardinal & Goldenrod*	*Brown Pelican & Magnolia*	*Chickadee & White Pine Cone and Tassel*	*Baltimore Oriole & Black-Eyed Susan*

	1982 continued	Un	U	PB/LP	#	FDC	Q
	State Birds & Flowers Issue, Apr. 14, Perf. 10½x11						
1953	20¢ Alabama	.40	.25			.75	13,339,900
1954	20¢ Alaska	.40	.25			.75	13,339,900
1955	20¢ Arizona	.40	.25			.75	13,339,900
1956	20¢ Arkansas	.40	.25			.75	13,339,900
1957	20¢ California	.40	.25			.75	13,339,900
1958	20¢ Colorado	.40	.25			.75	13,339,900
1959	20¢ Connecticut	.40	.25			.75	13,339,900
1960	20¢ Delaware	.40	.25			.75	13,339,900
1961	20¢ Florida	.40	.25			.75	13,339,900
1962	20¢ Georgia	.40	.25			.75	13,339,900
1963	20¢ Hawaii	.40	.25			.75	13,339,900
1964	20¢ Idaho	.40	.25			.75	13,339,900
1965	20¢ Illinois	.40	.25			.75	13,339,900
1966	20¢ Indiana	.40	.25			.75	13,339,900
1967	20¢ Iowa	.40	.25			.75	13,339,900
1968	20¢ Kansas	.40	.25			.75	13,339,900
1969	20¢ Kentucky	.40	.25			.75	13,339,900
1970	20¢ Louisiana	.40	.25			.75	13,339,900
1971	20¢ Maine	.40	.25			.75	13,339,900
1972	20¢ Maryland	.40	.25			.75	13,339,900

Mr. ZIP

The postal zoning system in the United States began in 1943 with the introduction of the one or two digit zone number. These numbers identified a delivery station of a metropolitan post office. On July 1, 1963, Mr. ZIP introduced the Zone Improvement Plan. This was a five-digit national coding system used to identify each postal delivery section. The first digit identifies one of ten geographical areas, with the second digit denoting a state, part of a heavily populated state, or two or three less populated states. The third digit designates a major metropolitan postal facility or sectional center, with the fourth and fifth digits picking up the original zone number.

The Federal German Post Office became the first to use the current postal code system to speed delivery. The function of a code system is to help in address scanning and the automated processing of mail, and to speed up mail sorting. Approximately 97 percent of all mail delivered in the United States uses the Zip Code. In 1974, the USPS issued a postage stamp (#1511) to publicize the numerical system.

The new improved version, ZIP + 4—a nine-digit code—will narrow the sorting down to individual streets, office buildings, and large users. Many collectors save the single stamps or block of four stamps with Mr. ZIP printed on the margins.

	1982 continued	Un	U	PB/LP	#	FDC	Q
1973	20¢ Massachusetts	.40	.25			.75	13,339,900
1974	20¢ Michigan	.40	.25			.75	13,339,900
1975	20¢ Minnesota	.40	.25			.75	13,339,900
1976	20¢ Mississippi	.40	.25			.75	13,339,900
1977	20¢ Missouri	.40	.25			.75	13,339,900
1978	20¢ Montana	.40	.25			.75	13,339,900
1979	20¢ Nebraska	.40	.25			.75	13,339,900
1980	20¢ Nevada	.40	.25			.75	13,339,900
1981	20¢ New Hampshire	.40	.25			.75	13,339,900
1982	20¢ New Jersey	.40	.25			.75	13,339,900
1983	20¢ New Mexico	.40	.25			.75	13,339,900
1984	20¢ New York	.40	.25			.75	13,339,900
1985	20¢ North Carolina	.40	.25			.75	13,339,900
1986	20¢ North Dakota	.40	.25			.75	13,339,900
1987	20¢ Ohio	.40	.25			.75	13,339,900
1988	20¢ Oklahoma	.40	.25			.75	13,339,900
1989	20¢ Oregon	.35	.25			.75	13,339,900
1990	20¢ Pennsylvania	.40	.25			.75	13,339,900
1991	20¢ Rhode Island	.40	.25			.75	13,339,900
1992	20¢ South Carolina	.40	.25			.75	13,339,900

Universal Postal Union

In the 19th century, figuring the cost of a letter mailed from the United States to another country was complicated. The rate depended on the U.S. domestic rate, sea postage, the rate of the receiving country, and the transit rate assessed by each country through which the letter traveled. The recipient of the letter usually paid all these fees. The receiving post office had to compute the postage due, then change this figure into gold centimes, a universal money exchange. This money had to be returned to the country where the letter originated. This led to postal agreements between individual countries, and sometimes sections of countries.

The basis of the Universal Postal Union (#1530-37) was that a letter written to another country usually prompts a letter in response. So in theory, the total amount of mail sent in one direction was the same as in the other.

This situation existed for almost 100 years, until Colombia complained at the 1969 UPU Congress that they received much more mail than they sent. They also stated that it cost them more money to deliver a letter in their country than it cost in an industrialized nation. A letter delivered to a remote area frequently was carried by train, bus, horse and boat before it reached its destination. In 1971, a system of balancing payments went into effect whereby "sender" countries pay other nations who receive more mail than they send to the "senders".

Massachusetts	Michigan	Minnesota	Mississippi	Missouri
USA 20c	USA 20c	USA 20c	USA 20c	USA 20c
Black-Capped Chickadee & Mayflower	*Robin & Apple Blossom*	*Common Loon & Showy Lady Slipper*	*Mockingbird & Magnolia*	*Eastern Bluebird & Red Hawthorn*
1973	1974	1975	1976	1977

Montana	Nebraska	Nevada	New Hampshire	New Jersey
USA 20c	USA 20c	USA 20c	USA 20c	USA 20c
Western Meadowlark & Bitterroot	*Western Meadowlark & Goldenrod*	*Mountain Bluebird & Sagebrush*	*Purple Finch & Lilac*	*American Goldfinch & Violet*
1978	1979	1980	1981	1982

New Mexico	New York	North Carolina	North Dakota	Ohio
USA 20c	USA 20c	USA 20c	USA 20c	USA 20c
Roadrunner & Yucca Flower	*Eastern Bluebird & Rose*	*Cardinal & Flowering Dogwood*	*Western Meadowlark & Wild Prairie Rose*	*Cardinal & Red Carnation*
1983	1984	1985	1986	1987

Oklahoma	Oregon	Pennsylvania	Rhode Island	South Carolina
USA 20c	USA 20c	USA 20c	USA 20c	USA 20c
Scissor-tailed Flycatcher & Mistletoe	*Western Meadowlark & Oregon Grape*	*Ruffed Grouse & Mountain Laurel*	*Rhode Island Red & Violet*	*Carolina Wren & Carolina Jessamine*
1988	1989	1990	1991	1992

South Dakota
USA 20c
Ring-Necked Pheasant &
Pasqueflower
1993

Tennessee
USA 20c
Mockingbird &
Iris
1994

Texas
USA 20c
Mockingbird &
Bluebonnet
1995

Utah
USA 20c
California Gull &
Sego Lily
1996

Vermont
USA 20c
Hermit Thrush &
Red Clover
1997

Virginia
USA 20c
Cardinal &
Flowering Dogwood
1998

Washington
USA 20c
American Goldfinch &
Rhododendron
1999

West Virginia
USA 20c
Cardinal &
Rhododendron Maximum
2000

Wisconsin
USA 20c
Robin &
Wood Violet
2001

Wyoming
USA 20c
Western Meadowlark &
Indian Paintbrush
2002

20c
USA
1782-1982·USA·THE·NETHERLANDS
2003

Library of Congress
USA 20c
2004

Wise shoppers
stretch dollars
Consumer
Education
USA 20c
2005

USA 20c
Solar energy   Knoxville World's Fair
USA 20c
Breeder reactor   Knoxville World's Fair
2006
2008

USA 20c
Synthetic fuels   Knoxville World's Fair
USA 20c
Fossil fuels   Knoxville World's Fair
2007
2009

Horatio Alger
USA 20c
2010

THE BARRYMORES
Performing Arts USA 20c
2012

Aging
together
USA
20c

	1982 continued	Un	U	PB/LP #	FDC	Q
1993	20¢ South Dakota	.40	.25		.75	13,339,900
1994	20¢ Tennessee	.40	.25		.75	13,339,900
1995	20¢ Texas	.40	.25		.75	13,339,900
1996	20¢ Utah	.40	.25		.75	13,339,900
1997	20¢ Vermont	.40	.25		.75	13,339,900
1998	20¢ Virginia	.40	.25		.75	13,339,900
1999	20¢ Washington	.40	.25		.75	13,339,900
2000	20¢ West Virginia	.40	.25		.75	13,339,900
2001	20¢ Wisconsin	.40	.25		.75	13,339,900
2002	20¢ Wyoming	.40	.25		.75	13,339,900
	Sheet of 50			20.00	25.00	
	Perf. 11					
2003	20¢ USA/Netherlands, Apr. 20	.40	.05	8.50 (20)	.75	109,245,000
2004	20¢ Library of Congress, Apr. 21	.40	.05	2.00 (4)	.75	112,535,000
	Perf. 10 Vert. Coil					
2005	20¢ Consumer Education, Apr. 27	.40	.05	1.10	.75	
	World's Fair Issue, Apr. 29, Perf. 11					
2006	20¢ Solar Energy	.40	.08		.75	31,160,000
2007	20¢ Synthetic Fuels	.40	.08		.75	31,160,000
2008	20¢ Breeder Reactor	.40	.08		.75	31,160,000
2009	20¢ Fossil Fuels	.40	.08		.75	31,160,000
	Block of 4, #2006-2009	1.60	.85	2.00 (4)	2.50	
2010	20¢ Horatio Alger, Apr. 30	.40	.05	2.00 (4)	.75	107,605,000
2011	20¢ Aging Together, May 21	.40	.05	2.00 (4)	.75	173,160,000
2012	20¢ The Barrymores, June 8	.40	.05	2.00 (4)	.75	107,285,000

Friend of Orphans

In New York in the late 1860s, an unknown writer, Horatio Alger Jr., became aware of the hundreds of young boys in that city who had been orphaned by the Civil War. They virtually lived on the streets, scrounging up food and shelter by performing odd jobs and taking advantage of what charity they could find.

Alger took up their cause and, in more than a hundred novels, wrote about street boys who, through a combination of "luck and pluck," managed to rise out of their poverty. His stories gave inspiration to his young audience and also served to dramatize the need for relief of their hardships.

Alger did more than write about the problem. For the rest of his life, he gave generously to various children's charities and devoted his time to being a busy, successful fund raiser for those charities. He himself informally adopted three of New York's orphans. Stamp #2010 depicts the homeless boys Horatio Alger championed.

1982

	1982 continued	Un	U	PB/LP #	FDC	Q
2013	20¢ Dr. Mary Walker, June 10	.40	.05	2.00 (4)	.75	109,040,000
2014	20¢ International Peace Garden, June 30	.40	.05	2.00 (4)	.75	183,270,000
2015	20¢ America's Libraries, July 13	.40	.05	2.00 (4)	.75	169,495,000
	Black Heritage Series, Aug. 2, Perf. 11x10½					
2016	20¢ Jackie Robinson	.40	.05	2.00 (4)	.75	164,235,000
	Perf. 11					
2017	20¢ Touro Synagogue, Aug. 22	.40	.05	8.50 (20)	.75	110,130,000
2018	20¢ Wolf Trap Farm Park, Sept. 1	.40	.05	2.00 (4)	.75	110,995,000
	American Architecture Issue, Sept. 30					
2019	20¢ Fallingwater	.40	.08		.75	41,335,000
2020	20¢ Illinois Institute of Technology	.40	.08		.75	41,335,000
2021	20¢ Gropius House	.40	.08		.75	41,335,000
2022	20¢ Dulles Airport	.40	.08		.75	41,335,000
	Block of 4, (#2019-2022)	1.60	.85	2.00 (4)	2.50	
2023	20¢ Francis of Assisi, Oct. 7	.40	.05	2.00 (4)	.75	174,180,000
2024	20¢ Ponce de Leon, Oct. 2	.40	.05	8.50 (20)	.75	110,261,000
2025	13¢ Puppy and Kitten, Nov. 3	.26	.06	1.30 (4)	.75	
2026	20¢ Christmas, Madonna and Child—Tiepolo, Oct. 28	.40	.05	8.50 (20)	.75	703,295,000
	Seasons Greetings Issue, Oct. 28					
2027	20¢ Sledding	.40	.05		.75	197,220,000
2028	20¢ Snowman	.40	.05		.75	197,220,000
2029	20¢ Skating	.40	.05		.75	197,220,000
2030	20¢ Tree	.40	.05		.75	197,220,000
	Block of 4, #2027-2030	1.60	.85	2.00 (4)	2.50	

Walter Gropius

By the time Walter Gropius (#2021) moved to the United States, he was already a legend among architects. As founder of the Bauhaus school in 1919, in Weimar, Germany, Gropius had revolutionized architecture with his vision of buildings as political statements.

Bauhaus was, most importantly, a philosophical movement. Its guiding principle was "functionalism," rejecting of all things "bourgeois." Functional building materials included steel, wood and glass; functional exteriors were white or beige. Ornamentation and color were discarded, and designs that affected individuality were considered elitist and antique. Gropius impressed his students with the idea that architecture, like post-monarchist Europe, was "starting from zero."

Mies van der Rohe and Le Corbusier were among the avant garde architects who taught at Bauhaus. With Nazi terrorism threatening the existence of his school, Gropius fled to a teaching position at Harvard University in 1937.

226

Dr. Mary Walker
Army Surgeon

Medal of Honor
USA 20c

2013

International Peace Garden
1932 1982   USA 20c

2014

America's
ABC
Libraries
XYZ
USA 20c
Legacies To Mankind

2015

Jackie Robinson

Black Heritage USA 20c

2016

Touro   USA 20c
Synagogue
Newport RI 1763

To bigotry,
no sanction,
To persecution,
no assistance.
George Washington

2017

Frank Lloyd Wright 1867-1959 Fallingwater Mill Run PA
Architecture USA 20c

Mies van der Rohe 1886-1969 Illinois Inst.Tech. Chicago
Architecture USA 20c

Walter Gropius 1883-1969 Gropius House Lincoln MA
Architecture USA 20c

Eero Saarinen 1910-1961 Dulles Airport Washington DC
Architecture USA 20c

2019
2021

2020
2022

USA 20c

Wolf Trap Farm Park
for the performing arts

2018

FRANCIS OF ASSISI 1182-1982 USA 20c

2023

Ponce de León   USA 20c

2024

USA 13c

2025

Christmas USA 20c

Tiepolo: National Gallery of Art

2026

Season's Greetings USA 20c

Season's Greetings USA 20c

Season's Greetings USA 20c

Season's Greetings USA 20c

2027
2029

2028
2030

2031

2032   2033   2035
         2034

2036

2037

Joseph Priestley
USA 20c

2038

2039

2040

2041

2042

2043

	Issues of 1983, Perf. 11	Un	U	PB/LP	#	FDC		Q
2031	20¢ Science & Industry, Jan. 19	.40	.05	2.00	(4)	.75		
	Balloon Issue, March 31							
2032	20¢ Intrepid	.40	.08			.75		
2033	20¢ Hot Air Balloons	.40	.08			.75		
2034	20¢ Hot Air Balloons	.40	.08			.75		
2035	20¢ Explorer	.40	.08			.75		
	Block of 4, #2032-2035	1.60	.85	2.00	(4)	2.50		
2036	20¢ Swedish-American Treaty,							
	March 24	.40	.05	2.00	(4)	.75		
2037	20¢ Civilian Conservation Corps,							
	March 24	.40	.05	2.00	(4)	.75		
2038	20¢ Joseph Priestley, April 13	.40	.05	2.00	(4)	.75		
2039	20¢ Voluntarism, April 5	.40	.05	8.50	(20)	.75		
2040	20¢ U.S./Germany Concord,							
	April 29	.40	.05	2.00	(4)	.75		
2041	20¢ Brooklyn Bridge, May 5	.40	.05	2.00	(4)	.75		
2042	20¢ TVA, May 18	.40	.05	8.50	(20)	.75		
2043	20¢ Physical Fitness, May 14	.40	.05	8.50	(20)	.75		

Counterfeits of Counterfeits

Occasionally forged stamps gain a special notoriety, either because of their interesting history or because of the closeness of the forgery to the original. Some philatelists even collect famous forgeries. And of course, whenever there is a demand for something, someone is tempted to make inauthentic copies. So every now and then, someone will make a counterfeit of a "true" counterfeit.

One curious case of this occurred after World War II. During the war, the Allied powers made counterfeits of German stamps as part of a campaign to do anything that might upset Germany's ability to wage war. Many different varieties of these propaganda stamps were printed, and after the war, stamp hobbyists sought them for their collections.

In the 1950s, it became clear that "unofficial" forgeries of the propaganda stamps had been on sale for quite awhile. In forgeries of regular issues, experts can usually detect some flaw, either because the actual stamp is easily obtainable for comparison, or because a description of the stamp is widely printed in catalogs or handbooks of stamps. It wasn't, however, until the mid-'50s that there were books which described the propaganda stamps in enough detail to let dealers and collectors know whether or not they had the true counterfeit or its forged copy.

	1983 continued	Un	U	PB/LP	#	FDC	Q
	Black Heritage Issues, June 9						
2044	20¢ Scott Joplin	.40	.05	2.00	(4)	.75	
2045	20¢ Medal of Honor, June 7	.40	.05	2.00	(4)	.75	
	American Sports Series, July 6, Perf. 10½x11						
2046	20¢ George Herman "Babe" Ruth	.40	.05	2.00	(4)	.75	
	Literary Arts Series, July 8, Perf. II						
2047	20¢ Nathaniel Hawthorne	.40	.05	2.00	(4)	.75	
	Summer Olympic Games, July 28						
2048	13¢ Discus	.26	.05			.75	
2049	13¢ High Jump	.26	.05			.75	
2050	13¢ Archery	.26	.05			.75	
2051	13¢ Boxing	.26	.05			.75	
	Block of 4, #2048-2051	1.05	.65	1.30	(4)	2.50	
2052	20¢ Treaty of Paris, Sept. 2	.40	.05	2.00	(4)	.75	
2053	20¢ Civil Service, Sept. 9	.40	.05	8.50	(20)	.75	
2054	20¢ Metropolitan Opera, Sept. 14	.40	.05	2.00	(4)	.75	
	American Inventors Issue, Sept. 14						
2055	20¢ Charles Steinmetz	.40	.05			.75	
2056	20¢ Edwin Armstrong	.40	.05			.75	
2057	20¢ Nikola Tesla	.40	.05			.75	
2058	20¢ Philo T. Farnsworth	.40	.05			.75	
	Block of 4, #2055-2058	1.60	.85			2.50	

Tennessee Valley Authority

Fifty years ago, the Tennessee Valley Authority revolutionized the power industry by selling electricity dirt cheap and urging people to use it with abandon. Half a century later, the Authority is spending millions of dollars studying alternative energy sources and promoting energy conservation.

What's been happening at the TVA?

The Authority was established in 1933 as an autonomous arm of the government, commissioned with developing the natural resources of the Tennessee Valley. This was done, in the first two decades, by building dams (20), reforestation (210,000 acres), soil-reclamation (on 68,000 farms), manufacturing new fertilizers, and building model towns, highways and industrial parks. By the early Fifties, TVA was the nation's largest power program, generating electricity for almost all of Tennessee, and parts of Kentucky, West Virginia, North Carolina, Georgia, Alabama and Mississippi.

The kilowatts came from the river, but soon consumers demanded more. So TVA switched to coal, and the Cumberland Plateau was ravaged with strip mines. When consumers demanded still more electricity, the TVA turned to the atom.

One nuclear plant is in operation today and several more are under construction. After a financial crisis in the Seventies, partly the result of atomic development, TVA has begun experimenting with solar power and other innovations.

2045

2044

2046

2047

2052

2048
2050

2049
2051

2054

2053

2055
2057

2056
2058

First American streetcar, New York City, 1832   Early electric streetcar, Montgomery, Ala., 1886

"Bobtail" horsecar, Sulphur Rock, Ark., 1926   St. Charles streetcar, New Orleans, La., 1923

2059
2061

2060
2062

Christmas USA 20c

Raphael, 1483-1983, National Gallery

2063

Season's Greetings USA 20c

2064

Martin Luther

1483-1983 USA 20c

2065

	1983 continued	Un	U	PB/LP	#	FDC	Q
	Streetcars Issue, Oct. 8						
2059	20¢ First American Streetcar	.40	.05			.75	
2060	20¢ Early Electric Streetcar	.40	.05			.75	
2061	20¢ "Bobtail" Horsecar	.40	.05			.75	
2062	20¢ St. Charles Streetcar	.40	.05			.75	
	Block of 4, #2059-2062	1.60	.85			2.50	
2063	20¢ Christmas Raphael, Oct. 28	.0	.05			.75	
2064	20¢ Christmas Santa Claus, Oct. 28	.40	.05			.75	
2065	20¢ Martin Luther, Nov. 11	.40	.05			.75	

Intrepid

In 1782, while France battled Britain to annex Gibraltar, a young Frenchman named Joseph Montgolfier was filling paper bags with smoke and watching them drift to the ceiling in his kitchen. He was testing his theory that a certain "gas" in smoke made air expand and rise. (In fact, it was hot air, not smoke, that lifted the balloons.) Delighted with his success, he dashed off a letter to the military authorities.

2032

"I possess a superhuman means of introducing our soldiers into Gibraltar's impregnable fortress. They may enter through the air. By making a bag large enough, it will be possible to introduce into Gibraltar an entire army, which, borne by the wind, will enter right above the heads of the English."

Thus the hot air balloon, from its beginnings, was recognized as an instrument of war. Some eighty years later, military balloons rose in America.

Union Army generals were skeptical about balloons, but aeronaut T.S.C. Lowe won President Lincoln's confidence in June, 1861. Lowe was convinced that balloons could be used for telegraphic communication. Taking a telegraph operator, a transmitter and half a mile of wire (attached to a land line which led to a local office), Lowe sailed up 500 feet in a moored balloon on the grounds of the Columbian Armory. He then dictated a message to the president—the first such message ever telegraphed from the air.

Within months, T.S.C. Lowe was Chief Aeronaut of the Union Army, commanding a fleet of balloons that included the Intrepid (#2032).

Alaska Statehood (20¢, #2066)

Type:	Commemorative
Date of Issue:	January 3, 1984
Place of Issue:	Fairbanks, Alaska
Designer:	Bill Bond
Printing:	Gravure
Colors:	Line Blue, Yellow, Red, Blue, Black

Besides highlighting the 25th anniversary of Alaskan statehood, this commemorative also observes the 200th anniversary of the first permanent settlement in the state and the 100th anniversary of the first civil government.

1984 Winter Olympics (20¢, #2067-2070)

Type:	Commemorative
Date of Issue:	January 6, 1984
Place of Issue:	Lake Placid, New York
Designer:	Robert Peak
Printing:	Gravure
Colors:	Yellow, Magenta, Cyan, Black

All U.S. stamps and stationery commemorating the 1984 Olympics were designed by Robert Peak of Scottsdale, Arizona.

This block features Ice Dancing, Alpine (Downhill) Skiing, Nordic (Cross-country) Skiing and Ice Hockey.

Federal Deposit Insurance Corporation
(20¢, #2071)

Type:	Commemorative
Date of Issue:	January 12, 1984
Place of Issue:	Washington, D.C.
Designer:	Michael David Brown
Printing:	Gravure
Colors:	Tan, Red, Blue, Rust, Green, Black

This stamp honors the 50th anniversary of the establishment of the Federal Deposit Insurance Corporation (FDIC) as an independent agency of the U.S. government.

Love (20¢, #2072)

Type: Special
Date of Issue: January 31, 1984
Place of Issue: Washington, D.C.
Designer: Bradbury Thompson
Printing: Intaglio and Gravure
Colors: Black and Red (Intaglio); Red, Orange,
                 Green, Blue, Violet (Gravure)

As with previous "Love" stamps (#1475 and #1951), this special-issue stamp will be available in larger quantities and for a longer period of time than commemorative issues. The stamp was designed for use on numerous special occasions, such as weddings, birthdays, anniversaries and, of course, on Valentine's Day.

Carter G. Woodson (20¢, #2073)

Type: Commemorative (Black Heritage Series)
Date of Issue: February 1, 1984
Place of Issue: Washington, D.C.
Designer: Jerry Pinkney
Printing: Gravure
Colors: Yellow, Red, Blue, Purple, Ochre

The latest addition to the Black Heritage USA Series (see also pages 34 and 35), this commemorative honors the "Father of Black History." Woodson overcame economic and social barriers to become the person most responsible for researching, writing and teaching about the heritage of black Americans during the early portion of this century. He also served as editor of the *Journal of Negro History,* a landmark publication in the field of black history.

Soil and Water Conservation (20¢, #2074)

Type: Commemorative
Date of Issue: February 6, 1984
Place of Issue: Denver, Colorado
Designer: Michael David Brown
Printing: Gravure
Colors: Tan, Red, Blue, Rust, Green, Black

Issued to honor the 50th anniversary of the soil and water conservation movement in the United States, this stamp focuses on the Soil Erosion Service, which, in 1934, began to work with farmers through demonstration projects. That same year, the Soil Conservation Service of the U.S. Department of Agriculture was signed into law.

Harry S. Truman (20¢, #1854)

Type:	Definitive (Great Americans Series)
Date of Issue:	January 26, 1984
Place of Issue:	Washington, D.C.
Designer:	Christopher Calle (after the official White House portrait)
Printing:	Intaglio
Colors:	Black

U.S. President

Lillian M. Gilbreth (40¢, #1861)

Type:	Definitive (Great Americans Series)
Date of Issue:	February 24, 1984
Place of Issue:	Montclair, New Jersey
Designer:	Ward Brackett
Printing:	Intaglio
Colors:	Green

Industrial Engineer

Richard Russell (10¢, #1846A)

Type:	Definitive (Great Americans Series)
Date of Issue:	May 31, 1984
Place of Issue:	Winder, Georgia
Designer:	Richard Sparks
Printing:	Intaglio
Colors:	Blue

U.S. Senator

Dr. Frank Laubach (30¢, #1858)

Type:	Definitive (Great Americans Series)
Date of Issue:	September 2, 1984
Place of Issue:	Benton, Pennsylvania
Designer:	Richard Sparks
Printing:	Gravure/Intaglio
Colors:	Green

Educator

Railroad Caboose (11¢, #1902—Coil)

Type:	Definitive (Transportation Series)
Date of Issue:	February 3, 1984
Place of Issue:	Rosemont, Illinois
Designer:	Jim Schleyer
Printing:	Intaglio
Colors:	Red

This is the 13th issue in the Transportation Series, which features early modes of transportation. The series was initiated in 1981 with the release of the 18¢ Surrey stamp (#1906). The caboose depicted on this stamp is similar to one used in the 1890s by a logging company railroad in the Sierra Nevada Mountains of California. The tiny cabooses were used to transport equipment and crews to and from tree felling sites.

Baby Buggy (7.4¢, #1899—Coil)

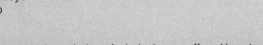

Type:	Definitive (Transportation Series)
Date of Issue:	April 7, 1984
Place of Issue:	San Diego, California
Designer:	Jim Schleyer
Printing:	Intaglio
Colors:	Brown

This stamp features a pen and ink rendering of a baby buggy offered by a toy company in its 1887 mail order catalog. This is the 14th stamp in the Transportation Series.

Federal Credit Union Act (20¢, #2075)

Type:	Commemorative
Date of Issue:	February 10, 1984
Place of Issue:	Salem, Massachusetts
Designer:	Michael David Brown
Printing:	Gravure
Colors:	Red, Blue, Rust, Green, Black

The stamp was issued in Salem, Massachusetts, the birthplace of Edward A. Filene, considered by many to be the father of the credit union movement in the United States. The stamp honors the 50th anniversary of the Credit Union Act, which enabled credit unions to organize under charters from the federal government. The first credit union in the U.S. was established under state charter in 1909 at Manchester, New Hampshire. Today, there are approximately 20,000 credit unions, with total assets of about $90 billion.

Orchids (20¢, #2076-2079)

Type:	Commemorative
Date of Issue:	March 5, 1984
Place of Issue:	Miami, Florida
Designer:	Manabu Saito
Printing:	Gravure
Colors:	Yellow, Magenta, Cyan, Black, Green

Orchids grow almost everywhere except the polar regions and the desert. Each of these stamps pictures a native American orchid.

Hawaii Statehood (20¢, #2080)

Type:	Commemorative
Date of Issue:	March 12, 1984
Place of Issue:	Honolulu, Hawaii
Designer:	Herb Kane
Printing:	Gravure
Colors:	Yellow, Magenta, Cyan, Black, Dark Blue

Hawaii is an archipelago in the North Pacific Ocean, almost 2,500 miles from the continental United States. Prior to being admitted as our 50th state, Hawaii had been a U.S. territory for more than 60 years.

National Archives (20¢, #2081)

Type:	Commemorative
Date of Issue:	April 16, 1984
Place of Issue:	Washington, D.C.
Designer:	Michael David Brown
Printing:	Gravure
Colors:	Brown, Red, Black

This stamp honors the work of our nation's archivists for their role in preserving the heritage of the U.S. at the National Archives. The National Archives contains many items of America's past.

1984 Summer Olympics (20¢, #2082-2085)

Type: Commemorative
Date of Issue: May 4, 1984
Place of Issue: Los Angeles, California
Designer: Robert Peak
Printing: Gravure
Colors: Yellow, Magenta, Cyan, Black

Issued at the site of the 1984 Summer Olympic
Games in Los Angeles, this block of four
features men's diving, women's long jump,
men's wrestling and women's canoeing
(kayaking). These are the last in the series of
stamps issued for the Winter and Summer
Olympics of 1984.

Louisiana World Exposition (20¢, #2086)

Type: Commemorative
Date of Issue: May 11, 1984
Place of Issue: New Orleans, Louisiana
Designer: Chuck Ripper
Printing: Gravure
Colors: Yellow, Magenta, Cyan, Black, Red

The Exposition, which opened in New Orleans on May 12, 1984, featured
"The World of Rivers—Fresh Water as a Source of Life." A variety of exhibits
spotlighted the rivers and ports of the world. Additionally, other pavilions
displayed technological and scientific breakthroughs.

Health Research (20¢, #2087)

Type: Commemorative
Date of Issue: May 17, 1984
Place of Issue: New York, New York
Designer: Tyler Smith
Printing: Gravure
Colors: Yellow, Red, Process Blue, Dark Blue, Silver

Health professionals have made dramatic strides with technical and medical
innovations which prevent disease or prolong life. Diseases such as polio,
smallpox and yellow fever are no longer incurable because of the dedication
of health researchers. The stamp design features laboratory equipment used
by researchers in performing their work.

Jim Thorpe (20¢, #2089)

Type:	Commemorative
Date of Issue:	May 24, 1984
Place of Issue:	Shawnee, Oklahoma
Designer:	Richard Gangel (from an early photograph)
Printing:	Intaglio
Colors:	Brown

Jim Thorpe was one of America's most versatile athletes. His feats on the track, football field and baseball diamond have become legendary. During the 1912 Summer Olympics in Stockholm, Thorpe became the first athlete to capture both the pentathlon and the decathlon. He was later stripped of these gold medals by Olympic officials when it was discovered that he had received $60 a month playing semi-pro baseball in North Carolina in 1910. However, a decision made in 1982 by the International Olympic Committee led to the return of the medals to Thorpe's family.

John McCormack (20¢, #2090)

Type:	Commemorative (Performing Arts Series)
Date of Issue:	June 6, 1984
Place of Issue:	Boston, Massachusetts
Designers:	Jim Sharpe (U.S.); Ron Mercer (Ireland)
Printing:	Gravure
Colors:	Yellow, Magenta, Green, Cyan, Black

This commemorative was jointly issued by the United States and Ireland to honor the 100th birthday of the Irish-American tenor, one of opera's greatest singers and a performer of ballads.

Douglas Fairbanks (20¢, #2088)

Type:	Commemorative (Performing Arts Series)
Date of Issue:	May 23, 1984
Place of Issue:	Denver, Colorado
Designer:	Jim Sharpe
Printing:	Gravure
Colors:	Yellow, Magenta, Cyan, Black

Fairbanks was noted for his dashing, swashbuckling roles which combined both his acting and athletic abilities. In 1919, he formed United Artists with Charlie Chaplin, D.W. Griffith and Mary Pickford. Together, they are credited with maintaining a standard of excellence which established the motion picture's status as a unique art form.

St. Lawrence Seaway (20¢, #2091)

Type:	Commemorative
Date of Issue:	June 26, 1984
Place of Issue:	Massena, New York
Designer:	Ernst Barenscher
Printing:	Gravure
Colors:	Silver, Blue, Green, Black

This stamp commemorates the 25th anniversary of the opening of the St. Lawrence Seaway and will be jointly issued by the U.S. and Canada (the Canadian design is different from the U.S.). The Seaway opened the industrial and agricultural heartlands of North America to deep-draft ocean-going vessels. The project forged the final link in the 2,342-mile waterway from Duluth, Minnesota, to the Atlantic Ocean by making passable a treacherous 190-mile stretch of the St. Lawrence River south of Montreal, Quebec.

Migratory Bird Hunting and Conservation Stamp Act (20¢, #2092)

Type:	Commemorative
Date of Issue:	July 2, 1984
Place of Issue:	Des Moines, Iowa
Designer:	Peter Cocci
Printing:	Intaglio
Colors:	Blue

Over the years, "Duck" stamps have become a whole area of specialty collecting. This commemorative features Jay Norwood "Ding" Darling's design for the original duck stamp of 1934, entitled "Mallards Dropping In." (For more information on Duck stamps, see pages 28-33.)

Roanoke Voyages (20¢, #2093)

Type:	Commemorative (Explorers' Series)
Date of Issue:	July 13, 1984
Place of Issue:	Manteo, North Carolina
Designer:	Charles Lundgren
Printing:	Gravure
Colors:	Yellow, Red, Blue, Brown, Black

This is the first in a new series on Explorers and honors the 400th anniversary of the Roanoke Voyages, begun in 1584 with a grant from Queen Elizabeth I to Walter Raleigh to establish an English colony in the New World.

1984 ISSUES

Herman Melville (20¢, #2094)

Type:	Commemorative (Literary Arts Series)
Date of Issue:	August 1, 1984
Place of Issue:	New Bedford, Massachusetts
Designer:	Bradbury Thompson
Printing:	Intaglio
Colors:	Green

This stamp is part of the Literary Arts Series, which includes John Steinbeck (#1773), Edith Wharton (#1832) and Nathaniel Hawthorne (#2047). Hawthorne, in fact, was Melville's neighbor and friend during a sojourn in Massachusetts. And it was Hawthorne who encouraged Melville to complete his masterpiece, *Moby Dick,* in 1851.

Horace A. Moses (20¢, #2095)

Type:	Commemorative
Date of Issue:	August 6, 1984
Place of Issue:	Bloomington, Indiana
Designer:	Dennis Lyall
Printing:	Intaglio
Colors:	Orange, Brown

Horace A. Moses was the founder in 1919 of the Junior Achievement movement to interest youngsters in developing business skills.

Smokey Bear (20¢, #2096)

Type:	Commemorative
Date of Issue:	August 13, 1984
Place of Issue:	Capitan, New Mexico
Designer:	Rudolph A. Wendelin
Printing:	Offset/Intaglio
Colors:	Yellow, Magenta, Cyan,
	Black (offset); Black (Intaglio)

Smokey Bear is the familiar symbol of the U.S. Forest Service's forest fire prevention campaign.

Roberto Clemente (20¢, #2097)

Type:	Commemorative (Sports Series)
Date of Issue:	August 17, 1984
Place of Issue:	Carolina, Puerto Rico
Designer:	Juan Lopez-Bonilla
Printing:	Gravure
Colors:	Grey, Tan, Brown, Red, Blue, Black

This is the fourth stamp in the Sports Series (Bobby Jones, Babe Zaharias and Babe Ruth are the others). It honors "Number 21" of the Pittsburgh Pirates, who played with a zeal that earned him the respect and admiration of millions.

Dogs (20¢)

Type:
Commemorative
Date of Issue:
September 7, 1984
Place of Issue:
New York, NY
Designer:
Roy Andersen
Printing:
Gravure
Colors:
Yellow, Magenta, Cyan, Black

This block of four honors the centennial year of the American Kennel Club.

Hispanic Americans (20¢)

Type: Commemorative

Other information not available at press time.

Crime Prevention (20¢, #2102)

Type:	Commemorative
Date of Issue:	September 26, 1984
Place of Issue:	Washington, D.C.
Designer:	Randall McDougall
Printing:	Gravure
Colors:	Yellow, Red, Blue, Black

Issued to commemorate Crime Prevention Month in the United States.

Family Unity (20¢)

Type:	Commemorative
Date of Issue:	October 1, 1984
Place of Issue:	Shaker Heights, Ohio
Designer:	Molly LaRue
Printing:	Gravure/Intaglio
Colors:	Red, Blue (Gravure); Black (Intaglio)

This design was a winner of the student stamp design contest conducted by the U.S. Postal Service. For more information, see pages 38-41.

Eleanor Roosevelt (20¢)

Type:	Commemorative
Date of Issue:	October 11, 1984
Place of Issue:	Hyde Park, New York
Designer:	Bradbury Thompson
Printing:	Intaglio
Colors:	Blue

This stamp was issued to honor the centennial of Eleanor Roosevelt's birth.

Nation of Readers (20¢)

Type:	Commemorative
Date of Issue:	October 16, 1984
Designer:	Bradbury Thompson
Printing:	Intaglio

This stamp was issued in recognition of America's love for the printed word.

Christmas (Traditional, 20¢)

Type:	Special
Date of Issue:	October 30, 1984
Place of Issue:	Washington, D.C.
Designer:	Bradbury Thompson
Printing:	Gravure

The painting pictured on this stamp is Fra Filippo Lippi's *Madonna and Child*, which is in the collection of the National Gallery in Washington.

Christmas (Contemporary, 20¢)

Type:	Special
Date of Issue:	October 30, 1984
Place of Issue:	Jamaica, New York
Designer:	Danny LaBoccetta
Printing:	Gravure

This year's Christmas (Contemporary) stamp was designed by a student from Jamaica, New York. Danny LaBoccetta drew a cheerful Santa with a sack of toys. This design was one of several chosen from more than half a million entries in a nationwide project sponsored by the U.S. Postal Service.

Vietnam Veterans Memorial (20¢)

Type:	Commemorative
Date of Issue:	November 13, 1984
Place of Issue:	Washington, D.C.
Designer:	Paul Calle
Printing:	Intaglio
Colors:	Blue, Green

This stamp recognizes the sacrifice of all those who served in Vietnam, and especially those whose names are inscribed on the Vietnam Veterans Memorial in Washington, D.C. The memorial contains the names of the 57,939 military personnel who gave their lives in Vietnam between 1959 and 1975.

1918-1935

C1

C2

C3

C3a

C4

C5

C6

C7

C10

C11

C12

C13

C14

C15

C18

C20

	Air Post Stamps	Un	U	PB/LP	#	FDC	Q
	For prepayment of postage on all mailable matter sent by airmail. All unwatermarked.						
	Issue of 1918, Perf. 11						
C1	6¢ Curtiss Jenny	130.00	45.00	1,700.00	(6)	*16,000.00*	3,395,854
C2	16¢ Curtiss Jenny	175.00	52.50	3,500.00	(6)	*16,000.00*	3,793,887
C3	24¢ Curtiss Jenny	175.00	65.00	950.00	(4)	*19,000.00*	2,134,888
C3a	Center Inverted	*110,000.00*					
	Issue of 1923						
C4	8¢ Wooden Propeller and						
	Engine Nose	55.00	20.00	825.00	(6)	500.00	6,414,576
C5	16¢ Air Service Emblem	175.00	50.00	5,000.00	(6)	850.00	5,309,275
C6	24¢ De Havilland Biplane	225.00	40.00	6,000.00	(6)	1,000.00	5,285,775
	Issue of 1926-27						
C7	10¢ Map of U.S.						
	and Two Mail Planes	6.00	.50	85.00	(6)	75.00	42,092,800
C8	15¢ olive brown (C7)	7.00	2.75	100.00	(6)	85.00	15,597,307
C9	20¢ yellow green (C7)	20.00	2.25	250.00	(6)	140.00	17,616,350
	Issue of 1927						
C10	10¢ Lindbergh's "Spirit of						
	St. Louis", June 18	15.00	3.00	240.00	(6)	25.00	20,379,179
C10a	Booklet pane of 3	140.00	*60.00*				
	Nos. C1-C10 inclusive were also available for ordinary postage.						
	Issue of 1928						
C11	5¢ Beacon on Rocky Mountains,						
	July 25	7.50	.65	80.00	(8)	45.00	106,887,675
C12	5¢ Winged Globe, Feb. 10	18.50	.45	275.00	(6)	15.00	97,641,200
	Graf Zeppelin Issue, Apr. 19						
C13	65¢ Zeppelin over Atlantic Ocean	450.00	350.00	4,500.00	(6)	2,400.00	93,536
C14	$1.30 Zeppelin between						
	Continents	1,000.00	650.00	11,000.00	(6)	1,600.00	72,428
C15	$2.60 Zeppelin Passing Globe	1,650.00	1,000.00	17,000.00	(6)	2,500.00	61,296
	Issued for use on mail carried on the first Europe-Pan-American round-trip flight of Graf Zeppelin, May 1930.						
	Issues of 1931-32, Perf. 10½x11						
C16	5¢ violet (C12)	10.00	.50	175.00	(4)	250.00	57,340,050
C17	8¢ olive bistre (C12)	4.00	.30	65.00	(4)	20.00	76,648,803
	Issue of 1933, Perf. 11						
C18	50¢ Century of Progress, Oct. 2	150.00	125.00	1,500.00	(6)	300.00	324,070
	Issue of 1934, Perf. 10½x11						
C19	6¢ dull orange (C12), July 1	4.50	.12	35.00	(4)	*200.00*	302,205,100
	Issue of 1935, Perf. 11						
C20	25¢ Transpacific, Nov. 22	2.50	1.75	40.00	(6)	35.00	10,205,400

	Issue of 1937	Un	U	PB/LP	#	FDC	Q
C21	20¢ The "China Clipper," over the						
	Pacific, Feb. 15	20.00	2.25	225.00	(6)	40.00	12,794,600
C22	50¢ carmine (C21)	19.00	6.50	210.00	(6)	40.00	9,285,300
	Issue of 1938						
C23	6¢ Eagle Holding Shield,						
	Olive Branch, and Arrows, May 14	.65	.06	11.00	(4)	20.00	349,946,500
	Issue of 1939						
C24	30¢ Transatlantic, May 16	19.00	1.50	325.00	(6)	45.00	19,768,150
	Issues of 1941-44, Perf. 11x10½						
C25	6¢ Twin-motor Transport Plane,						
	1941	.18	.05	1.00	(4)	2.25	4,476,527,700
C25a	Booklet pane of 3	6.50	1.00				
	Singles No. C25a are imperf. at sides or imperf. at sides and bottom.						
C26	8¢ olive green (C25), 1944	.25	.05	1.50	(4)	3.75	1,744,876,650
C27	10¢ violet (C25), 1941	2.00	.20	16.00	(4)	7.00	67,117,400
C28	15¢ brown carmine (C25), 1941	4.50	.35	22.00	(4)	10.00	78,434,800
C29	20¢ bright green (C25), 1941	3.25	.30	20.00	(4)	10.00	42,359,850
C30	30¢ blue (C25), 1941	4.00	.30	21.00	(4)	16.00	59,880,850
C31	50¢ orange (C25), 1941	22.50	4.00	150.00	(4)	40.00	11,160,600
	Issue of 1946						
C32	5¢ DC-4 Skymaster, Sept. 25	.12	.05	.75	(4)	2.00	864,753,100
	Issues of 1947, Perf. 10½x11						
C33	5¢ DC-4 Skymaster, Mar. 26	.12	.05	.75	(4)	2.00	971,903,700
	Perf. 11x10½						
C34	10¢ Pan American Union Building,						
	Washington, D.C., Aug. 30	.30	.06	2.50	(4)	2.00	207,976,550
C35	15¢ Statue of Liberty/						
	N.Y. Skyline, Aug. 20	.35	.05	2.85	(4)	2.75	756,186,350
C36	25¢ Plane over San Francisco-						
	Oakland Bay Bridge, July 30	1.60	.12	7.50	(4)	3.50	132,956,100
	Issues of 1948						
	Coil Stamp, Perf. 10 Horizontally						
C37	5¢ carmine (C33), Jan. 15	2.00	1.10	13.50		2.00	Unlimited
	Perf. 11x10½						
C38	5¢ New York City, July 31	.18	.18	20.00	(4)	1.75	38,449,100
	Issues of 1949						
	Perf. 10½x11						
C39	6¢ carmine (C33), Jan. 18	.18	.05	.85	(4)	1.50	5,070,095,200
C39a	Booklet pane of 6	13.50	5.00				
	Perf. 11x10½						
C40	6¢ Alexandria 200th Anniv., May 11	.18	.10	.95	(4)	1.25	75,085,000
	Coil Stamp, Perf. 10 Horizontally						
C41	6¢ carmine (C33), Aug. 25	4.50	.05	20.00		1.25	Unlimited
	Universal Postal Union Issue, Perf. 11x10½						
C42	10¢ Post Office Dept. Bldg., Nov. 18	.35	.35	3.50	(4)	1.75	21,061,300

C21 C23 C24

C25 C32 C33

C34 C35 C36

C38 C40 C42

C43

C44

C45

C46

C47

C48

C49

C51

C53

C54

C55

C56

C57

C58

C59

C60

	1949 continued	Un	U	PB/LP	#	FDC	Q
C43	15¢ Globe and Doves Carrying						
	Messages, Oct. 7	.50	.50	3.00	(4)	2.25	36,613,100
C44	25¢ Boeing Stratocruiser						
	and Globe, Nov. 30	.85	.85	11.00	(4)	2.75	16,217,100
C45	6¢ Wright Brothers, Dec. 17	.20	.10	1.00	(4)	3.75	80,405,000
	Issue of 1952						
C46	80¢ Diamond Head, Honolulu,						
	Hawaii, Mar. 26	12.50	1.50	80.00	(4)	17.50	18,876,800
	Issue of 1953						
C47	6¢ Powered Flight, May 29	.16	.10	.85	(4)	1.50	78,415,000
	Issue of 1954						
C48	4¢ Eagle in Flight, Sept. 3	.12	.08	5.00	(4)	.75	50,483,600
	Issue of 1957						
C49	6¢ Air Force, Aug. 1	.20	.10	1.50	(4)	1.75	63,185,000
	Issues of 1958						
C50	5¢ rose red (C48), July 31	.22	.15	5.00	(4)	.80	72,480,000
	Perf. 10½x11						
C51	7¢ Silhouette of Jet Liner, July 31	.22	.05	1.30	(4)	.75	532,410,300
C51a	Booklet pane of 6	16.50	6.50				1,326,960,000
	Coil Stamp, Perf. 10 Horizontally						
C52	7¢ blue (C51)	4.50	.20	22.50		.90	157,035,000
	Issues of 1959, Perf. 11x10½						
C53	7¢ Alaska Statehood, Jan. 3	.25	.12	1.50	(4)	.65	90,055,200
	Perf. 11						
C54	7¢ Balloon Jupiter, Aug. 17	.25	.12	1.50	(4)	1.10	79,290,000
	Issued for the 100th anniversary of the carrying of mail by the balloon Jupiter from Lafayette to Crawfordsville, Indiana.						
	Perf. 11x10½						
C55	7¢ Hawaii Statehood, Aug. 21	.25	.12	1.50	(4)	1.00	84,815,000
	Perf. 11						
C56	10¢ Pan-American Games, Aug. 27	.40	.40	5.00	(4)	.90	38,770,000
	Issue of 1959-66						
C57	10¢ Liberty Bell, June 10, 1960	3.00	1.00	15.00	(4)	1.50	39,960,000
C58	15¢ Statue of Liberty, Jan. 13, 1961	.75	.06	4.00	(4)	1.10	Unlimited
C59	25¢ Abraham Lincoln, Apr. 22, 1960	.75	.06	4.00	(4)	1.50	Unlimited
	Issue of 1960, Perf. 10½x11						
C60	7¢ Jet Airliner (C51), Aug. 12	.30	.05	1.50	(4)	.70	289,460,000
C60a	Booklet pane of 6	22.50	7.00				
	Coil Stamp, Perf. 10 Horizontally						
C61	7¢ carmine (C60), Oct. 22	8.00	.25	50.00		1.00	87,140,000

1961-1973

	Issue of 1961, Perf. 11	Un	U	PB/LP	#	FDC	Q
C62	13¢ Liberty Bell, June 28, 1961	.65	.10	7.00	(4)	.80	Unlimited
C63	15¢ Statue of Liberty, Jan. 13, 1961	.40	.08	2.25	(4)	1.00	Unlimited
	No. C63 has a gutter between the two parts of the design; No. C58 does not.						
	Issue of 1962, Perf. 10½x11						
C64	8¢ Jetliner over Capitol, Dec. 5	.22	.05	1.10	(4)	.60	Unlimited
	Booklet pane of 5 + label	7.50	1.25				
	Coil Stamp, Perf. 10 Horizontally						
C65	8¢ carmine (C64), Dec. 5	.50	.08	4.00		.80	Unlimited
	Issue of 1963, Perf. 11						
C66	15¢ Montgomery Blair, May 3	1.40	.75	11.00	(4)	1.35	42,245,000
	Issues of 1963-64, Perf. 11x10½						
C67	6¢ Bald Eagle, July 12, 1963	.20	.15	4.00	(4)	.50	Unlimited
	Perf. 11						
C68	8¢ Amelia Earhart, July 24, 1963	.40	.15	4.50	(4)	2.50	63,890,000
C69	8¢ Robert H. Goddad, Oct. 5, 1964	1.20	.15	7.50	(4)	2.75	65,170,000
	Issues of 1967						
C70	8¢ Alaska Purchase, Mar. 30	.45	.20	7.00	(4)	.70	64,710,000
C71	20¢ "Columbia Jays" by Audubon,						
	Apr. 26	1.50	.15	10.00	(4)	2.00	165,430,000
	Issues of 1968, Perf. 11x10½						
C72	10¢ 50-Star Runway, Jan. 5	.30	.05	2.25	(4)	.60	Unlimited
C72b	Booklet pane of 8	4.00	.75				
C72c	Booklet pane of 5 + label	2.50	.75				
C73	10¢ carmine (C72), Coil, Perf. 10	.50	.05			.60	Unlimited
	Air Mail Service Issue, Perf. 11						
C74	10¢ Curtiss Jenny, May 15	.60	.15	8.00	(4)	1.50	74,180,000
C75	20¢ U.S.A. and Jet, Nov. 22	1.00	.06	6.50	(4)	1.10	Unlimited
	Issue of 1969						
C76	10¢ Moon Landing, Sept. 9	.30	.15	3.50	(4)	3.50	152,364,800
	Issues of 1971-73, Perf. 10½x11, 11x10½						
C77	9¢ Plane, May 15, 1971	.22	.15	3.00	(4)	.50	Unlimited
C78	11¢ Silhouette of Jet, May 7, 1971	.30	.05	1.35	(4)	.50	Unlimited
C78a	Booklet pane of 4 + 2 labels	1.50	.40				
C79	13¢ Winged Airmail Envelope,						
	Nov. 16, 1973	.32	.10	1.65	(4)	.55	Unlimited
C79a	Booklet pane of 5 + label,						
	Dec. 27, 1973	1.35	.70				
	Perf. 11						
C80	17¢ Statue of Liberty, July 13, 1971	.55	.15	2.75	(4)	.60	Unlimited
	Perf. 11x10½						
C81	21¢ red, blue and black (C75)						
	May 21, 1971	.55	.10	2.75	(4)	.75	Unlimited

1961-1973

C62

C63

C64

C66

C67

C68

C69

C70

C71

C72

C74

C75

C76

C77

C78

C79

C80

C81

1972-1980

C84

C85

C86

C87

C88

C89

C90

C97

C91
C92

C93
C94

C95
C96

C98

C99

C100

	1971-1973 continued	Un	U	PB/LP #	FDC	Q
	Coil Stamps, Perf. 10 Vertically					
C82	11¢ Silhouette of Jet (C78),					
	May 7, 1971	.40	.06	1.65	.50	Unlimited
C83	13¢ red (C79), Dec. 27, 1973	.40	.10	1.75	.50	
	Issues of 1972, Perf. 11					
C84	11¢ City of Refuge, May 3	.30	.15	2.75 (4)	.65	78,210,000
	Perf. 11x10½					
C85	11¢ Skiing and Olympic Rings,					
	Aug. 17	.30	.15	3.50 (10)	.50	96,240,000
	Issue of 1973					
C86	11¢ De Forest Audions, July 10	.30	.15	1.75 (4)	.50	58,705,000
	Issues of 1974, Perf. 11					
C87	18¢ Statue of Liberty, Jan. 11	.45	.45	2.50 (4)	.65	Unlimited
C88	26¢ Mt. Rushmore National					
	Memorial, Jan. 2	.60	.15	2.85 (4)	.85	Unlimited
	Issue of 1976					
C89	25¢ Plane & Globes, Jan. 2	.60	.18	2.50 (4)	.85	
C90	31¢ Plane, Globes & Flag, Jan. 2	.62	.10	3.10 (4)	1.10	
	Issues of 1978, Wright Brothers Issue, Sept. 23					
C91	31¢ Orville & Wilbur Wright	.85	.15	3.10 (4)	1.15	
C92	31¢ Orville & Wilbur Wright	.85	.15	3.10 (4)	1.15	
	Pair, #C91-C92	1.75	.65		2.30	
	Issues of 1979, Octave Chanute Issue, March 29					
C93	21¢ Octave Chanute	.85	.32	2.10 (4)	1.00	
C94	21¢ Octave Chanute	.85	.32	2.10 (4)	1.00	
	Pair, #C93-C94	1.75	.75		2.00	
	Wiley Post Issue, Nov. 20					
C95	25¢ Wiley Post	.85	.35	2.50 (4)	1.00	
C96	25¢ Wiley Post	.85	.35	2.50 (4)	1.00	
	Pair, #C95-C96	1.75	.85	2.50	2.00	
	Olympic Games Issue					
C97	31¢ High Jump	.70	.30	8.75 (12)	1.15	47,200,000
	Issues of 1980					
C98	40¢ Philip Mazzei, Oct. 13	.90	.30	11.00 (12)	1.35	
C99	28¢ Blanche Stuart Scott, Dec. 30	.70	.15	7.75 (12)	1.10	
C100	35¢ Glenn Curtiss, Dec. 30	.70	.15	10.00 (12)	1.25	

		Un	U	PB/LP	#	FDC	Q
C101	28¢ Gymnastics	.56	.28			1.10	
C102	28¢ High Jump	.56	.28			1.10	
C103	28¢ Basketball	.56	.28			1.10	
C104	28¢ Soccer	.56	.28			1.10	
	Block of 4, #C101-C104	2.25	2.00	2.75	(4)	3.00	
	Olympics Issues, April 8						
C105	40¢ Shotput	.80	.40			1.35	
C106	40¢ Gymnastics	.80	.40			1.35	
C107	40¢ Swimming	.80	.40			1.35	
C108	40¢ Weightlifting	.80	.40			1.35	
	Block of 4, #C105-C108	3.25	2.75	4.00	(4)	3.75	
	Olympics Issues, Nov. 4						
C109	35¢ Fencing	.70	.35				
C110	35¢ Bicycling	.70	.35				
C111	35¢ Volleyball	.70	.35				
C112	35¢ Pole Vault	.70	.35				
	Block of 4, #C109-C112	3.00	1.85				
	Air Post Special Delivery Stamps						
	Issue of 1934, Perf. 11						
CE1	16¢ dark blue (CE2)	1.00	.95	30.00	(6)	25.00	
	For imperforate variety see No. 771.						
	Issue of 1936						
CE2	16¢ Great Seal of United States	.50	.25	12.00	(4)	17.50	

The Father of Rocketry

Robert Goddard was a visionary who was not appreciated in his own country. His work was well known to German and Russian rocket scientists, who followed his early experiments with keen interest. Yet when he tried to interest the U.S. military men in the potential value of his rockets, they did not have the foresight to realize the usefulness of these space vehicles. Among his achievements, Goddard was the first to develop a rocket motor using liquid fuels, successfully fired a liquid fuel rocket, developed gyro steering apparatus for rockets, unfolded the concept of the two-stage rocket, and demonstrated mathematically the use of rocket power to reach extreme altitudes and to head for the Moon.

It took a private foundation, The Guggenheim, to finance his experiments at Roswell, New Mexico, from 1930 to 1941. Even with the United States at war, the worth of rocketry went unheeded. When the U.S. troops captured some of the German rocket documents, they found Goddard's papers among them. The story is told that an American intelligence officer had to ask "Who is this Goddard?"

The U.S. Postal Service honored Robert Goddard with an air mail postage stamp on October 5, 1964 (#C69); the first day city was Roswell, N. M.

1983, 1934-1936

C101   C102
C103   C104

C105   C106
C107   C108

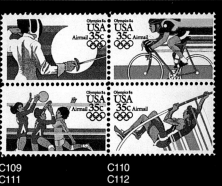

C109   C110
C111   C112

CE1

CE2

		Un	U	PB/LP	#	FDC	Q
	Special Delivery Stamps.						
	Unwmkd., Issue of 1885, Perf. 12						
E1	10¢ Messenger Running	275.00	30.00	*15,000.00*	(8)	*8,000.00*	
	Issue of 1888						
E2	10¢ blue (E3)	275.00	7.50	*15,000.00*	(8)		
	Issue of 1893						
E3	10¢ Messenger Running	185.00	14.00	*9,000.00*	(8)		
	Issue of 1894, Line under "Ten Cents"						
E4	10¢ Messenger Running	775.00	17.50	*16,500.00*	(6)		
	Issue of 1895, Wmkd. (191)						
E5	10¢ blue (E4)	150.00	2.50	*5,500.00*	(6)		
	Issue of 1902						
E6	10¢ Messenger on Bicycle	100.00	2.50	*3,250.00*	(6)		
	Issue of 1908						
E7	10¢ Mercury Helmet and						
	Olive Branch	65.00	27.50	*1,200.00*	(6)		
	Issue of 1911, Wmdk. (190)						
E8	10¢ ultramarine (E6)	100.00	4.00	*3,000.00*	(6)		
	Issue of 1914, Perf. 10						
E9	10¢ ultramarine (E6)	200.00	5.25	*5,750.00*	(6)		
	Unwmkd., Issue of 1916						
E10	10¢ ultramarine (E6)	350.00	21.00	*7,500.00*	(6)		
	Issue of 1917, Perf. 11						
E11	10¢ ultramarine (E6)	17.00	.30	300.00	(6)		
	Issue of 1922						
E12	10¢ Postman and Motorcycle	27.50	.15	525.00	(6)	550.00	
	Issue of 1925						
E13	15¢ Postman and Motorcycle	21.00	.65	325.00	(6)	275.00	
E14	20¢ Post Office Truck	3.50	1.75	50.00	(6)	150.00	
	Issue of 1927, Perf. 11x10½						
E15	10¢ Postman and Motorcycle	.70	.05	6.50	(4)	100.00	
	Issue of 1931						
E16	15¢ orange (E12)	.80	.08	6.50	(4)	135.00	
	Issue of 1944						
E17	13¢ Postman and Motorcycle	.65	.06	5.00	(4)	12.00	
E18	17¢ Postman and Motorcycle	5.00	2.25	30.00	(4)	12.00	
	Issue of 1951						
E19	20¢ black (E14)	2.00	.12	12.00	(4)	5.00	
	Issue of 1954-57						
E20	20¢ Delivery of Letter	.60	.08	4.50	(4)	3.00	
E21	30¢ Delivery of Letter	.90	.05	5.25	(4)	2.25	
	Issue of 1969-71, Perf. 11						
E22	45¢ Arrows	2.25	.20	14.50	(4)	3.50	
E23	60¢ Arrows	1.20	.12	6.00	(4)	3.50	

E1

E3

E4

E6

E7

E12

E13

E14

E15

E17

E18

E20

E21

E22

E23

259

1879-1959

F1

FA1

JQ1

JQ2

J2

J19

J25

J33

J69

J78

J88

J98

J101

		Un	U	PB/LP	#	FDC		Q

Registration Stamp

Issued for the prepayment of registry; not usable for postage. Sale discontinued May 28, 1913.

Issue of 1911, Perf. 12, Wmkd. USPS (190)

		Un	U	PB/LP	#	FDC	Q
F1	10¢ Bald Eagle	85.00	4.50	*2,100.00*	(6)	*9,000.00*	

Certified Mail Stamp

For use on first-class mail for which no indemnity value is claimed, but for which proof of mailing and proof of delivery are available at less cost than registered mail.

Issue of 1955, Perf. 10½x11

		Un	U	PB/LP	#	FDC	Q
FA1	15¢ Letter Carrier	.50	.30	6.25	(4)	3.25	54,460,300

		Un	U

Postage Due Stamps

For affixing by a postal clerk to any mail to denote amount to be collected from addressee because of insufficient prepayment of postage.

Printed by American Bank Note Company Issue of 1879, Design of J2, Perf. 12, Unwmd.

		Un	U
J1	1¢ brown	22.50	5.00
J2	2¢ Figure of Value	150.00	4.00
J3	3¢ brown	17.50	2.50
J4	5¢ brown	225.00	20.00
J5	10¢ brown	300.00	8.00
J6	30¢ brown	125.00	20.00
J7	50¢ brown	190.00	30.00

Special Printing

		Un	U
J8	1¢ deep brown	*5,000.00*	—
J9	2¢ deep brown	*3,250.00*	—
J10	3¢ deep brown	*3,000.00*	—
J11	5¢ deep brown	*2,500.00*	—
J12	10¢ deep brown	*1,450.00*	—
J13	30¢ deep brown	*1,450.00*	—
J14	50¢ deep brown	*1,450.00*	

Regular Issue of 1884-89, Design of J19

		Un	U
J15	1¢ red brown	25.00	2.50
J16	2¢ red brown	32.50	2.50
J17	3¢ red brown	400.00	75.00
J18	5¢ red brown	185.00	7.25
J19	10¢ Figure of Value	140.00	3.50
J20	30¢ red brown	80.00	20.00
J21	50¢ red brown	900.00	110.00

Issue of 1891-93, Design of J25

		Un	U
J22	1¢ bright claret	7.50	.50
J23	2¢ bright claret	10.00	.45
J24	3¢ bright claret	22.50	2.75
J25	5¢ Figure of Value	25.00	2.75
J26	10¢ bright claret	50.00	6.50
J27	30¢ bright claret	200.00	70.00
J28	50¢ bright claret	225.00	75.00

Printed by the Bureau of Engraving and Printing, Issue of 1894, Design of J33, Perf. 12

		Un	U
J29	1¢ vermillion	400.00	65.00
J30	2¢ vermillion	175.00	27.50

Parcel Post Postage Due Stamps

For affixing by a postal clerk to any parcel post package to denote the amount to be collected from the addressee because of insufficient prepayment of postage.

Beginning July 1, 1913, these stamps were valid for use as regular postage due stamps.

Issue of 1912, Design of JQ1 and JQ5, Perf. 12

		Un	U
JQ1	1¢ Figure of Value	10.00	3.00
JQ2	2¢ dark green	85.00	15.00
JQ3	5¢ dark green	12.50	3.50
JQ4	10¢ dark green	165.00	35.00
JQ5	25¢ Figure of Value	80.00	3.50

1895-1959

		Un	U	PB/LP	#	FDC	Q
J31	1¢ deep claret	15.00	3.00	375.00	(6)		
J32	2¢ deep claret	12.50	1.75	325.00	(6)		
J33	3¢ Figure of Value	50.00	15.00	850.00	(6)		
J34	5¢ deep claret	55.00	20.00	950.00	(6)		
J35	10¢ deep rose	50.00	10.00	850.00	(6)		
J36	30¢ deep claret	175.00	40.00				
J37	50¢	400.00	85.00				
	Issue of 1895, Design of J33, Wmkd. (191)						
J38	1¢ deep claret	4.00	.30	190.00	(6)		
J39	2¢ deep claret	4.00	.20	190.00	(6)		
J40	3¢ deep claret	25.00	1.00	425.00	(6)		
J41	5¢ deep claret	25.00	1.00	450.00	(6)		
J42	10¢ deep claret	27.50	2.00	550.00	(6)		
J43	30¢ deep claret	225.00	15.00	3,750.00	(6)		
J44	50¢ deep claret	150.00	16.50	2,250.00	(6)		
	Issue of 1910-12, Design of J33, Wmkd. (190)						
J45	1¢ deep claret	17.50	2.00	400.00	(6)		
J46	2¢ deep claret	17.50	.15	350.00	(6)		
J47	3¢ deep claret	300.00	10.00	3,850.00	(6)		
J48	5¢ deep claret	40.00	2.50	600.00	(6)		
J49	10¢ deep claret	45.00	6.00	1,150.00	(6)		
J50	50¢ deep claret	550.00	55.00	6,500.00	(6)		
	Issue of 1914-15, Design of J33, Perf. 10						
J52	1¢ carmine lake	35.00	6.00	550.00	(6)		
J53	2¢ carmine lake	20.00	.20	350.00	(6)		
J54	3¢ carmine lake	325.00	8.50	4,500.00	(6)		
J55	5¢ carmine lake	17.50	1.50	285.00	(6)		
J56	10¢ carmine lake	27.50	.85	675.00	(6)		
J57	30¢ carmine lake	125.00	12.00	2,350.00	(6)		
J58	50¢ carmine lake	4,500.00	300.00	30,000.00	(6)		
	Issue of 1916, Design of J33, Unwmkd.						
J59	1¢ rose	800.00	130.00	7,250.00	(6)		
J60	2¢ rose	60.00	3.00	800.00	(6)		
	Issue of 1917, Design of J33, Perf. 11						
J61	1¢ carmine rose	1.50	.08	40.00	(6)		
J62	2¢ carmine rose	1.25	.05	35.00	(6)		
J63	3¢ carmine rose	6.50	.08	100.00	(6)		
J64	5¢ carmine	6.50	.08	95.00	(6)		
J65	10¢ carmine rose	9.00	.20	125.00	(6)		
J66	30¢ carmine rose	45.00	.40	575.00	(6)		
J67	50¢ carmine rose	60.00	.12	750.00	(6)		

	Issue of 1925, Design of J33	Un	U	PB/LP	#	FDC	Q
J68	½¢ dull red	.50	.06	11.00	(6)		
	Issue of 1930-31, Design of J69						
J69	½¢ Figure of Value	3.50	.70	35.00	(6)		
J70	1¢ carmine	2.50	.15	27.50	(6)		
J71	2¢ carmine	3.50	.15	40.00	(6)		
J72	3¢ carmine	20.00	1.00	240.00	(6)		
J73	5¢ carmine	20.00	1.50	225.00	(6)		
J74	10¢ carmine	35.00	.50	400.00	(6)		
J75	30¢ carmine	120.00	1.00	1,000.00	(6)		
J76	50¢ carmine	135.00	.30	1,150.00	(6)		
	Design of J78						
J77	$1 carmine	30.00	.06	275.00	(6)		
J78	$5 "FIVE" on $	45.00	.12	375.00	(6)		
	Issue of 1931-56, Design of J69, Perf 11x10½						
J79	½¢ dull carmine	1.25	.08	22.50	(4)		
J80	1¢ dull carmine	.15	.05	2.00	(4)		
J81	2¢ dull carmine	.15	.05	2.00	(4)		
J82	3¢ dull carmine	.25	.05	3.00	(4)		
J83	5¢ dull carmine	.35	.05	4.00	(4)		
J84	10¢ dull carmine	1.10	.05	8.50	(4)		
J85	30¢ dull carmine	8.50	.08	45.00	(4)		
J86	50¢ dull carmine	9.50	.06	57.50	(4)		
	Perf. 10½x11						
J87	$1 scarlet, same design as J78	45.00	.20	325.00	(4)		
	Issue of 1959, Perf. 11x10½, Design of J88 and J98						
J88	½¢ Figure of Value	1.25	.85	125.00	(4)		
J89	1¢ carmine rose	.05	.05	.50	(4)		
J90	2¢ carmine rose	.06	.05	.60	(4)		
J91	3¢ carmine rose	.07	.05	.70	(4)		
J92	4¢ carmine rose	.08	.05	1.25	(4)		
J93	5¢ carmine rose	.10	.05	.75	(4)		
J94	6¢ carmine rose	.12	.05	1.40	(4)		
J95	7¢ carmine rose	.14	.06	1.60	(4)		
J96	8¢ carmine rose	.16	.05	1.75	(4)		
J97	10¢ carmine rose	.20	.05	1.25	(4)		
J98	30¢ Figure of Value	.70	.05	5.50	(4)		
J99	50¢ carmine rose	1.10	.05	6.50	(4)		
	Design of J101						
J100	$1 carmine rose	2.00	.05	10.00	(4)		
J101	$5 Outline Figure of Value	8.00	.15	40.00	(4)		
	Design of J88						
J102	11¢ carmine rose	.22	.05	1.10	(4)		
J103	13¢ carmine rose	.26	.05	1.30	(4)		

1873-1911

O7    O14   O18    O34    O44

O52   O57   O76   O91   

O71

 O93   O95   O101    O114   O121

O127   O128   O129   O130

   O132   O133   O135   

264

Official Stamps

The franking privilege having been abolished as of July 1, 1873, these stamps were provided for each of the departments of Government for the prepayment on official matter.

These stamps were supplanted on May 1, 1879 by penalty envelopes and on July 5, 1884 were declared obsolete.

Designs are as follows: Post Office officials, figures of value and department name; all other departments, various portraits and department names.

Issues of 1873
Printed by the Continental Bank Note Co. Thin Hard Paper
Department of Agriculture: Yellow

		Un	U
O1	1¢ Franklin	55.00	30.00
O2	2¢ Jackson	37.50	13.50
O3	3¢ Washington	30.00	3.50
O4	6¢ Lincoln	40.00	12.50
O5	10¢ Jefferson	95.00	47.50
O6	12¢ Clay	130.00	70.00
O7	15¢ Webster	130.00	70.00
O8	24¢ Winfield Scott	90.00	47.50
O9	30¢ Hamilton	150.00	85.00

Executive Dept.

		Un	U
O10	1¢ carmine, Franklin	225.00	85.00
O11	2¢ Jackson	150.00	70.00
O12	3¢ carmine, Washington	175.00	60.00
O13	6¢ carmine, Lincoln	275.00	140.00
O14	10¢ Jefferson	235.00	140.00

Dept. of the Interior: Vermilion

		Un	U
O15	1¢ Franklin	15.00	2.25
O16	2¢ Jackson	12.00	1.50
O17	3¢ Washington	20.00	1.50
O18	6¢ Lincoln	15.00	1.50
O19	10¢ Jefferson	12.50	3.50
O20	12¢ Clay	18.50	2.50
O21	15¢ Webster	37.50	7.25
O22	24¢ W. Scott	27.50	5.50
O23	30¢ Hamilton	37.50	5.75
O24	90¢ Perry	85.00	12.50

Dept. of Justice: Purple

		Un	U
O25	1¢ Franklin	32.50	17.50
O26	2¢ Jackson	57.50	20.00
O27	3¢ Washington	60.00	7.00
O28	6¢ Lincoln	52.50	10.00
O29	10¢ Jefferson	60.00	25.00

		Un	U
O30	12¢ Clay	35.00	12.00
O31	15¢ Webster	95.00	47.50
O32	24¢ W. Scott	275.00	120.00
O33	30¢ Hamilton	250.00	85.00
O34	90¢ Perry	375.00	175.00

Navy Dept: Ultramarine

		Un	U
O35	1¢ Franklin	30.00	10.00
O36	2¢ Jackson	20.00	8.00
O37	3¢ Washington	24.00	3.00
O38	6¢ Lincoln	20.00	4.50
O39	7¢ Stanton	150.00	60.00
O40	10¢ Jefferson	26.00	10.00
O41	12¢ Clay	37.50	8.25
O42	15¢ Webster	65.00	22.50
O43	24¢ W. Scott	65.00	30.00
O44	30¢ Hamilton	55.00	12.50
O45	90¢ Perry	275.00	80.00

Post Office Dept: Black

		Un	U
O47	1¢ Figure of Value	7.25	3.00
O48	2¢ Figure of Value	7.00	2.50
O49	3¢ Figure of Value	2.50	.75
O50	6¢ Figure of Value	7.00	1.65
O51	10¢ Figure of Value	32.50	16.50
O52	12¢ Figure of Value	17.50	3.75
O53	15¢ Figure of Value	20.00	6.50
O54	24¢ Figure of Value	25.00	8.25
O55	30¢ Figure of Value	25.00	7.00
O56	90¢ Figure of Value	40.00	11.00

Dept. of State

		Un	U
O57	1¢ dark green Franklin	35.00	10.00
O58	2¢ dark green Jackson	80.00	25.00
O59	3¢ bright green Washington	30.00	7.50
O60	6¢ bright green Lincoln	25.00	7.50
O61	7¢ dark green Stanton	55.00	15.00
O62	10¢ dark green Jefferson	35.00	12.50
O63	12¢ dark green Clay	70.00	27.50
O64	15¢ dark green Webster	55.00	15.00
O65	24¢ dark green W. Scott	150.00	75.00
O66	30¢ Hamilton	135.00	60.00

	Un	U
1873 continued		
O67 90¢ dark green Perry	300.00	120.00
O68 $2 green and black		
Seward	500.00	225.00
O69 $5 green and black		
Seward	4,000.00	2,000.00
O70 $10 green and black		
Seward	2,500.00	1,300.00
O71 $20 Seward	2,150.00	1,100.00
Treasury Dept.: Brown		
O72 1¢ Franklin	12.00	1.75
O73 2¢ Jackson	18.00	1.75
O74 3¢ Washington	10.00	1.00
O75 6¢ Lincoln	17.50	1.00
O76 7¢ Stanton	35.00	11.00
O77 10¢ Jefferson	35.00	3.50
O78 12¢ Clay	35.00	1.50
O79 15¢ Webster	35.00	3.25
O80 24¢ W. Scott	165.00	55.00
O81 30¢ Hamilton	50.00	3.25
O82 90¢ Perry	55.00	3.00
War Dept.: Rose		
O83 1¢ Franklin	50.00	3.25
O84 2¢ Jackson	45.00	5.00
O85 3¢ Washington	42.50	1.00
O86 6¢ Lincoln	200.00	4.00
O87 7¢ Stanton	45.00	25.00
O88 10¢ Jefferson	14.00	3.00
O89 12¢ Clay	40.00	2.00
O90 15¢ Webster	12.00	1.20
O91 24¢ W. Scott	12.50	1.75
O92 30¢ Hamilton	13.00	1.50
O93 90¢ Perry	35.00	10.00

Issues of 1879
Printed by the American Bank Note Co. Soft, Porous Paper, Dept. of Agriculture: Yellow

	Un	U
O94 1¢ Franklin, issued		
without gum	*1,350.00*	—
O95 3¢ Washington	160.00	25.00
Dept. of the Interior: Vermilion		
O96 1¢ Franklin	110.00	60.00
O97 2¢ Jackson	2.50	.75
O98 3¢ Washington	2.00	.60

	Un	U
O99 6¢ Lincoln	3.00	1.00
O100 10¢ Jefferson	27.50	17.50
O101 12¢ Clay	50.00	30.00
O102 15¢ Webster	115.00	60.00
O103 24¢ W. Scott	1,000.00	—
Dept. of Justice: Bluish Purple		
O106 3¢ Washington	40.00	17.50
O107 6¢ Lincoln	100.00	60.00
Post Office Dept.: Black		
O108 3¢ Figure of Value	6.50	1.40
Treasury Dept.: Brown		
O109 3¢ Washington	21.00	2.50
O110 6¢ Lincoln	42.50	17.50
O111 10¢ Jefferson	60.00	15.00
O112 30¢ Hamilton	675.00	135.00
O113 90¢ Perry	700.00	135.00
War Dept.: Rose Red		
O114 1¢ Franklin	1.75	.75
O115 2¢ Jackson	2.75	1.00
O116 3¢ Washington	2.75	.65
O117 6¢ Lincoln	2.50	.70
O118 10¢ Jefferson	13.50	6.00
O119 12¢ Clay	10.00	1.75
O120 30¢ Hamilton	35.00	25.00

Official Postal Savings Mail, Perf. 12
These stamps were used to prepay postage on official correspondence of the Postal Savings Division of the Post Office Department. Discontinued Sept. 23, 1914

	Un	U
Issues of 1911, Wmkd. (191)		
O121 2¢ Official Postal Savings	9.00	1.10
O122 50¢ Official Postal Savings	100.00	32.50
O123 $1 Official Postal Savings	95.00	9.50
Wmkd. (190)		
O124 1¢ Official Postal Savings	4.00	1.00
O125 2¢ Official Postal Savings	30.00	3.50
O126 10¢ Official Postal Savings	8.50	1.00
Issues of 1983		
O127 1¢ Official Mail U.S.A.	.05	—
O128 4¢ Official Mail U.S.A.	.08	—
O129 13¢ Official Mail U.S.A.	.26	—
O130 17¢ Official Mail U.S.A.	.34	—
O132 1.00 Official Mail U.S.A.	2.00	—
O133 5.00 Official Mail U.S.A.	10.00	—
O135 20¢ Official Mail U.S.A.	.40	—

1861-1863

1

2

3

5

6

5

8

9

11

13

14

	Un	U
General Issues, All Imperf.		
Issue of 1861: Lithographed, Unwatermarked		
1 5¢ Jefferson Davis	195.00	110.00
2 10¢ Thomas Jefferson	250.00	200.00
Issue of 1862		
3 2¢ Andrew Jackson	600.00	725.00
4 5¢ blue J. Davis (6)	125.00	105.00
5 10¢ Thomas Jefferson	900.00	625.00
Typographed		
6 5¢ J. Davis		
(London print)	12.00	20.00
7 5¢ blue (6) (local print)	16.00	17.00
Issues of 1863, Engraved		
8 2¢ Andrew Jackson	67.50	285.00

Thick or Thin Paper		
9 10¢ Jefferson Davis	800.00	650.00
10 10¢ blue (9), (with		
rectangular frame)	3,500.00	1,750.00
Prices of No. 10 are for copies showing parts of lines on at least two sides of frame.		
11 10¢ Jefferson Davis,		
die A	13.00	15.00
12 10¢ blue J. Davis,		
die B (11)	14.00	16.00
Dies A and B differ in that B has an extra line outside its corner ornaments.		
13 20¢ George Washington	47.50	*275.00*
Issue of 1862, Typographed		
14 1¢ John C. Calhoun		
(This stamp was never		
put in use.)	135.00	—

		Un	U

Newspaper Stamps
Perf. 12, Issues of 1865
Printed by the National Bank Note Co.,
Thin, Hard Paper, No Gum, Unwmkd.,
Colored Borders

		Un	U
PR1	5¢ Washington	135.00	—
PR2	10¢ Franklin	75.00	—
PR3	25¢ Lincoln	75.00	—

White Border, Yellowish Paper

PR4	5¢ light blue (PR1)	30.00	25.00

Reprints of 1875
Printed by the Continental Bank Note Co.,
Hard, White Paper, No Gum

PR5	5¢ dull blue (PR1),		
	white border	55.00	—
PR6	10¢ dark bluish green,		
	(PR2), colored border	32.50	—
PR7	25¢ dark carmine		
	(PR3), colored border	65.00	—

Issue of 1880
Printed by the American Bank Note Co.,
Soft, Porous Paper, White Border

PR8	5¢ dark blue (PR1)	110.00	—

Issue of 1875
Printed by the Continental Bank Note Co.,
Thin, Hard Paper

PR9-PR15; "Statue of Freedom" (PR15)

PR9	2¢ black	8.00	8.00
PR10	3¢ black	11.00	11.00
PR11	4¢ black	9.00	9.00
PR12	6¢ black	12.50	12.50
PR13	8¢ black	17.50	17.50
PR14	9¢ black	40.00	40.00
PR15	10¢ Statue of Freedom	17.50	15.00

PR16-PR23: "Justice" (PR18)

PR16	12¢ rose	40.00	30.00
PR17	24¢ rose	50.00	35.00
PR22	84¢ rose	150.00	95.00
PR23	96¢ rose	110.00	85.00
PR24	$1.92 Ceres	130.00	90.00
PR25	$3 "Victory"	175.00	110.00
PR26	$6 Clio	325.00	150.00
PR27	$9 Minerva	425.00	185.00
PR28	$12 Vesta	500.00	250.00
PR29	$24 "Peace"	500.00	275.00
PR30	$36 "Commerce"	550.00	325.00
PR31	$48 red brown Hebe		
	(PR78)	700.00	425.00

		Un	U
PR32	$60 violet Indian		
	Maiden (PR79)	700.00	375.00

Special Printing, Hard, White Paper,
Without Gum

PR33-PR39: Statue of Freedom (PR15)

PR33	2¢ gray black	60.00	—
PR34	3¢ gray black	65.00	—
PR35	4¢ gray black	80.00	—
PR36	6¢ gray black	110.00	—
PR37	8¢ gray black	130.00	—
PR38	9¢ gray black	150.00	—
PR39	10¢ gray black	185.00	—

PR40-PR47: "Justice" (PR18)

PR40	12¢ pale rose	210.00	—
PR41	24¢ pale rose	275.00	—
PR42	36¢ pale rose	375.00	—
PR43	48¢ pale rose	425.00	—
PR44	60¢ pale rose	500.00	—
PR45	72¢ pale rose	650.00	—
PR46	84¢ pale rose	675.00	—
PR47	96¢ pale rose	800.00	—
PR48	$1.92 dark brown		
	Ceres (PR24)	2,400.00	—
PR49	$3 vermilion "Victory"		
	(PR25)	5,000.00	—
PR50	$6 ultra. Clio (PR26)	6,000.00	—
PR51	$9 yel. Minerva		
	(PR27)	11,000.00	—
PR52	$12 bl. grn. Vesta		
	(PR28)	10,000.00	—
PR53	$24 dark gray violet		
	"Peace" (PR29)	—	—
PR54	$36 brown rose		
	"Commerce" (PR30)	—	—
PR55	$48 red brown Hebe		
	(PR78)	—	—
PR56	$60 violet Indian		
	Maiden (PR79)	—	—

All values of this issue Nos. PR33 to
PR56 exist imperforate but were not
regularly issued.

1879-1895

		Un	U
Issue of 1879, Printed by the American Bank Note Co., Soft, Porous Paper			
PR57-PR62: Statue of Freedom (PR15)			
PR57	2¢ black	4.00	3.50
PR58	3¢ black	5.00	4.50
PR59	4¢ black	5.00	4.50
PR60	6¢ black	10.50	9.00
PR61	8¢ black	10.50	9.00
PR62	10¢ black	10.50	9.00
PR63-PR70: "Justice" (PR18)			
PR63	12¢ red	30.00	20.00
PR64	24¢ red	30.00	18.50
PR65	36¢ red	110.00	85.00
PR66	48¢ red	80.00	50.00
PR67	60¢ red	60.00	50.00
PR68	72¢ red	145.00	90.00
PR69	84¢ red	110.00	75.00
PR70	96¢ red	80.00	55.00
PR71	$1.92 pale brown Ceres (PR24)	65.00	50.00
PR72	$3 red vermilion "Victory" (PR25)	65.00	50.00
PR73	$6 blue Clio (PR26)	110.00	75.00
PR74	$9 org. Minerva (PR27)	70.00	50.00
PR75	$12 yellow green Vesta (PR28)	110.00	75.00
PR76	$24 dark violet "Peace" (PR29)	145.00	100.00
PR77	$36 Indian red "Commerce" (PR30)	185.00	120.00
PR78	$48 Hebe	250.00	150.00
PR79	$60 Indian Maiden	275.00	150.00

All values of the 1879 issue except Nos. PR63 to PR66 and PR68 to PR70 exist imperforate but were not regularly issued.

Issue of 1883 Special Printing			
PR80	2¢ intense black Statue of Freedom (PR15)	130.00	—
Regular Issue of 1885			
PR81	1¢ black Statue of Freedom (PR15)	5.50	3.50

		Un	U
PR82-PR89: "Justice" (PR18)			
PR82	12¢ carmine	17.50	8.50
PR83	24¢ carmine	20.00	12.50
PR84	36¢ carmine	30.00	15.00
PR85	48¢ carmine	40.00	25.00
PR86	60¢ carmine	60.00	35.00
PR87	72¢ carmine	70.00	40.00
PR88	84¢ carmine	140.00	85.00
PR89	96¢ carmine	100.00	70.00

All values of the 1885 issue exist imperforate but were not regularly issued.

Issue of 1894 Printed by the Bureau of Engraving and Printing, Soft Wove Paper			
PR90-PR94: Statue of Freedom (PR90)			
PR90	1¢ Statue of Freedom	25.00	—
PR91	2¢ intense black	25.00	—
PR92	4¢ intense black	35.00	—
PR93	6¢ intense black	750.00	—
PR94	10¢ intense black	65.00	—
PR95-PR99: "Justice" (PR18)			
PR95	12¢ pink	300.00	—
PR96	24¢ pink	275.00	—
PR97	36¢ pink	1,750.00	—
PR98	60¢ pink	1,750.00	—
PR99	96¢ pink	2,750.00	—
PR100	$3 sclt. "Victory" (PR25)	4,000.00	—
PR101	$6 pl. blue Clio (PR26)	4,750.00	3,000.00
Issue of 1895, Unwmkd. PR102-PR105: Statue of Freedom (PR116)			
PR102	1¢ black	17.50	5.00
PR103	2¢ black	18.50	5.00
PR104	5¢ black	25.00	8.50
PR105	10¢ black	55.00	25.00
PR106	25¢ cme "Justice" (PR118)	75.00	25.00
PR107	50¢ cme. "Justice" (PR119)	175.00	75.00
PR108	$2 sclt. "Victory" (PR120)	200.00	45.00
PR109	$5 ultra Clio (PR121)	325.00	135.00

PR15   PR18   PR24   PR25   PR26

PR27   PR28   PR29   PR30   PR78

PR79   PR90   PR116   PR118   PR119

PR120   PR121   PR122   PR123   PR124

Q1

Q2

Q3

Q4

Q5

Q6

Q7

Q8

Q9

Q10

Q11

Q12

QE1

QE2

QE3

QE4

		Un	U
PR110	$10 green Vesta		
	(PR122)	300.00	150.00
PR111	$20 slate "Peace"		
	(PR123)	575.00	275.00
PR112	$50 dull rose		
	"Commerce" (PR124)	600.00	275.00
PR113	$100 purple Indian		
	Maiden (PR125)	675.00	325.00

Issue of 1895-97
Wmkd. (191), Yellowish Gum

PR114-PR117: Statue of Freedom (PR116)

		Un	U
PR114	1¢ black	2.50	2.00
PR115	2¢ black	2.50	1.50
PR116	5¢ black	4.00	3.00
PR117	10¢ black	2.50	2.00
PR118	25¢ "Justice"	4.00	3.75
PR119	50¢ "Justice"	5.00	3.50
PR120	$2 "Victory"	7.50	8.50
PR121	$5 Clio	17.50	20.00
PR122	$10 Vesta	15.00	25.00
PR123	$20 "Peace"	16.00	27.50
PR124	$50 "Commerce"	17.50	27.50
PR125	$100 Indian Maiden	20.00	35.00

In 1899, the Government sold 26,989 sets of these stamps, but, as the stock of the high values was not sufficient to make up the required number, the $5, $10, $20, $50 and $100 were reprinted. These are virtually indistinguishable from earlier printings.

Parcel Post Stamps

Issued for the prepayment of postage on parcel post packages only.

Beginning July 1, 1913, these stamps were valid for all postal purposes.

Issue of 1912-13, Perf. 12

		Un	U
Q1	1¢ Post Office Clerk	4.00	.90
Q2	2¢ City Carrier	4.50	.70
Q3	3¢ Railway Postal Clerk	11.00	5.00
Q4	4¢ Rural Carrier	30.00	2.15
Q5	5¢ Mail Train	30.00	1.25
Q6	10¢ Steamship and		
	Mail Tender	45.00	1.75
Q7	15¢ Automobile		
	Service	75.00	9.00
Q8	20¢ Airplane Carrying		
	Mail	150.00	17.50
Q9	25¢ Manufacturing	85.00	4.50
Q10	50¢ Dairying	250.00	35.00
Q11	75¢ Harvesting	80.00	25.00
Q12	$1 Fruit Growing	450.00	20.00

Special Handling Stamps

For use on parcel post packages to secure the same expeditious handling accorded to first class mail matter.

Issue of 1925-29, Design of QE3, Perf. 11

		Un	U
QE1	10¢ Special Handling	1.60	.90
QE2	15¢ Special Handling	1.75	.90
QE3	20¢ Special Handling	2.25	1.75
QE4	25¢ Special Handling	22.50	7.50

With First Day Cancellations

The Postal Service offers Souvenir Pages for new stamps. The series began with a page for the Yellowstone Park Centennial stamp issued March 1, 1972. The pages feature one or more stamps tied by the first day cancel, technical data and information on the subject of the issue. More than just collectors' items, Souvenir Pages make wonderful show and conversation pieces. Souvenir Pages are issued in limited editions. For information on becoming a subscriber, see the postal card following page 288.

1972

1	Yellowstone Park,	$100.00
1a	Family Planning (sold only with FD cancellation by USPS at INTERPEX '72 show in NYC),	$300.00
2	Cape Hatteras,	$100.00
3	Fiorello La Guardia,	$100.00
4	City of Refuge,	$100.00
5	Wolf Trap Farm,	$25.00
5a	Wolf Trap Farm with star,	$50.00
6	Colonial Craftsman, (4),	$25.00
7	Mount McKinley,	$35.00
8	Olympic Games, (4),	$20.00
9	Parent Teachers Association,	$10.00
10	Wildlife Conservation, (4),	$12.00
11	Mail Order,	$10.00
12	Osteopathic Medicine,	$10.00
13	Tom Sawyer,	$10.00
14	Benjamin Franklin,	$9.00
15	Christmas, (2),	$15.00
16	Pharmacy,	$8.00
17	Stamp Collecting,	$9.00

1973

18	Eugene O'Neill Coil,	$15.00
19	Love,	$10.00
20	Pamphleteer,	$8.00
21	George Gershwin,	$8.00
22	Posting Broadside,	$7.00
23	Copernicus,	$6.00
24	Postal Service Employees, (10),	$10.00
25	Harry S. Truman,	$5.00
26	Postrider,	$8.00
27	Giannini,	$6.00
28	Boston Tea Party, (4),	$10.00
29	Progress in Electronics, (4),	$9.00
30	Robinson Jeffers,	$4.00
31	Lyndon B. Johnson,	$4.00
32	Henry O. Tanner,	$4.00
33	Willa Cather,	$4.00
34	Colonial Drummer,	$7.00
35	Angus Cattle,	$4.00
36	Christmas, (2),	$8.00

37	13¢ Airmail sheet stamp,	$3.50
38	10¢ Crossed Flags,	$3.50
39	Jefferson Memorial,	$3.50
40	13¢ Airmail Coil,	$3.50

1974

41	Mount Rushmore,	$4.00
42	ZIP Code,	$3.50
42a	ZIP Code with error date,	$400.00
43	Statue of Liberty,	$4.00
44	Elizabeth Blackwell,	$3.50
45	Veterans of Foreign Wars,	$3.50
46	Robert Frost,	$3.50
47	EXPO '74,	$3.50
48	Horse Racing,	$3.50
49	Skylab,	$6.00
50	Universal Postal Union, (8),	$8.00
51	Mineral Heritage, (4),	$6.00
52	Fort Harrod,	$3.50
53	Continental Congress, (4),	$6.00
54	Chautauqua,	$3.50
55	Kansas Wheat,	$3.50
56	Energy Conservation,	$3.50
57	6.3¢ Bulk Rate, (2),	$4.00
58	Sleepy Hollow,	$3.50
59	Retarded Children,	$3.50
60	Christmas, (3),	$7.00

1975

61	Benjamin West,	$3.00
62	Pioneer,	$6.00
63	Collective Bargaining,	$4.00
64	Sybil Ludington,	$3.50
65	Salem Poor,	$3.50
66	Haym Salomon,	$3.50
67	Peter Francisco,	$3.50
68	Mariner,	$6.00
69	Lexington & Concord,	$4.00
70	Paul Laurence Dunbar,	$3.00
71	D.W. Griffith,	$3.00
72	Bunker Hill,	$4.00
73	Military Uniforms, (4),	$7.00
74	Apollo Soyuz, (2),	$7.00
75	International Women's Year,	$3.50
76	Postal Bicentennial, (4),	$5.00
77	World Peace Through Law,	$3.00

78	Banking & Commerce, (2),	$3.50
79	Christmas, (2),	$5.00
80	Francis Parkman,	$2.50
81	Freedom of the Press,	$3.00
82	Old North Church,	$3.50
83	Flag & Independence Hall,	$3.00
84	Freedom to Assemble,	$3.00
85	Liberty Bell Coil,	$3.00
86	American Eagle & Shield,	$3.00

1976

87	Spirit of '76, (3),	$5.00
87a	Spirit of '76 with error cancellation,	$400.00
88	25¢ & 31¢ Airmails, (2),	$3.50
89	Interphil,	$3.00
90	Fifty State Flag Series,	$45.00
91	Freedom to Assemble Coil,	$3.00
92	Telephone Centennial,	$3.00
93	Commercial Aviation,	$3.00
94	Chemistry,	$3.00
95	7.9¢ Bulk Rate,	$3.00
96	Benjamin Franklin,	$3.00
97	Bicentennial SS,	$50.00
98	Declaration of Independence, (4),	$6.00
99	Olympics, (4),	$7.00
100	Clara Maass,	$2.50
101	Adolph S. Ochs,	$2.50
102	Christmas, (3),	$5.00
103	7.7¢ Bulk Rate,	$3.00

1977

104	Washington at Princeton,	$3.00
105	$1 Vending Machine Booklet Pane, perf. 10,	$27.50
106	Sound Recording,	$3.00
107	Pueblo Art, (4),	$4.00
108	Lindbergh Flight,	$3.50
109	Colorado Centennial,	$3.00
110	Butterflies, (4),	$4.00
111	Lafayette,	$3.00
112	Skilled Hands, (4),	$4.00
113	Peace Bridge,	$2.50
114	Herkimer at Oriskany,	$3.00
115	Alta, California,	$2.50
116	Articles of Confederation,	$2.50

117	Talking Pictures,	$3.00
118	Surrender at Saratoga,	$3.00
119	Energy, (2),	$3.00
120	Christmas Mailbox,	$3.00
121	Christmas, Valley Forge,	$3.00
122	Petition for Redress Coil, (2),	$3.00
123	Petition for Redress sheet stamp,	$3.00
124	1¢, 2¢, 3¢, 4¢ Americana,	$3.00

1978

125	Carl Sandburg,	$2.50
126	Indian Head Penny,	$3.00
127	Captain Cook, Anchorage,	$4.00
128	Captain Cook, Honolulu,	$4.00
129	Harriet Tubman,	$2.50
130	American Quilts, (4),	$3.50
131	16¢ Statue of Liberty,	$3.50
132	Sandy Hook Lighthouse,	$3.50
133	American Dance, (4),	$3.50
134	French Alliance,	$2.50
135	Dr. Papanicolaou,	$2.50
136	"A" Stamp, (2),	$3.00
137	Jimmie Rodgers,	$2.50
138	CAPEX '78, (SS),	$6.00
139	Oliver Wendell Holmes,	$2.50
140	Photography,	$2.50
141	Fort McHenry Flag, (2),	$3.50
142	George M. Cohan,	$2.50
143	Rose Booklet single,	$2.50
144	8.4¢ Bulk Rate,	$3.00
145	Viking Missions,	$4.00
146	Remote Outpost,	$4.00
147	American Owls, (4),	$3.50
148	Wright Brothers, (2),	$3.50
149	American Trees,	$3.50
150	Hobby Horse,	$3.00

151	Andrea della Robbia,	$3.00
152	$2 Kerosene Lamp,	$8.50

1979

153	Robert F. Kennedy,	$2.50
154	Martin Luther King, Jr.,	$2.50
155	International Year of the Child,	$2.50
156	John Steinbeck,	$2.50
157	Albert Einstein,	$3.00
158	Octave Chanute, (2),	$3.50
159	Pennsylvania Toleware, (4),	$3.50
160	American Architecture, (4),	$3.50
161	Endangered Flora, (4),	$3.50
162	Seeing Eye Dogs,	$2.50
163	$1 Americana,	$8.00
164	Special Olympics,	$3.00
165	$5 Americana,	$25.00
166	30¢ Americana,	$5.00
167	Olympics,	$3.00
168	50¢ Americana,	$5.00
169	John Paul Jones,	$3.00
170	15¢ Olympic, (4),	$5.50
171	Gerard David Madonna,	$3.00
172	Santa Claus,	$3.00
173	3.1¢ Coil,	$3.00
174	31¢ Olympic,	$6.00
175	Will Rogers,	$3.00
176	Vietnam Veterans,	$3.00
177	Wiley Post,	$4.00

1980

178	W. C. Fields,	$3.50
179	Winter Olympics, (4),	$5.50
180	Windmills Booklet,	$5.50
181	Benjamin Banneker,	$2.50
182	Letter Writing, (6),	$4.00
183	1¢ Quill Pen Coil,	$2.50
184	Frances Perkins,	$2.50
185	Dolley Madison,	$2.50
186	Emily Bissell,	$2.50

187	3.5¢ Non-Profit Bulk Rate Coil,	$4.00
188	Helen Keller/ Anne Sullivan,	$2.50
189	Veterans Administration,	$2.50
190	General Bernardo de Galvez,	$2.50
191	Coral Reefs, (4),	$3.00
192	Organized Labor,	$2.50
193	Edith Wharton,	$2.50
194	American Education,	$2.50
195	Northwest Indian Masks, (4),	$4.00
196	Architecture, (4),	$4.00
197	Phillip Mazzei,	$3.00
198	Stained Glass Window,	$3.00
199	Antique Toys,	$3.00
200	19¢ Sequoyah,	$2.00
201	28¢ Scott A/M,	$2.50
202	35¢ Curtiss A/M,	$2.50

1981

203	Everett Dirksen,	$2.00
204	Whitney M. Young,	$2.00
205	"B" Sheet & Coil,	$2.50
206	"B" Booklet Pane,	$2.50
207	12¢ Americana S & C,	$3.50
208	Flowers Block, (4),	$3.00
209	18¢ Flag Sheet & Coil,	$2.50
210	18¢ Flag Booklet Pane,	$3.00
211	American Red Cross,	$2.00
212	George Mason,	$2.00
213	Savings & Loan,	$2.00
214	Animals Booklet Pane,	$4.50
215	18¢ Surrey Coil,	$2.00
216	Space Achievement, (8),	$7.50
217	17¢ Rachel Carson,	$2.00
218	35¢ Dr. Charles Drew,	$2.50
219	Professional Management,	$2.00

Jim Thorpe
Commemorative Stamp

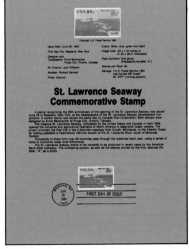

St. Lawrence Seaway
Commemorative Stamp

220	17¢ Electric Car Coil,	$2.50
221	Wildlife Habitat, (4),	$3.00
222	International Year Disabled,	$2.00
223	Edna St. Vincent Millay,	$2.00
224	Alcoholism,	$2.00
225	Architecture, (4),	$3.00
226	Zaharis,	$2.50
227	Bobby Jones,	$2.50
228	Frederic Remington,	$2.00
229	"C" Sheet/Coil,	$2.50
230	"C" Booklet,	$4.00
231	18¢/20¢ Hoban, (2),	$2.50
232	Yorktown, (2),	$2.50
233	Teddybear-Christmas,	$2.50
234	Art-Christmas '81,	$2.50
235	John Hanson,	$2.00
236	20¢ Pumper, Coil	$2.50
237	Desert Plant, (4),	$3.00
238	9.3¢ Wagon, (3),	$2.00
239	20¢ Reg + Coil,	$2.50
240	20¢ Booklet,	$3.00

1982

241	Sheep Booklet,	$4.00
242	20¢ Ralph Bunche,	$2.00
243	13¢ Crazy Horse,	$2.00
244	37¢ Millikan,	$2.50
245	Roosevelt, FD.,	$2.00
246	20¢ LOVE,	$2.50
247	5.9¢ Bicycle, (4),	$2.00
248	20¢ Washington,	$2.00
249	10.9¢ Cab Coil,	$2.00
250	Birds & Flowers,	$30.00
250a	Birds & Flowers with all 10½ x 11 Perfs,	$60.00
250b	Birds & Flowers with all 11 x 11 Perfs,	$60.00
251	Netherlands,	$2.00
252	Library of Congress,	$2.00
253	20¢ Consumer Coil,	$2.00
254	World's Fair, (4),	$3.00
255	Horatio Alger,	$2.00

256	2¢ Locomotive Coil,	$2.00
257	20¢ Aging,	$2.00
258	20¢ Barrymores,	$2.00
259	Mary Walker,	$2.00
260	Peace Garden,	$2.00
261	America's Libraries,	$2.00
262	Jackie Robinson,	$2.50
263	Stagecoach,	$2.00
264	Touro Synagogue,	$2.00
265	Wolf Trap,	$2.00
266	Architecture, (4),	$2.50
267	Francis of Assisi,	$2.00
268	Ponce de Leon,	$2.00
269	Snow Scenes, (4),	$3.00
270	Art-Christmas,	$2.00
271	Kitten & Puppy,	$2.00
272	Igor Stravinsky,	$2.00

1983

273	Officials (7 stamps-3 pgs),	$22.50
274	Science,	$2.00
275	Sleigh Coil,	$2.00
276	Sweden,	$2.00
277	Handcar Coil,	$2.00
278	Ballooning (4),	$3.50
279	Civilian Conservation Corps,	$2.00
280	40¢ Olympics (4),	$4.00
281	Priestley,	$2.00
282	Voluntarism,	$2.00
283	German Immigrants,	$2.00
284	Physical Fitness,	$2.00
285	Brooklyn Bridge,	$2.00
286	Tennessee Valley Authority,	$2.00
287	Carl Schurz,	$2.00
288	Medal of Honor,	$2.00
289	Scott Joplin,	$2.00
290	Thomas H. Gallaudet,	$2.00
291	28¢ Olympics (4),	$3.00
292	Pearl S. Buck,	$2.00
293	Babe Ruth,	$3.00
294	Nathaniel Hawthorne,	$2.00

295	Henry Clay,	$2.00
296	13¢ Olympics (4),	$3.00
297	$9.35 Eagle,	$20.00
297a	$9.35 Eagle Booklet Pane of 3,	$50.00
298	Omnibus,	$2.00
299	Treaty of Paris,	$2.00
300	Civil Service,	$2.00
301	Metropolitan Opera,	$2.00
302	Inventors (4),	$3.00
303	Dorothea Dix,	$2.00
304	Streetcars (4),	$3.00
305	Motorcycle Coil,	$2.00
306	Contemporary Christmas,	$2.00
307	Art Masterpiece Christmas,	$2.00
308	35¢ Olympic (4),	$3.50
309	Martin Luther,	$2.00
310	Flag Booklet Pane,	$4.00

1984*

311	Alaska,	$2.00
312	Winter Olympics, (4)	$3.00
313	FDIC,	$2.00
314	Truman,	$2.00
315	LOVE,	$2.00
316	Carter G. Woodson,	$2.00
317	Railroad Caboose Coil	$2.00
318	Soil & Water Conservation,	$2.00
319	Credit Union,	$2.00
320	Lillian Gilbreth,	$2.00
321	Orchids, (4)	$2.50
322	Hawaii,	$2.00
323	Baby Buggy Coil,	$2.00
324	National Archives,	$2.00
325	Summer Olympics, (4)	$3.00
326	New Orleans World's Fair,	$2.00
327	Health Research,	$2.00
328	Douglas Fairbanks,	$2.00
329	Jim Thorpe,	$2.00
330	Richard Russell,	$2.00
331	St. Lawrence Seaway,	$2.00
332	Duck Stamp 50th Anniversary,	$2.00
333	Roanoke Voyages,	$2.00
334	Dr. Frank Laubach,	$2.00
335	Herman Melville,	$2.00
336	Horace Moses,	$2.00
337	Smokey Bear,	$2.00
338	Roberto Clemente,	$2.00
339	Dogs, (4)	$2.50
340	Crime Prevention,	$2.00
341	John McCormack,	$2.00
342	Family Unity,	$2.00
343	Eleanor Roosevelt,	$2.00
344	Nation of Readers,	$2.00
345	Santa Claus,	$2.00
346	Madonna & Child,	$2.00
347	Vietnam Veterans Memorial,	$2.00

Orchids Commemorative Stamps

*Numbers for 1984 subject to change.

The Postal Service offers American Commemorative Panels for each new commemorative stamp and special Christmas stamp issued. The series first began September 20, 1972, with the issuance of the Wildlife Commemorative Panel and will total over 235 panels by the end of 1984. The panels feature stamps in mint condition complemented by reproductions of steel line engravings and stories behind the commemorated subject. For further information, please see page 289.

1972

1	Wildlife,	$16.00
2	Mail Order,	$16.00
3	Osteopathic Medicine,	$16.00
4	Tom Sawyer,	$16.00
5	Pharmacy,	$16.00
6	Christmas 1972,	$20.00
7	'Twas the Night Before Christmas,	$20.00
8	Stamp Collecting,	$16.00

1973

9	Love,	$16.00
10	Pamphleteers,	$20.00
11	George Gershwin,	$20.00
12	Posting Broadside,	$20.00
13	Copernicus,	$16.00
14	Postal People,	$20.00
15	Harry S. Truman,	$23.50
16	Post Rider,	$26.50
17	Boston Tea Party,	$52.50
18	Electronics,	$16.00
19	Robinson Jeffers,	$16.00

20	Lyndon B. Johnson,	$23.50
21	Henry O. Tanner,	$16.00
22	Willa Cather,	$16.00
23	Drummer,	$26.50
24	Angus Cattle,	$16.00
25	Christmas 1973,	$20.00
26	Christmas Needlepoint,	$20.00

1974

27	Veterans of Foreign Wars,	$16.00
28	Robert Frost,	$16.00
29	EXPO '74,	$20.00
30	Horse Racing,	$16.00
31	Skylab,	$20.00
32	Universal Postal Union,	$23.50
33	Mineral Heritage,	$16.00
34	Fort Harrod,	$16.00
35	Continental Congress,	$16.00
36	Chautauqua,	$16.00
37	Kansas Wheat,	$16.00

38	Energy Conservation,	$16.00
39	Sleepy Hollow,	$16.00
40	Retarded Children,	$16.00
41	Christmas "The Road-Winter",	$20.00
42	Christmas Angel Altarpiece,	$20.00

1975

43	Benjamin West,	$16.00
44	Pioneer,	$20.00
45	Collective Bargaining,	$16.00
46	Contributors to the Cause,	$20.00
47	Mariner,	$20.00
48	Lexington & Concord,	$20.00
49	Paul Laurence Dunbar,	$16.00
50	D. W. Griffith,	$16.00
51	Bunker Hill,	$20.00
52	Military Services,	$20.00
53	Apollo Soyuz,	$20.00

277

54	World Peace Through Law,	$16.00
55	International Women's Year,	$16.00
56	Postal Bicentennial,	$20.00
57	Banking and Commerce,	$16.00
58	Early Christmas Card,	$20.00
59	Christmas Madonna,	$20.00

1976

60	Spirit of '76,	$20.00
61	Interphil 76,	$20.00
62	State Flags,	$33.00
63	Telephone, Centennial,	$16.00
64	Commercial Aviation,	$16.00
65	Chemistry,	$16.00
66	Benjamin Franklin,	$22.00
67	Declaration of Independence,	$20.00
68	Olympics,	$20.00
69	Clara Maas,	$20.00
70	Adolph S. Ochs,	$16.00
71	Currier Winter Pastime,	$20.00
72	Copley Nativity,	$20.00

1977

73	Washington at Princeton,	$23.50
74	Sound Recording,	$29.00
75	Pueblo Art,	$135.00
76	Lindbergh Flight,	$135.00
77	Colorado Centennial,	$29.00
78	Butterflies,	$33.00
79	Lafayette,	$29.00
80	Skilled Hands,	$29.00
81	Peace Bridge,	$29.00
82	Herkimer at Oriskany,	$29.00

83	Alta, California,	$29.00
84	Articles of Confederation,	$29.00
85	Talking Pictures,	$29.00
86	Surrender at Saratoga,	$29.00
87	Energy Conservation & Development,	$29.00
88	Christmas, Washington at Valley Forge,	$33.00
89	Christmas, Rural Mailbox,	$33.00

1978

90	Carl Sandburg,	$20.00
91	Captain Cook,	$33.00
92	Harriet Tubman,	$20.00
93	American Quilts,	$29.00
94	American Dance,	$20.00
95	French Alliance,	$27.50
96	Dr. Papanicolaou,	$20.00
97	Jimmie Rodgers,	$20.00
98	Photography,	$20.00
99	George M. Cohan,	$20.00
100	Viking Missions,	$33.00
101	American Owls,	$29.00
102	American Trees,	$29.00
103	Madonna and Child,	$20.00
104	Christmas Hobby Horse,	$20.00

1979

105	Robert F. Kennedy,	$20.00
106	Martin Luther King, Jr.	$20.00
107	Year of the Child,	$20.00
108	John Steinbeck,	$20.00
109	Albert Einstein,	$27.50
110	Pennsylvania Toleware,	$20.00
111	American Architecture,	$20.00
112	Endangered Flora,	$20.00
113	Seeing Eye Dogs,	$20.00

114	Special Olympics,	$20.00
115	John Paul Jones,	$33.00
116	15¢ Olympic Games,	$26.50
117	Virgin and Child,	$20.00
118	Santa Claus,	$20.00
119	Will Rogers,	$19.00
120	Vietnam Veterans,	$23.50
121	10¢, 31¢ Olympic Games,	$26.50

1980

122	W.C. Fields,	$20.00
123	Winter Olympics,	$26.50
124	Benjamin Banneker,	$20.00
125	Frances Perkins,	$20.00
126	Emily Bissell,	$20.00
127	Helen Keller/ Anne Sullivan,	$20.00
128	Veterans Administration,	$20.00
129	General Bernardo de Galvez,	$20.00
130	Coral Reefs,	$20.00
131	Organized Labor,	$20.00
132	Edith Wharton,	$20.00
133	American Education,	$20.00
134	Northwest Indian Masks,	$25.00
135	American Architecture,	$20.00
136	Christmas Stained Glass Window,	$20.00
137	Christmas Antique Toys,	$20.00

1981

138	Everett Dirksen,	$16.00
139	Whitney Moore Young,	$16.00
140	American Flowers,	$16.00
141	American Red Cross,	$16.00
142	Savings & Loan,	$16.00
143	Space Achievement,	$20.00

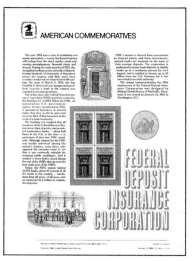

AMERICAN COMMEMORATIVES

AMERICAN COMMEMORATIVES

SOUVENIR CARDS

These cards were issued as souvenirs of the philatelic gatherings at which they were distributed by the United States Postal Service, its predecessor the United States Post Office Department, or the Bureau of Engraving and Printing. They were not valid for postage.

For information regarding current availability of souvenir cards, send postal card following page 288.

A forerunner of the souvenir cards is the 1938 Philatelic Truck souvenir sheet which the Post Office Department issued and distributed in various cities visited by the Philatelic Truck. It shows the White House, printed in blue on white paper. Issued with and without gum. Price with gum, $80, without gum, $10.

**United States Post Office
& United States Postal Service**

1960 Barcelona, 1st International Philatelic Congress, Mar. 26-Apr. 5. Enlarged vignette, Landing of Columbus from No. 231. Printed in black. 400.00

1968 EFIMEX, International Philatelic Exhibition, Nov. 1-9, Mexico City, Card of 1. No. 292, inscribed in Spanish. 6.00

1970 PHILYMPIA, London International Stamp Exhibition, Sept. 18-26. Card of 3. Nos. 548-550. 4.50

1971 EXFILIMA 71, 3rd Inter-American Philatelic Exhibition, Nov. 6-14, Lima, Peru. Card of 3. Nos. 1111 and 1126, Peru No. 360. Card inscribed in Spanish. 3.50

1972 BELGICA 72, Brussels International Philatelic Exhibition, June 24-July 9. Brussels, Belgium. Card of 3. Nos. 914, 1026 and 1104. Card inscribed in Flemish and French. 3.50
OLYMPIA PHILATELIC MÜNCHEN 72, Aug. 18-Sept. 10, Munich, Germany. Card of 4. Nos. 1460-1462 and C85. Card inscribed in German. 3.75
EXFILBRA 72, 4th Inter-American Philatelic Exhibition, Aug. 26-Sept. 2, Rio de Janeiro, Brazil. Card of 3. No. C14, Brazil Nos. C18-C19. Card inscribed in Portuguese. 3.50
NATIONAL POSTAL FORUM VI, Aug. 28-30, Washington, D.C. Card of 4. No. 1396. 3.50

1973 IBRA 73 Internationale Briefmarken Ausstellung, May 11-20, Munich, Germany. With one No. C13. 4.00
APEX 73, International Airmail Exhibition, July 4-7, Manchester, England. Card of 3. Newfoundland No. C4, U.S. No. C3a and Honduras No. C12. 3.50
POLSKA 73, Swiatowa Wystawa Filatelistyczna, Aug. 19-Sept. 2, Poznan, Poland. Card of 3. No. 1488 and Poland Nos. 1944-1945. Card inscribed in Polish. 4.00
POSTAL PEOPLE CARD, Card of 10 (#1489-1498) distributed to Postal Service employees. Not available to public. 14x11". $75.00 (est.)

1974 HOBBY, The Hobby Industry Association of America Convention and Trade Show, February 3-6, Chicago, Illinois. Card of 4. Nos. 1456-1459. 4.00
INTERNABA, International Philatelic Exhibition, June

7-16, Basel, Switzerland. Card of 8, strip of Nos. 1530-1537. Card inscribed in 4 languages. 4.00
STOCKHOLMIA 74, International frimarksutstallning, September 21-29, Stockholm, Sweden. Card of 3. No. 836, Sweden Nos. 300 and 765. Card inscribed in Swedish. 4.50
EXFILMEX 74 UPU, Philatelic Exposition Inter-Americana, October 26-November 3, Mexico City, Mexico. Card of 2. No. 1157 and Mexico No. 910. Card inscribed in Spanish and English. 4.50

1975 ESPANA 75, World Stamp Exhibition, Apr. 4-13, Madrid, Spain. Card of 3. Nos. 233, 1271 and Spain No. 1312. Card inscribed in Spanish. 4.00
ARPHILA 75, June 6-16, Paris, France. Card of 3. Nos. 1187, 1207 and France No. 1117. Card inscribed in French. 3.50

1976 WERABA 76, Third International Space Stamp Exhibition, April 1-4, Zurich, Switzerland. Card of 2. Nos. 1434 and 1435 se-tenant. 4.00
BICENTENNIAL EXPOSITION on Science and Technology, May 30-Sept. 6. Kennedy Space Center, Fla. Card of 1. No. C76. 5.50
COLORADO STATEHOOD CENTENNIAL, August 1, Card of 3. Nos. 743, 288 and 1670. 5.00
HAFNIA 76, International Stamp Exhibition, Aug. 20-29, Copenhagen, Denmark. Card of 2. No. 5 and Denmark No. 2. Card inscribed in Danish and English. 5.00
ITALIA 76, International Philatelic Exhibition, Oct. 14-24, Milan, Italy. Card of 3. No. 1168 and Italy Nos. 578 and 601. Card inscribed in Italian. 4.00
NORDPOSTA 76, North German Stamp Exhibition, Oct. 30-31, Hamburg, Germany. Card of 3. No. 689 and Germany Nos. B366 and B417. Card inscribed in German. 4.00

1977 AMPHILEX 77, International Philatelic Exhibition, May 26-June 5, Amsterdam, Netherlands. Card of 3. No. 1027 and Netherlands Nos. 41 and 294. Card inscribed in Dutch. 4.50
SAN MARINO 77, International Philatelic Exhibition, Aug. 28-Sept. 4, San Marino, Card of 3. Nos. 1-2 and San Marino No. 1. Card inscribed in Italian. 5.00

NO POSTAGE
NECESSARY IF
MAILED IN THE
UNITED STATES

OFFICIAL BUSINESS
Penalty for Private Use $300

BUSINESS REPLY MAIL
First Class, Permit No. 73026, Washington, D.C.

United States Postal Service
Philatelic Sales Division
Washington, DC 20265-9980

WANT TO KNOW ABOUT ALL THE STAMPS AND PRODUCTS YOUR U.S. POSTAL SERVICE OFFERS?

*You can "sign up" to receive a **FREE** copy of the Philatelic Catalog. This bimonthly catalog will keep you up-to-date on the currently available stamp issues and philatelic products...give you the opportunity to have stamps, postal cards, collecting kits and more delivered right to your home! When you order from it, you will automatically receive copies for the balance of the year.*

*Your Philatelic Catalog is **FREE** when you send in this card. Neatly print your name and address below and drop this card in the mail. No postage necessary.*

Information which you provide will be protected and only disclosed in accordance with the Privacy Act of 1974.

Mr./Mrs./Ms.

_____

Initials   Last Name

_____

Street address
(Include P.O. Box, R.D. Route, etc. where appropriate)

City   State   ZIP CODE

Please Print Legibly

Please detach at perforation.

El Servicio Postal de los Estados Unidos se complace en emitir esta tarjeta conmemorativa en honor de ESPAÑA 84, la exhibición filatélica internacional que se está celebrando en Madrid.

La tarjeta representa una réplica del sello de 40 céntimos en homenaje a Cristóbal Colón, que fue emitido en 1930. El dibujo representa una vista de la Niña, la Pinta y la Santa María, las embarcaciones que utilizó Colón en su viaje del descubrimiento del Nuevo Mundo.

En la parte derecha de la tarjeta hay reproducido el sello de cuatro centavos estadounidense de la Serie Colombiana, que se emitió en 1893 en honor del 400 aniversario del Descubrimiento de América por Colón. El sello reproduce las tres carabelas de la flota de Colón.

William F. Bolger
Postmaster General

© UNITED STATES POSTAL SERVICE 1984

BANGKOK 83

กรุงเทพมหานคร ประเทศไทย
4 - 13 สิงหาคม

องค์การไปรษณีย์แห่งสหรัฐอเมริกา มีความยินดีเข้าร่วมเพื่อเป็นเกียรติ แก่นิทรรศการ "กรุงเทพมหานคร 2526" โดยการออกบัตรไปรษณีย์ที่ระลึกนี้สำหรับ ผู้ที่นิยมสะสมดวงตราไปรษณีย์

บัตรไปรษณีย์นี้จัดพิมพ์ขึ้นเพื่อเป็นอนุสรณ์สำหรับนิทรรศการการสะสมดวงตรา ไปรษณีย์ระหว่างประเทศ ซึ่งจัดขึ้นที่กรุงเทพมหานคร เพื่อเป็นเกียรติและเฉลิมฉลอง วาระครบรอบ 100 ปี ของการออกดวงตราไปรษณีย์เป็นครั้งแรกในประเทศไทย บัตรไปรษณีย์นี้มีรูปดวงตราไปรษณีย์รุ่นแรกของไทย ซึ่งผลิตออกมาเมื่อปี พ. ศ. 2426 เพื่อเป็นเกียรติแก่พระบาทสมเด็จพระจุลจอมเกล้าเจ้าอยู่หัว รัชกาลที่ 5 อยู่ด้วย

นอกจากนี้ บัตรไปรษณีย์นี้ ยังมีดวงตราไปรษณีย์เป็นรูปธนบัตร 2 เซนต์ ที่สหรัฐอเมริกาผลิตออกมาเมื่อ 100 ปีมาแล้ว เพื่อเป็นเกียรติแก่ประธานาธิบดี จอร์จ วอชิงตัน

William F. Bolger
Postmaster General

© UNITED STATES POSTAL SERVICE 1983

JOINT STAMP ISSUES
FEDERAL REPUBLIC OF GERMANY AND UNITED STATES OF AMERICA
APRIL 29, 1983

Die Postverwaltungen der Vereinigten Staaten von Amerika und der Bundesrepublik Deutschland würdigen die 300-Jahrfeier des Beginns der deuschen Einwanderung in die Vereinigten Staaten durch die gleichzeitige Herausgabe je einer Sonderbriefmarke, die das Segelschiff "Concord" zeigt.

Im Jahre 1683 verliess die "Concord" London. An Bord befanden sich 13 Familien, die auf der Suche nach religiöser Freiheit von Krefeld, einer Stadt im heutigen Nordrhein-Westfalen, den Weg in die Neue Welt angetreten hatten. Die Einwanderer waren am 24. Juli 1683 in London aufgebrochen und landeten am 6. Oktober 1683 in Philadelphia. Sie kauften Land in Pennsylvania und gründeten die Stadt Germantown, die heute ein Stadtteil von Philadelphia ist.

Die Herausgabe dieser Briefmarke ehrt den Mut, die Ausdauer und die Zielstrebigkeit jener ersten Einwanderer und all derer, die ihnen folgen sollten. Die amerikanische und die deutsche Briefmarke wurden beide von Richard Schlecht, einem Amerikaner deutscher Abstammung aus Arlington in Virginia, entworfen. Da kein Bild der "Concord" aufzufinden war, beruht der Entwurf der Marke auf vorhandenen Beschreibungen des Schiffes.

The United States Postal Service and the Postal Administration of the Federal Republic of Germany are commemorating the tricentennial of German immigration to the United States by the joint issuance of postage stamps featuring the **Concord**.

In 1683, the **Concord** sailed from London, carrying 13 families making their way to the New World from Krefeld, which is now in North-Rhine Westphalia, in search of religious freedom. The immigrants sailed on July 24, 1683, and landed in Philadelphia on October 6, 1683. They purchased land in Pennsylvania to build the community of Germantown, which today is part of Philadelphia.

The issuance of these stamps salutes the courage, stamina and motivation of those first immigrants and all who followed in their footsteps. Both the U. S. and German stamps were designed by Richard Schlecht of Arlington, Virginia, who is an American of German descent. Since a picture of the **Concord** was not available, his design is based upon written descriptions of the ship.

William F. Bolger
Postmaster General

1978 ROCPEX 78, International Philatelic Exhibition, Mar. 20-29, Taipei, Taiwan. Card of 6. Nos. 1706-1709 and Taiwan No. 1812 and 1816. Card inscribed in Chinese. 4.00

NAPOSTA 78, Philatelic Exhibition, May 20-25, Frankfurt, Germany. Card of 3. Nos. 555, 563 and Germany No. 1216. Card inscribed in German. 4.00

1979 BRASILIANA 79, International Philatelic Exhibition, Sept. 15-23, Rio de Janeiro, Brazil. Card of 3 Nos. C91—C92 (C92a) and Brazil No. A704. Card inscribed in Portuguese. 4.00

JAPEX 79, International Philatelic Exhibition, Nov. 2-4, Tokyo, Japan. Card of 2. Nos. 1158 and Japan No. A674. Card inscribed in Japanese. 4.00

1980 LONDON 80—IPEX, May 6-14, London, England. Card of 1. U.S. 2c 1907 No. 329. Card inscribed in English. 4.00

NORWEX 80—IPEX, June 13-22, Oslo, Norway. 1975 Norway stamp and two 1925 Nos. 620-621 (Norse-American issue). Card inscribed in Norwegian. 4.00

ESSEN 80—IPEX, Nov. 15-19, Essen, West Germany. Card of 2. 1954 West German and No. 1014 Gutenberg Bible. Card inscribed in German. 4.00

1981 WIPA 81, May 22-31, Vienna, Austria. Card of 2. 1967 Austria and No. 1252 American Music. NSCM, National Stamp Collecting Month. Oct. 1981. Issued to call attention to special month for stamp collectors. Card of 2. Nos. 245 and 1918. Card inscribed in English. 4.00

PHILATOKYO 81, International Philatelic Exhibition, Oct. 9-18, Tokyo, Japan. Card of 2. Nos. 1531 and Japan No. 800. Card inscribed in Japanese. 4.00

NORDPOSTA 81, North German Stamp Exhibition, Nov. 7-8, Hamburg, Germany. Card of 2. Nos. 923 and Germany 9NB133. Card inscribed in German. 4.00

1982 CANADA 82 International Philatelic Youth Exhibition, May 20-24, Toronto, Ontario, Canada. Card of 2. 1869 U.S. Eagle and Shield and 1859 Canadian Beaver. 4.00

PHILEXFRANCE 82. June 11-21, Paris, France. Card of 2. 1978 U.S. French Alliance and 1976 French commemoration of American Bicentennial. 4.00

ESPAMER 82, Oct. 12-17, San Juan, Puerto Rico. Card of 3. Nos. 810 and 1437 and the U.S. Ponce de Leon 1982 issue. 4.00

NSCM, National Stamp Collecting Month. October. Issued to call attention to special month for stamp collectors. Card of 1. No. C3a. 4.00

1983 Sweden/U.S. March 24, Philadelphia, PA. Card of 3. U.S. Nos. 958 and 2036. Sweden No. 1453. 4.00

German/U.S., April 29, Germantown, PA. Card of 2. U.S. No. 2040 and German No. 1397. 4.00

TEMBAL '83, May 21-29, Basil, Switzerland. Card of 2 in German. U.S. No. C71 and Switzerland No. 3L1. 4.00

BRASILIANA '83. July 29-August 7. Rio de Janeiro, Brazil. Card of 2, in Portuguese. U.S. No. 1 and Brazil No. 1. 4.00

BANGKOK '83. August 4-13, Bangkok, Thailand. Card of 2, in Thai. U.S. No. 210 and Thailand No. 1. 4.00

NSCM, National Stamp Collecting Month. Card of 1. U.S. No. 293. 4.00

1984 ESPANA 84. International Exhibition. April 27-May 6. Madrid, Spain. Card of 2, in Spanish. U.S. No. 233. Spain 1930 issue of 40-centimo tribute to Christopher Columbus. 2.00

SALON DER PHILATELIE. International Philatelic Exhibition. June 19-26. Hamburg. Federal Republic of Germany. Card of 2, in English, French and German. U.S. No. C66. German 1949 issue honoring Heinrich von Stephan, initiator of the first UPU Congress. NSCM, Ntl. Stamp Collecting Month. Card of 1. 4.00

AUSIPEX 84

PHILAKOREA 84

Bureau of Engraving and Printing

1954 POSTAGE STAMP DESIGN EXHIBITION, National Philatelic Museum, Mar. 13. Philadelphia. Card of 4. Monochrome views of Washington, D.C. Inscribed: "Souvenir sheet designed, engraved and printed by members, Bureau, Engraving and Printing./Reissued by popular request". 625.00

1966 SIPEX, 6th International Philatelic Exhibition, May 21-30, Washington, D.C. Card of 3. Multicolored views of Washington, D.C. Inscribed "Sixth International Philatelic Exhibition/Washington, D.C./Designed, Engraved, and Printed by Union Members of Bureau of Engraving and Printing". 210.00

1969 SANDIPEX, San Diego Philatelic Exhibition, July 16-20, San Diego, Cal. Card of 3. Multicolored views of Washington, D.C. Inscribed: "Sandipex—San Diego 200th Anniversary—1769-1969". 80.00
ASDA National Postage Stamp Show, Nov. 21-23, 1969, New York. Card of 4. No. E4. 30.00

1970 INTERPEX, Mar. 13-15, New York. Card of 4. Nos. 1027, 1035, C35 and C38. 55.00
COMPEX, Combined Philatelic Exhibition of Chicagoland, May 29-31, Chicago. Card of 4. No. C18. 20.00
HAPEX, American Philatelic Society Convention, Nov. 5-8, Honolulu, Hawaii. Card of 3. Nos. 799, C46 and C55. 25.00

1971 INTERPEX, Mar. 12-14, New York. Card of 4. No. 1193. Background includes Nos. 1331-1332, 1371 and C76. 5.00
WESTPEX, Western Philatelic Exhibition, Apr. 23-25, San Francisco. Card of 4. Nos. 740, 852, 966 and 997. 4.50
NAPEX 71, National Philatelic Exhibition, May 21-23, Washington, D.C. Card of 3. Nos. 990, 991, 992. 4.50
TEXANEX 71, Texas Philatelic Association and American Philatelic Society conventions, Aug. 26-29, San Antonio, Tex. Card of 3. Nos. 938, 1043 and 1242. 4.50
ASDA National Postage Stamp Show, Nov. 19-21, New York. Card of 3. Nos. C13-C15. 4.50
ANPHILEX '71, Anniversary Philatelic Exhibition, Nov. 26-Dec. 1, New York. Card of 2. Nos. 1-2. 4.50

1972 INTERPEX, Mar. 17-19, New York. Card of 4. No. 1173. Background includes Nos. 976, 1434-1435 and C69. 4.00
NOPEX, Apr. 6-9, New Orleans. Card of 4. No. 1020. Background includes Nos. 323-327. 3.50
SEPAD 72, Oct. 20-22, Philadelphia. Card of 4. No. 1044. 3.50
ASDA National Postage Stamp Show, Nov. 17-19, New York. Card of 4. Nos. 883, 863, 868 and 888. 3.00
STAMP EXPO, Nov. 24-26, San Francisco. Card of 4. No. C36. 3.00

1973 INTERPEX, March 9-11, New York. Card of 4. No. 976. 4.00
COMPEX 73, May 25-27, Chicago. Card of 4. No. 245. 4.00
NAPEX 73, Sept. 14-16, Washington, D.C. Card of 4. No. C3. Background included Nos. C4-C6. 3.50
ASDA National Postage Stamp Show, Nov. 16-18, New York. Card of 4. No. 908. Foreground includes Nos. 1139-1144. 4.00
STAMP EXPO NORTH, Dec. 7-9, San Francisco. Card of 4. No. C20. 4.00

1974 MILCOPEX, March 8-10, Milwaukee, Wisconsin. Card of 4. No. C43. Background depicts U.P.U. monument at Berne, Switzerland. 5.00

1975 NAPEX 75, May 9-11, Washington, D.C. Card of 4. No. 708. 14.00
INTERNATIONAL WOMEN'S YEAR. Card of 3. Nos. 872, 878 and 959. Reproduction of 1886 dollar bill. 35.00
ASDA National Postage Stamp Show, Nov. 21-23, New York. Bicentennial series. Card of 4. No. 1003. "...and maintain the liberty which we have derived from our ancestors." 57.50

1976 INTERPHIL 76, Seventh International Philatelic Exhibition, May 29-June 6, Philadelphia. Bicentennial series. Card of 4. No. 120. "that all men are created equal." 9.50
STAMP EXPO 76, June 11-13, Los Angeles. Bicentennial series. Card of 4. Nos. 1351, 1352, 1345 and 1348 se-tenant vertically. "when we assumed the soldier, we did not lay aside the citizen". 6.50

1977 MILCOPEX, Milwaukee Philatelic Society, Mar. 4-6, Milwaukee. Card of 2. Nos. 733 and 1128. 5.00
ROMPEX 77, Rocky Mountain Philatelic Exhibition, May 20-22, Denver. Card of 4. No. 1001. 4.00
PURIPEX 77, Silver Anniversary Philatelic Exhibit, Sept. 2-5, San Juan, Puerto Rico. Card of 4. No. 801. 5.00
ASDA National Postage Stamp Show, Nov. 15-20, New York. Card of 4. No. C45. 4.50

1978 CENJEX 78, Federated Stamp Clubs of New Jersey, 30th annual exhibition, June 23-25, Freehold, N.J. Card of 9. Nos. 646, 680, 689, 1086, 1716 and 4 No. 785. 5.00

1980 NAPEX 80, July 4-6, Washington, D.C. Card of 4. No. 573. 5.00
ASDA National Postage Stamp Show, Sept. 25-28, New York. Card of 4. No. 962. 5.00

1981 STAMP EXPO 81, South International Stamp Collectors Society, Mar. 20-22, Anaheim, Cal. Card of 4. No. 1287. 5.00

1982 MILCOPEX, March 5-7, Milwaukee, Wisconsin. Card of 4. No. 1136. 5.00
ESPAMER 82, Oct. 12-17, San Juan, Puerto Rico. Card of 1. No. 244. 5.00

1983 TEXANEX-TOPEX 83, June 17-19, San Antonio, Texas. Card of 2. Nos. 776 and 1660. 5.00
NORTHEASTERN 83, Oct. 21-23, Boston, Mass. Card of 2, Nos. 718 and 719. 5.00

1984 STAMP EXPO 84 SOUTH, April 27-29, Los Angeles, California. Card of 4, U.S. Nos. 1791-1794. 3.00.
ESPANA 84, April 27-May 6, Madrid, Spain. Card of 4, U.S. No. 241 as a block of 4. 3.00.
COMPEX 84, May 25-27, Rosemont, Illinois. Card of 4, U.S. No. 728 as a block of 4. 3.00

Over the years, the U.S. Postal Service has published a number of limited edition philatelic products issued to commemorate various philatelic and other events. These current market values were determined through various dealers who carry these products.

Commemorative Mint Sets	Original Price	Current Market Value
1968	$ 2.50	$22.50
1969	2.50	28.50
1970	2.50	14.95
1971	2.50	7.95
1972	3.00	7.95
1973	3.00	7.95
1974	3.50	7.95
1975	3.50	7.95
1976	3.50	7.95
1977	4.50	7.95
Bicentennial Mint Set With Souvenir Sheets	$11.80	$25.00
Without Souvenir Sheets	7.50	9.95
1980 Olympics Mint Set	6.50	9.95
Prominent Americans Series Mint Set	12.00	22.50
Women's Mint Set	3.00	6.00
Americana Series Mint Set	14.00	19.50
Fifty Birds and Flowers Mint Set Hardbound	17.00	17.00
Softbound	11.00	11.00
American Wildlife Album	3.50	3.50

POSTAL CARD VALUES

All prices are for postal cards in mint condition.

Scott #		Mint Card
	1873-98 Issues	
UX1	1¢ Liberty, brown, Lrg USPOD	225.00
UX3	1¢ Liberty, brown, Sml USPOD	50.00
UX4	1¢ Liberty, black, Wmkd	1,250.00
UX5	1¢ Liberty, black, Unwmkd	40.00
UX6	2¢ Liberty, blue	12.50
UX7	1¢ Jeff., black, faces L	40.00
UX8	1¢ Jeff., brown, faces L	25.00
UX9	1¢ Jeff., black, faces R	8.00
UX10	1¢ Grant, black	22.50
UX11	1¢ Grant, blue	8.50
UX12	1¢ Jeff., black	22.00
UX13	2¢ Jeff., black	*80.00*
UX14	1¢ Jeff., black	17.50
UX15	1¢ Adams, black	25.00
UX16	2¢ Adams, black	5.50
UX17	1¢ McKinley, black	*5,000.00*
UX18	1¢ McKinley, Oval	6.00
UX19	1¢ McKinley	22.50
UX20	1¢ McKinley, black	32.50
UX21	1¢ McKinley, blue	80.00
UX22	1¢ McKinley, blue	10.00
UX23	1¢ Lincoln, red	5.00
UX24	1¢ McKinley, red	6.00
UX25	2¢ Grant	1.00
UX26	1¢ Lincoln, green	5.50
UX27	1¢ Jeff., die I	.25
UX28	1¢ Lincoln, green	6.00
UX29	2¢ Jeff., die I	27.50
UX30	2¢ Jeff., die II	15.00
UX31	1¢ on 2¢ Jeff., red	*2,750.00*
UX32	1¢ on 2¢ Jeff., red	35.00
UX33	1¢ on 2¢ Red, die II	5.00
UX34	1¢ on 2¢ Jeff., red	300.00
UX35	1¢ on 2¢ Jeff., red	150.00
UX36	1¢ on 2¢ Grant red	*3,500.00*
UX37	3¢ McKinley	2.00
	1951-58 Issues	
UX38	2¢ Franklin	.30
UX39	2¢ on 1¢ Jeff., green	.50
UX40	2¢ on 1¢ Linc., green	.60
UX41	2¢ on 1¢ Jeff., dk. gr.	3.50
UX42	2¢ on 1¢ Linc., dk. gr.	4.50
UX43	2¢ Lincoln, carmine	.25
UX44	2¢ FIPEX	.25
UX45	4¢ Liberty	.75
UX46	3¢ Liberty	.40
UX47	2¢ & 1¢ Frank, rose	140.00
	1962-68 Issues	
UX48	4¢ Lincoln, precan	.25
UX49	7¢ "USA"	1.25
UX50	4¢ Customs	.40
UX51	4¢ Social Security	.40
UX52	4¢ Coast Guard	.30
UX53	4¢ Census	.30
UX54	8¢ "USA"	1.00
UX55	5¢ Lincoln	.25
UX56	5¢ Women Marines	.35
	1970-72 Issues	
UX57	5¢ Weather Service	.30
UX58	6¢ Paul Revere	.25
UX59	10¢ "USA"	1.50
UX60	6¢ Hospitals	.25
UX61	6¢ Constellation	.30
UX62	6¢ Monument Valley	.30
UX63	6¢ Gloucester	.30
UX64	6¢ John Hanson	.25
	1973-77 Issues	
UX65	6¢ Liberty	.25
UX66	8¢ Samuel Adams	.25
UX67	12¢ Visit USA	.35
UX68	7¢ Charles Thomson	.25
UX69	9¢ Witherspoon	.25
UX70	9¢ Caesar Rodney	.25
UX71	9¢ Court House	.25
UX72	9¢ Nathan Hale	.25
	1978-79 Issues	
UX73	10¢ Music Hall	.25
UX74	(10¢) John Hancock	.25
UX75	10¢ John Hancock	.25
UX76	14¢ Cutter "Eagle"	.30
UX77	10¢ Molly Pitcher	.25
UX78	10¢ G. R. Clark	.25
UX79	10¢ Pulaski	.25
UX80	10¢ Olympics	.50
UX81	10¢ Iolani Palace	.25
	1980-81 Issues	
UX82	14¢ Winter Olympics	.50
UX83	10¢ Salt Lake Temple	.22
UX84	10¢ Rochambeau	.22
UX85	10¢ King's Mountain	.22
UX86	19¢ Golden Hinde	.42
UX87	10¢ Cowpens	.22
UX88	(12¢) Eagle	.28
UX89	12¢ Isaiah Thomas	.28
UX90	12¢ N. Greene	.28
UX91	12¢ Lewis & Clark	.28
UX92	(13¢) Morris	.30
UX93	13¢ Morris	.30
	1982 Issues	
UX94	13¢ F. Marion	.30
UX95	13¢ La Salle	.30
UX96	13¢ Music Academy	.30
UX97	13¢ St. Louis P.O.	.30
	1983 Issues	
UX98	13¢ Georgia	.30
UX99	13¢ Old P. Office	.30
UX100	13¢ Yachting	.30

*Prices in italic indicate infrequent sales or lack of adequate pricing information.

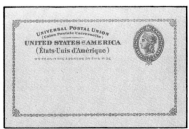

Philatelic Societies

American Air Mail Society
102 Arbor Rd.
Cinnaminson, NJ 08077-3859

Specializes in aerophilately, and periodically presents the Conrath Award to a member of the society in the name of Walter Conrath, one of its founders.

American First Day Cover Society
Mrs. Monte Eiserman
Membership Chairman
14359 Chadbourne
Houston, TX 77079-6611

American Philatelic Society
Box 8000
State College, PA 16801-8000

A full complement of services and resources for the philatelist. Membership offers: American Philatelic Research Library; expertizing service; estate advisory service; translation services; a stamp theft committee which functions as a clearing house for stamp theft information; a speakers' bureau and a monthly journal, "The American Philatelist," sent to all members.

American Stamp Dealer's Association
5 Dakota Dr.
Suite 102
Lake Success, NY 11042-1109

Association of dealers engaged in every facet of philately, with eleven regional chapters nation wide. Sponsors national and local shows, seminars for member and non-member dealers, credit information service, monthly newsletter and ASDA membership directory.

American Topical Association
3306 No. 50th Street
Milwaukee, WI 53216-3299

A service organization concentrating on the specialty of topical collecting. Offers handbooks on specific topics; an exhibition award; *Topical Time,* a bi-monthly publication dealing with topical interest areas; a slide and film loan service; information, translation, biography and sales services; and an heirs' estate service.

Black American Philatelic Society
% Walt Robinson
9101 Taylor Street
Landover, MD 20785-2554

For collectors interested in the study of black Americans on postage stamps.

Bureau Issues Association
Box 1125
Falls Church, VA 22041-0125

Collectors Club, Inc.
22 East 35th Street
New York, NY 10016-3806

Regular services include library and reading rooms, a publication and lectures on philatelic subjects. The group also honors a great American collector annually and actively supports national and international exhibitions.

Council of Philatelic Organizations
P.O. Box 3492
North New Hyde Park Station
New Hyde Park, NY 11040-0801

A non-profit organization comprised of more than 200 national, regional and local stamp clubs, organizations, societies and philatelic business firms. The objective of COPO is to promote and encourage the hobby of stamp collecting. Membership is open only to organizations; COPO uses a variety of methods to promote stamp collecting including an on-going publicity campaign, a quarterly newsletter and joint sponsorship (with the USPS) of National Stamp Collecting Month. For more information on COPO send a stamped, self-addressed envelope requesting a copy of "COPO is Everyone."

Errors, Freaks and Oddities Collectors Club
Box 1125
Falls Church, VA 22041-0125

Includes an exhibit critique service.

Junior Philatelists of America
Box 195
Minetto, NY 13115-0195

Provides an auction department, library service, tape and slide service, stamp identification and translation services. Publishes a bi-monthly, illustrated publication titled the *Philatelic Observer.*

Maximum Card Study Club
Bill Kelleher
Box 375
Bedford, MA 01730-0375

Mobile Post Office Society
5030 Aspen Drive
Omaha, NE 68157-2267

A non-profit organization concentrating on transit markings and the history of postal transit routes. The Society is engaged in documenting and recording transit postal history by publishing books, catalogs and monographs, as well as a semi-monthly journal.

Modern Postal History Association
% Psychology Department
Pace University
Pleasantville, NY 10570-2799

National Association of Precancel Collectors
5121 Park Blvd.
Wildwood, NJ 08260-1454

The Perfins Club
2163 Cumbre Place
El Cajon, CA 92020-1005

Send SASE for information.

Philatelic Foundation
270 Madison Ave.
New York, NY 10016-0656

A non-profit organization known for its excellent expertization service. The Foundation's broad resources, including extensive reference collections, 5,000-volume library and Expert Committee, provide collectors with comprehensive consumer protection. It also publishes educational information. Slide and cassette programs are available on such subjects as the Pony Express, Provisionals, Confederate Postal History and special programs for beginning collectors.

Plate Block Collector Club
Box 937
Homestead, FL 33090-0937

Plate Number Society
9600 Colesville Rd.
Silver Spring, MD 20901-3144

Postal History Society
Box 20
Bayside, NY 11361-0020

Post Mark Collectors Club
Wilma Hinrichs
4200 SE. Indianola Rd.
Des Moines, IA 50320-1555

Precancel Stamp Society
David A. Coates, Secretary
2500 Wisconsin Avenue, N.W. #829
Washington, D.C. 20007-4561

Souvenir Card Collectors Society
Box 7116
Rochester, MN 55903-7116

United Postal Stationery Society
Mrs. J. Thomas
Box 48
Redlands, CA 92373-0601

U.S. Souvenir Page Society
1138 Princeton Drive
Richardson, TX 75081-3615

**The United States Possessions
Philatelic Society**
141 Lyford Drive
Tiburon, CA 94920-1652

The Universal Ship Cancellation Society
P.O. Box 13
New Britain, CT 06050-0013
    Specializing in naval ship cancellations.

Catalogs

Brookman Price List of U.S. Stamps
91 South 9th Street
Minneapolis, MN 55402-3295

Catalogue of United States Souvenir Cards
The Washington Press
2 Vreeland Rd.
Florham Park, NJ 07932-1587

First Day Cover Catalogue (U.S.-U.N.)
The Washington Press
2 Vreeland Rd.
Florham Park, NJ 07932-1587

Perfins of the World
9801 Dewey Drive
Garden Grove, CA 92641-1344

Souvenir Pages Price List
(Please send self-addressed stamped envelope
to receive current listings.)
Charles D. Simmons
P.O. Box 6238
Buena Park, CA 90622-6238

**Noble Official Catalog of United States Bureau
Precancels, 64th Edition**
P.O. Box 931
Winter Park, FL 32789-0931

Stamps of the World 1982 Catalogue
Stanley Gibbons Publications. Available through
dealers only. All the stamps of the world from 1840 to
date. Over 1,900 pages feature more than 200,000
stamps (47,900 illustrations) from over 200 issuing
countries.

Commemorative Panel Price List
(Please send self-addressed stamped envelope
to receive current listings.)
Frank Riolo
P.O. Box 1540
Delray Beach, FL 33447-1540

Fleetwoods Standard First Day Cover Catalog
Unicover Corporation
Cheyenne, WY 82008-0001

Harris Illustrated Postage Stamp Catalog
H.E. Harris & Co., Inc.
Boston, MA 02117-0810

Minkus New World Wide Stamp Catalogue
116 West 32nd Street
New York, NY 10001-3284

American Air Mail Catalogue
American Air Mail Society
Cinnaminson, NJ 08077-3859

Scott Standard Postage Stamp Catalogue
3 East 57th St.
New York, NY 10022-2562

U.S. Postal Card Catalog, 1980
Box 48
Redlands, CA 92373-0601

Magazines and Newspapers

Linn's Stamp News
Box 29
Sidney, OH 45365-0029

Mekeel's Weekly Stamp News
Box 1660
Portland, ME 04104-1660

Minkus Stamp Journal
41 West 25th Street
New York, NY 10010-2021

Scott's Monthly Stamp Journal
3 East 57th St.
New York, NY 10022-2562

Stamps
153 Waverly Place
New York, NY 10014-3849

Stamp Collector
Box 10
Albany, OR 97321-0006

Stamp Review
1839 Palmer Ave.
Larchmont, NY 10538-3099

1983 DEFINITIVE MINT SETS

For The Complete Collector

A relative newcomer to the world of stamps, the Definitive Mint Set was first offered in 1980 and has, in that short period of time, become a philatelic article of considerable importance and in great demand. With its introduction, collectors now have the special opportunity to acquire one of every postal item issued by the USPS during the year. Then, too, the Set is issued in a limited edition printing of 170,000 (compared to a production of 1.2 million for the Commemorative Mint Set), which offers added appeal to many collector enthusiasts.

For 1983, the Definitive Set is particularly impressive: a 24-page, four-color album contains 9 regular stamp issues, 5 coil stamp pairs and 10 different postal stationery items, each to be mounted in plastic protectors and accompanied by illustrations, photographs and articles relevant to the featured topic.

The 1983 Definitive Mint Set is available for $6.25 at more than 15,000 Post Offices nationwide, through all Philatelic Centers, and by mail order from the Postal Service's Philatelic Sales Division, Washington, D.C. 20265-9997. For additional information, send the postal card following page 288.

AMERICAN COMMEMORATIVE PANELS

A Treasured Tradition

In 1972, the Postal Service inaugurated a great philatelic tradition: the limited edition of American Commemorative Panels. Since that time, the panels have been offered annually to honor each new commemorative issue for that year. First in the continuing series was the famous Wildlife Commemorative Panel.

Commemorative Panels represent the highest standards of stamp art and the engraver's craft. Each one highlights newly issued, mint condition stamps on an 8½" x 11¼" page. Then, the stamps are enhanced by intaglio-printed reproductions of historical engravings (many over 100 years old) and are accompanied by carefully researched, informative articles on the commemorative subject. The finished display is a work of art in itself—worthy of framing, exhibiting and sharing.

Beginning in 1982, complete annual sets of the Commemorative Panel series, produced as a limited edition, were made available on an advance subscription basis only. Subscriptions are for a full year beginning each January. For additional information write the Philatelic Sales Division, Commemorative Panel Program, Washington, D.C. 20265-9993.

Discover the "Hobby of a Lifetime"

Stamp collecting! It's educational, exciting, challenging...and fun! You've heard about it and you're eager to join the ranks of 20,000,000 Americans who enjoy the world's most popular hobby. But where and how do you start? With the U.S. Postal Service Stamp Collecting Kits. Available at your local post office, these Kits offer an inexpensive introduction to the world of stamps.

Every USPS Kit contains four essential tools: a color-illustrated album with background information and display space for each stamp; a selection of genuine, colorful stamps ready for mounting; a convenient packet of mounting hinges; and *Introduction to Stamp Collecting*.

Your local post office may have additional Stamp Collecting Kits beyond those shown here. Be sure to ask. Since availability may vary, you may also wish to check more than one post office.

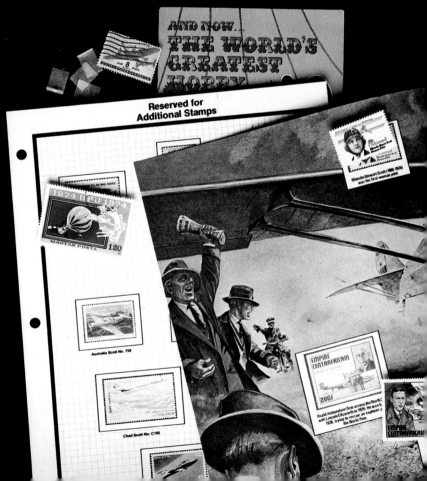

USPS Stamp Collecting Kits to be issued during the next few months include these interesting topics: Soccer, Costumes, Automobiles and The 1984 Summer Games.

And in early 1985...the 1985 U.S. Commemorative Stamp Collecting Kit will be available at your local post office with information on such 1985 issues as the Duck Decoys block of four and stamps honoring our Korean War Veterans and World War I Veterans.

1984 United States Commemorative Stamp Collecting Kit is now available at your local post office. It contains 7 U.S. commemorative stamps comprising 4 issues (Alaska, Winter Olympics, Federal Deposit Insurance Corporation and Carter G. Woodson), a full-color album describing all 1984 U.S. commemoratives, stamp mounts and the booklet *Introduction to Stamp Collecting*. $3.00

Lasting Value for All Collectors

U.S. Postal Service Commemorative Mint Sets are more than just a collection of all commemorative stamps issued in one year—the sets are fun, informative and valuable (see page 284 for current values of past Commemorative Mint Sets). Each year's complete set of commemoratives includes protection sleeves or individual plastic mounts to help preserve and display your stamps. The attractive folders feature concise background on the subjects of commemoration, the stamp artists and other philatelic information. Mint Sets launch the new collector in an absorbing, often lifelong, avocation. Experienced enthusiasts also value the Sets as adjuncts to their own collecting efforts. Commemorative Mint Sets are available at your local post office.

1983 Commemorative Mint Set—The 1983 set consists of 26 issues totalling 47 separate stamps, including the 16 stamps issued during 1983 to commemorate the 1984 Olympic Games. Also notable in 1983: joint issues with Sweden and the Federal Republic of Germany, the Treaty of Paris which represents the last stamp in the Bicentennial issues, and new issues on the Black Heritage and American Sports series. $12.50.

1984 Commemorative Mint Set—Consists of commemorative stamps comprising all 1984 issues, including blocks of four for the Winter Olympics, Orchids, the Summer Olympics, and Dogs. Also included are the Christmas stamps. $11.00

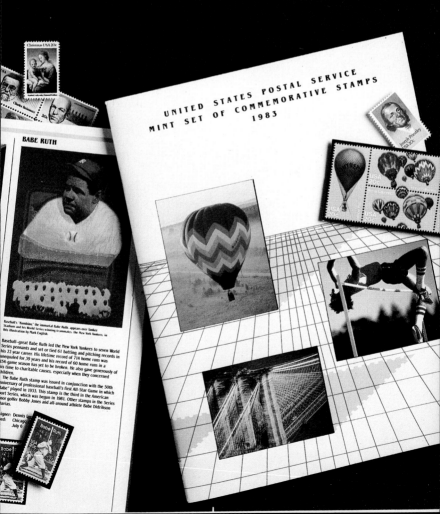

PHILATELIC CENTERS

In addition to the more than 15,000 postal facilities authorized to sell philatelic products, the U.S. Postal Service also maintains more than 343 Philatelic Centers located in major population centers throughout the country.

These Philatelic Centers have been developed to serve stamp collectors and make it convenient for them to acquire an extensive range of all current postage stamps, postal stationery and philatelic products issued by the Postal Service.

All Centers listed here are located at the Main Post Office unless otherwise indicated.

Alabama
351 North 24th Street
Birmingham, AL 35203

101 Holmes N.W.
Huntsville, AL 35804

250 St. Joseph
Mobile, Al 36601

Downtown Station
135 Catoma Street
Montgomery, AL 31604

1313 22nd Avenue
Tuscaloosa, AL 35401

Alaska
College Branch
3350 College Road
Fairbanks, AK 99708

Downtown Station
3rd & C Street
Anchorage, AK 99510

Arizona
Osborn Station
3905 North 7th Avenue
Phoenix, AZ 85013

1501 South Cherrybell
Tucson, AZ 85726

Arkansas
30 South 6th Street
Fort Smith, AR 72901

100 Reserve
Hot Springs National
Park, AR 71901

310 East Street
Jonesboro, AR 72401

600 West Capitol
Little Rock, AR 72201

California
200 Allston Way
Berkeley, CA 94504

Downtown Station
135 East Olive Street
Burbank, CA 91502

315 G. Street
Davis, CA 95616

8111 East Firestone
Downey, CA 90241

Cutten Station
3901 Walnut Drive
Eureka, CA 95501

1900 E Street
Fresno, CA 93706

313 E. Broadway
Glendale, CA 91209

Hillcrest Station
303 E. Hillcrest
Inglewood, CA 90311

300 Long Beach Blvd.
Long Beach, CA 90801

300 N. Los Angeles St.
Los Angeles, CA 90012

Terminal Annex
900 N. Alameda
Los Angeles, CA 90052

Village Station
11000 Wilshire Blvd.
Los Angeles, CA 90024

El Viejo Station
1125 I Street
Modesto, CA 95354

Civic Center Annex
201 13th Street
Oakland, CA 94612

211 Brooks
Oceanside, CA 92054

281 E. Colorado Blvd.
Pasadena, CA 91109

1647 Yuba St.
Redding, CA 96001

1201 North Catalina
Redondo Beach. CA
90277

Downtown Station
3890 Orange St.
Riverside, CA 92501

2000 Royal Oaks Drive
Sacramento, CA 95813

Base Line Station
1164 North E Street
San Bernardino, CA
92410

2535 Midway Drive
San Diego, CA 92199

7th and Mission Sts.
San Francisco, CA 94101

1750 Meridian Drive
San Jose, CA 95101

Spurgeon Station
615 North Bush
Santa Ana, CA 92701

836 Anacada Street
Santa Barbara, CA 93102

4245 West Lane
Stockton, CA 95208

15701 Sherman Way
Van Nuys, CA 91408

396 South California St.
West Covina, CA 91790

Colorado
1905 15th St.
Boulder, CO 80302

201 E. Pikes Peak
Colorado Springs, CO
80901

241 N. 4th St.
Grand Junction, CO
81501

1823 Stout Street
Denver, CO 80202

421 N. Main Street
Pueblo, CO 81003

Connecticut
141 Weston Street
Hartford, CT 06101

11 Silver Street
Middletown, CT 06457

141 Church Street
New Haven, CT 06510

27 Masonic Street
New London, CT 06320

421 Atlantic Street
Stamford, CT 06904

135 Grand Street
Waterbury, CT 06701

Delaware
55 The Plaza
Dover, DE 19801

Federal Station
110 E. Main St.
Newark, DE 19711

11th and Market Streets
Wilmington, DE 19801

District of Columbia
L'Enfant Plaza Philatelic
Center
U.S. Postal Service
Headquarters
475 L'Enfant Plaza
West, SW
Washington, DC 20260

Harriet Tubman
Philatelic Center
North Capitol Street and
Massachusetts Avenue
Washington, DC 20013

National Visitors Center
Union Station
50 Massachusetts
Ave., N.E.
Washington, DC 20002

Headsville Station
National Museum of
American History
Smithsonian Institution
Washington, DC 20560

Florida
824 Manatee Ave. West
Bradenton, FL 33506

100 South Belcher Road
Clearwater, FL 33515

1900 West Oakland Park
Boulevard
Fort Lauderdale, FL
33310

401 S.E. 1st Avenue
Gainesville, FL 32601

1801 Polk Street
Hollywood, FL 33022

1110 Kings Road
Jacksonville, FL 32201

210 North Missouri Ave.
Lakeland, FL 33802

118 North Bay Drive
Largo, FL 33540

2200 NW 72nd Avenue
Miami, FL 33101

1200 Goodlette Rd. North
Naples, FL 33940

400 Southwest First Ave.
Ocala, FL 32678

46 East Robinson Street
Orlando, FL 32801

1400 West Jordan Street
Pensacola, FL 32501

3135 First Avenue North
Saint Petersburg, FL
33730

Open Air Station
76 4th St. N.
Saint Petersburg, FL
33701

1661 Ringland Blvd.
Sarasota, FL 33578

5201 Spruce Street
Tampa, FL 33630

801 Clematis Street
West Palm Beach, FL
33401

Georgia
115 Hancock Avenue
Athens, GA 30601

Downtown Station
101 Marietta Street
Atlanta, GA 30304

Perimeter Branch
4400 Ashford-
Dunwoody Road
Atlanta, GA 30346

General Mail Facility
3916 Milgen Road
Columbus, GA 31908

364 Green Street
Gainesville, GA 30501

451 College Street
Macon, GA 31201

2 North Fahm Street
Savannah, GA 31401

Hawaii
3600 Aolele Street
Honolulu, HI 96819

Idaho
770 South 13th Street
Boise, ID 83708

Illinois
909 West Euclid Avenue
Arlington Heights, IL
60004

Moraine Valley Station
7401 100th Place
Bridgeview, IL 60455

433 West Van Buren St.
Chicago, IL 60607

Loop Station
211 South Clark Street
Chicago, IL 60604

1000 East Oakton
Des Plaines, IL 60018

1101 Davis St.
Evanston, IL 60204

2350 Madison Ave.
Granite City, IL 62040

2000 McDonough St.
Joliet, IL 60436 .

901 Lake Street
Oak Park, IL 60301

123 Indianwood
Park Forest, IL 60466

211-19th Street
Rock Island, IL 61201

Schaumburg Station
450 W. Roselle Road
Roselle, IL 60194

2105 E. Cook St.
Springfield, IL 62703

Edison Square Station
1520 Washington
Waukegan, IL 60085

Indiana
North Park Branch
44923 1st Avenue
Evansville, IN 47710

Fort Wayne Postal
Facility
1501 S. Clinton Street
Fort Wayne, IN 46802

5530 Sohl Street
Hammond, IN 46320

125 West South Street
Indianapolis, IN 46206

2719 South Webster
Kokomo, IN 46901

3450 State Road 26. E
Lafayette, IN 47901

424 South Michigan
South Bend, IN 46624

30 N. 7th Street
Terre Haute, IN 47808

Iowa
615 6th Avenue
Cedar Rapids, IA 52401

1165 Second Avenue
Des Moines, IA 50318

320 6th Street
Sioux City, IA 51101

Kansas
1021 Pacific
Kansas City, KS 66110

434 Kansas Avenue
Topeka, KS 66603

Downtown Station
401 North Market
Wichita, KS 67202

Kentucky
1088 Nadino Blvd.
Lexington, KY 40511

St. Mathews Station
4600 Shelbyville Road
Louisville, KY 40207

Louisiana
1724 Bank Drive
Alexandria, LA 71301

1715 Odom St.
Alexandria, LA 71301

750 Florida Street
Baton Rouge, LA 70821

1105 Moss Street
Lafayette, LA 70501

3301 17th Street
Metairie, LA 70004

501 Sterlington Road
Monroe, LA 71201

701 Loyola Avenue
New Orleans, LA 70113

Vieux Carre Station
1022 Iberville Street
New Orleans, LA 70112

2400 Texas Avenue
Shreveport, LA 71102

Maine
40 Western Avenue
Augusta, ME 04330

202 Harlow Street
Bangor, ME 04401

125 Forest Avenue
Portland, ME 04101

Maryland
900 E. Fayette Street
Baltimore, MD 21233

201 East Patrick Street
Frederick, MD 21701

6411 Baltimore Avenue
Riverdale, MD 20840

U.S. Route 50 and
Naylor Road
Salisbury, MD 21801

Massachusetts
Post Office and
Courthouse Bldg.
Boston, MA 02109

120 Commercial Street
Brockton, MA 02401

7 Bedford Street
Burlington, MA 01803

330 Cocituate Road
Framingham, MA 01701

385 Main Street
Hyannis, MA 02601

Post Office Square
Lowell, MA 01853

212 Fenn Street
Pittsfield, MA 01201

Long Pond Road
Plymouth, MA 02360

Quincy Branch
47 Washington Street
Quincy, MA 02169

2 Margin Street
Salem, MA 01970

74 Elm Street
West Springfield, MA
01089

462 Washington St.
Woburn, MA 01888

4 East Central Street
Worcester, MA 01603

Michigan
2075 W. Stadium Blvd.
Ann Arbor, MI 48106

26200 Ford Road
Dearborn Heights, MI
48127

1401 West Fort Street
Detroit, MI 48233

250 East Boulevard Dr.
Flint, MI 48502

225 Michigan Avenue
Grand Rapids, MI 49501

200 South Otsego
Jackson, MI 49201

Downtown Station
315 West Allegan
Lansing, MI 48901

200 West 2nd Street
Royal Oak, MI 48068

30550 Gratiot Street
Roseville, MI 48066

1233 South Washington
Saginaw, MI 48605

Minnesota
2800 West Michigan
Duluth, MN 55806

1st and Marquette Ave.
Minneapolis, MN 55401

Downtown Station
102 S. Broadway
Rochester, MN 55904

The Pioneer Postal
Emporium
133 Endicott Arcade
St. Paul, MN 55101

Mississippi
2421-13th Street
Gulfport, MS 39501

245 East Capitol
Jackson, MS 32905

500 West Miln Street
Tupelo, MS 38801

Missouri
315 Pershing Road
Kansas City, MO 64108

Northwest Plaza Station
500 Northwest Plaza
St. Ann, MO 63074

8th and Edmond
St. Joseph, MO 64501

Clayton Branch
7750 Maryland
St. Louis, MO 63105

H.S. Jewell Station
870 Boonville Ave.
Springfield, MO 65801

Montana
841 South 26th
Billings, MT 59101

Nebraska
700 R Street
Lincoln, NE 68501

204 W. South Front St.
Grand Island, NE 68801

1124 Pacific
Omaha, NE 68108

Nevada
1001 Circus Circus Dr.
Las Vegas, NV 89114

200 Vassar Street
Reno, NV 89510

New Hampshire
South Main Street
Hanover, NH 03755

80 Daniel Street
Portsmouth, NH 03801

955 Goffs Falls Road
Manchester, NH 03103

New Jersey
1701 Pacific Avenue
Atlantic City, NJ 08401

3 Miln Street
Cranford, NJ 07016

Belimawr Branch
Haag Ave. & Benigno
Boulevard
Gloucester, NJ 08031

Route 35 & Hazlet Ave.
Hazlet, NJ 07730

150 Ridgedale
Morristown, NJ 07960

Federal Square
Newark, NJ 07102

86 Bayard Street
New Brunswick, NJ
08901

194 Ward Street
Paterson, NJ 07510

171 Broad Street
Red Bank, NJ 07701

757 Broad Ave.
Ridgefield, NJ 07657

76 Huyler Street
South Hackensack, NJ
07606

680 Highway #130
Trenton, NJ 08650

155 Clinton Road
West Caldwell, NJ 07006

41 Greenwood Avenue
Wykoff, NJ 07481

New Mexico
Main Post Office
1135 Broadway NE
Albuquerque, NM 87101

200 E. Las Cruces Ave.
Las Cruces, NM 88001

New York
General Mail Facility
30 Old Karner Road
Albany, NY 12212

Empire State Plaza
Station
Albany, NY 12220

115 Henry Street
Binghampton, NY 13902

Bronx General Post
Office
149th Street & Grand
Concourse
Bronx, NY 10401

Parkchester Station
1449 West Avenue
Bronx, NY 10462

Riverdale Station
5951 Riverdale Avenue
Bronx, NY 10471

Throggs Neck Station
3630 East Tremont Ave.
Bronx, NY 10465

Wakefield Station
4165 White Plains Rd.
Bronx, NY 10466

Bayridge Station
5501 7th Avenue
Brooklyn, NY 11229

Brooklyn General
Post Office
271 Cadman Plaza East
Brooklyn, NY 11201

Greenpoint Station
66 Meserole Avenue
Brooklyn, NY 11222

Homecrest Station
2002 Avenue U
Brooklyn, NY 11229

Kensington Station
421 McDonald Avenue
Brooklyn, NY 11218

1200 William Street
Buffalo, NY 14240

Downtown Station
255 Clemens Ave.
Elmira, NY 14901

Rte. 9
Clifton Park, NY 12065

1836 Mott Avenue
Far Rockaway, NY 11691

41-65 Main Street
Flushing, NY 11351

Ridgewood Station
869 Cypress Avenue
Flushing, NY 11385

Old Glenham Road
Glenham, NY 12527

16 Hudson Avenue
Glens Falls, NY 12801

185 West John Street
Hicksville, NY 11802

88-40 164th Street
Jamaica, NY 11431

Ansonia Station
1980 Broadway
New York, NY 10004

Bowling Green Station
25 Broadway
New York, NY 10004

Church Street Station
90 Church Street
New York, NY 10007

Empire State Station
350 Fifth Avenue
New York, NY 10001

F.D.R. Station
909 Third Avenue
New York, NY 10022

Grand Central Station
45th St. & Lexington Ave.
New York, NY 10017

Madison Square Station
149 East 23rd Street
New York, NY 10010

New York General
Post Office
33rd and 8th Avenue
New York, NY 10001

Rockefeller Center
Station
610 Fifth Avenue
New York, NY 10020

Times Square Station
340 West 42nd Street
New York, NY 10036

Franklin & S. Main Sts.
Pearl River, NY 10965

55 Mansion Street
Poughkeepsie, NY 12601

1335 Jefferson Road
Rochester, NY 14692

Rockville Centre Main
Post Office
250 Merrick Road
Rockville Centre, NY
11570

25 Route 11
Smithtown, NY 11787

550 Manor Road
Staten Island, NY 10314

New Springville Station
2843 Richmond Ave.
Staten Island, NY 10314

5640 East Taft Road
Syracuse, NY 13220

10 Broad Street
Utica, NY 13503

143 Grand Street
White Plains, NY 10602

North Carolina
West Asheville Station
1300 Patton Avenue
Asheville, NC 28806

Eastway Station
3065 Eastway Drive
Charlotte, NC 28205

301 Green Street
Fayetteville, NC 28302

310 New Bern Avenue
Raleigh, NC 27611

North Dakota
657 2nd Avenue North
Fargo, ND 58102

Ohio
675 Wolf Ledges Pkwy.
Akron, OH 44309

2650 N. Cleveland Ave.
Canton, OH 44701

Fountain Square Station
5th and Walnut Street
Cincinnati, OH 45202

301 W. Prospect Ave.
Cleveland, OH 44101

850 Twin Rivers Drive
Columbus, OH 43216

1111 East 5th Street
Dayton, OH 45401

200 North Diamond St.
Mansfield, OH 44901

200 North 4th Street
Steubenville, OH 43952

435 S. St. Clair Street
Toledo, OH 46301

99 South Walnut Street
Youngstown, OH 44503

Oklahoma
101 East First
Edmond, OK 73034

115 West Broadway
Enid, OK 73701

102 South 5th
Lawton, OK 73501

525 West Okmulgee
Muskogee, OK 74401

129 West Gray
Norman, OK 73069

76320 SW 5th
Oklahoma City, OK
73125

333 West 4th
Tulsa, OK 74101

12 South 5th
Yukon, OK 73099

Oregon
520 Willamette Street
Eugene, OR 97401

751 N.W. Hoyt
Portland, OR 97208

Pennsylvania
Lehigh Valley Branch
Airport Rd. & Route 22
Bethlehem, PA 18001

535 Wood St.
Bethlehem, PA 18016

Beaver Drive Industrial
Park
Dubois, PA 15801

442-456 Hamilton St.
Allentown, PA 18101

Griswold Plaza
Erie, PA 16501

238 S. Pennsylvania Ave.
Greensburg, PA 15601

10th and Markets Sts.
Harrisburg, PA 17105

111 Franklin Street
Johnstown, PA 15901

Downtown Station
48-50 W. Chestnut St.
Lancaster, PA 17603

1 W. Washington Street
Kennedy Square
New Castle, PA 16101

30th and Market Sts.
Philadelphia, PA 19104

B. Free Franklin Station
316 Market Street
Philadelphia, PA 19106

William Penn Annex
Station
9th and Chestnut Sts.
Philadelphia, PA 19107

Seventh Avenue &
Grant Street
Pittsburgh, PA 15219

59 North 5th Street
Reading, PA 19603

North Washington Ave.
& Linden St.
Scranton, PA 18503

237 South Frazer Street
State College, PA 16801

300 S. Main St.
Wilkes Barre, PA 18701

200 S. George Street
York, PA 17405

Puerto Rico
San Juan General
Post Office
Roosevelt Avenue
San Juan, PR 00936

Plaza Las Americas
Station
San Juan, PR 00938

Rhode Island
24 Corliss Street
Providence, RI 02904

South Carolina
4290 Daley Avenue
Charleston, SC 29411

1601 Assembly Street
Columbia, SC 29201

600 West Washington
Greenville, SC 29602

South Dakota
500 East Boulevard
Rapid City, SD 57701

320 S. 2nd Avenue
Sioux Falls, SD 57101

Tennessee
General Mail Facility
6050 Shallowford Road
Chattanooga, TN 37422

1000 Georgia Avenue
Chattanooga, TN 37402

Tom Murray Station
133 Tucker Street
Jackson, TN 38301

501 West Main Avenue
Knoxville, TN 37901

Colonial Finance Unit
4695 Southern Avenue
Memphis, TN 38124

555 South Third
Memphis, TN 38101

Crosstown Finance Unit
1520 Union Street
Memphis, TN 38104

901 Broadway
Nashville, TN 37202

Texas
2300 South Ross
Amarillo, TX 79105

300 East South Street
Arlington, TX 76010

300 East 9th
Austin, TX 78710

300 Willow
Beaumont, TX 77704

809 Nueces Bay
Corpus Christi, TX 78408

400 North Ervay Street
Dallas, TX 75221

5300 East Paisano Dr.
El Paso, TX 79910

251 West Lancaster
Avenue
Fort Worth, TX 76101

408 Main Street
Hereford, TX 79045

401 Franklin Avenue
Houston, TX 77201

411 "L" Avenue
Lubbock, TX 79408

601 E. Pecan
McAllen, TX 78501

100 East Wall
Midland, TX 79702

10410 Perrin Beitel Road
San Antonio, TX 78284

615 East Houston
San Antonio, TX 78205

2211 North Robinson
Texarkana, TX 75501

221 West Ferguson
Tyler, TX 75702

800 Franklin
Waco, TX 76701

1000 Lamar Street
Wichita Falls, TX 76307

Utah
1760 West 2100 South
Salt Lake City, UT 84119

Vermont
1 Elmwood Avenue
Burlington, VT 05401

151 West Street
Rutland, VT 05701

Virginia
1155 Seminole Trail
Charlottesville, VA 22906

1425 Battlefield Blvd.,
North
Chesapeake, VA 23320

Merrified Branch
8409 Lee Highway
Fairfax, VA 22116

600 Granby Street
Norfolk, VA 23501

Tyson's Corner Branch
Tyson's Corner Shopping
Center
McLean, VA 22102

Thomas Corner Station
6274 East Virginia Beach
Blvd.
Norfolk, VA 23502

1801 Brook Road
Richmond, VA 23232

419 Rutherford Ave. NE
Roanoke, VA 24022

London Bridge Station
550 1st Colonial Road
Virginia Beach, VA 23454

Washington
Crossroads Station
15800 N.E. 8th
Bellevue, WA 98008

315 Prospect St.
Bellingham, WA 98225

2828 West Sylvester
Pasco, WA 99301

301 Union Street
Seattle, WA 98101

West 904 Riverside
Spokane, WA 99210

1102 A Street
Tacoma, WA 98402

205 West Washington
Ave.
Yakima, WA 98903

West Virginia
301 North Street
Bluefield, WV 24701

Lee and Dickinson St.
Charleston, WV 25301

500 West Pike Street
Clarksburg, WV 26301

1000 Virginia Street
Huntington, WV 25704

217 King Street
Martinsburg, WV 25401

Wisconsin
325 East Walnut
Green Bay, WI 54301

3902 Milwaukee St.
Madison, WI 53707

345 West St. Paul Ave.
Milwaukee, WI 53203

Wyoming
2120 Capitol Avenue
Cheyenne, WY 82001

IMPORTANT NOTE: This Index covers all issues from the 1893 Columbian Exposition issues (#230) through 1983. Listings in italic typeface refer to Definitive or Regular issues. The numbers in parentheses ( ) refer to the page number on which the stamp appears.

INDEX

INDEX

INDEX